ALSO BY SAMUEL DASH

The Eavesdroppers

CHIEF
COUNSEL

*Inside the
Ervin Committee—
The Untold Story
of Watergate*

Samuel Dash

CHIEF COUNSEL

Inside the Ervin Committee– The Untold Story of Watergate

Random House
New York

Library of Congress Cataloging in Publication Data

Dash, Samuel.
Chief counsel.

1. Watergate Affair, 1972–   —Personal narratives.
2. United States. Congress. Senate. Select Committee
on Presidential Campaign Activities. 3. Dash, Samuel.
4. Lawyers—Washington, D. C.—Biography. 5.Wash-
ington, D. C.—Biography. I. Title.
E860.D36   364.1′32′0973   76–14171
ISBN 0–394–40853–5

Manufactured in the United States of America

2 4 6 8 9 7 5 3

To Sara

Acknowledgments

I am indebted to many for this book. I could not have lived the experiences about which I have written without the aid of a remarkably able and dedicated staff. I am especially grateful to David Dorsen, a former assistant chief counsel of the committee, for reading the entire manuscript from the point of view of one who worked by my side during most of the committee's investigations. I have benefited from his wise advice.

I could not contemplate publishing this book without first showing the manuscript to Senator Sam J. Ervin, Jr. He took on this assignment with the same thoroughness and enthusiasm he exhibited in dealing with the important matters before the Senate Watergate committee. I was soon receiving letters from him containing helpful suggestions amid references to poetry. His delightful letters commenting on the book reflected his special humanity and sense of decency.

From the very beginning of this project my favorite author, James A. Michener, encouraged, indeed urged me, to persevere in completing it. When the manuscript was completed, Mr. Michener interrupted his own research on another of his fascinating writing adventures to read it and offered invaluable advice and instruction. For this I am deeply grateful to him.

My administrative assistant with the Senate committee, Carolyn Andrade, kept my papers and files in such good order that I have been able to readily recapture the details of significant events. And it was only due to the extraordinary patience, good nature and skill of my Georgetown University Law Center secretary, Mary Ann DeRosa, that the many revisions of the manuscript were typed and sent to my editor and others within the unreasonable deadlines I set.

Alan U. Schwartz, my legal representative, demonstrated faith in this book when I needed it most and brought me together with Random House. I have only praise for my relationship with Random House. At every stage of the development of this book their talented staff have displayed professionalism, sensitivity and enthusiasm. I am especially thankful for the guidance of my editor Robert D. Loomis. I have learned much from him about writing. Though at times he cut deeply, he was always responsive to my conerns about content and factual integrity and was never doctrinaire. In addition, I benefited from the editing assistance of James Wilcox and Sono Rosenberg.

Finally, and most important, I had the support, encouragement and, when necessary, prodding of my wife, Sara. Her contribution was much more than that of a rooter. Sara read and reread the manuscript, often revealing to me weaknesses in the text that prompted rewriting. She also aided me in recalling events I had overlooked. This truly was a joint venture for us.

Contents

Part One

1

A Call from Sam Ervin

IT WAS THE SECOND WEEK OF JANUARY 1973 WHEN WATERGATE touched me personally. Spring semester had just begun at Georgetown University Law Center where I taught a class in criminal procedure. My secretary buzzed me on the intercom and told me that a Professor Arthur Miller from George Washington University Law School was on line 2.

"I don't know if you remember me," said the voice on the other end of the line, "but the last time we saw each other was about twelve years ago when you visited us here to make up your mind whether you wanted to join our faculty. Frankly, Sam, I wish you had."

I remembered the visit to the school, but I did not remember Arthur Miller, specifically. "Oh yes," I said. "How are you?"

"Fine," replied Professor Miller. "But I'm not calling to reminisce. I want to talk to you about something very confidential. It's important that you keep to yourself what I will say to you, at least for the time being.

"I have been working with Senator Ervin on the Hill for a number of years on constitutional questions. The senator has been chosen to head up the Senate investigation of the Watergate scandal. No one knows yet whether it will be through one of his regular committees or through a special committee set up just for that purpose. But there is a lot of work that has to be done in advance preparation for this investigation. Research memos on a lot of legal issues, such as executive privilege, immunity, contempt of Congress and so on. Would you be available to take on a consultant role to help out?"

I had been trying to avoid new obligations, since I was already overloaded. In addition to my class in criminal procedure, I directed the Institute of Criminal Law and Procedure at the Law Center and we had a number of research projects under way. There were a dozen or more other commitments that I had made. I mentioned a number of them to Miller and suggested that I was probably too busy for Senator Ervin's needs.

"Sam, this is going to be really big," he urged. "Will you think it over and call me back?"

I told him I would, thanked him for calling me and hung up. I thought I would let a couple of days go by and then call up Miller and turn him down. My busy schedule had taken me out of the country during the summer of 1972, when the Watergate bugging had occurred. On my return I found that facts were sparse about the Watergate matter, although the details of the odd political burglary were themselves well known. On June 17, 1972, five men, possessing photographic and wiretapping equipment, had been caught by District of Columbia police inside the Democratic National Committee headquarters at the Watergate Office Building. One of the men was quickly identified as James McCord, security chief for the Committee to Re-Elect the President (CRP). Shortly afterwards two additional men were arrested and charged with complicity in the break-in. One was E. Howard Hunt, a White House aide; and the other, G. Gordon Liddy, counsel for the Finance Committee to Re-Elect the President.

Speculation was rife about the involvement of the White House or CRP in the Watergate burglary. But by September 1972 the highest campaign official indicted by the grand jury on charges resulting from the break-in had been G. Gordon Liddy. And there was no evidence touching the President himself, or his White House staff or anyone directing the President's reelection campaign. But there still was suspicion that higher-ups were involved.

Senator Edward Kennedy had begun a preliminary investigation of the Watergate matter through his Administrative Practices Subcommittee. Democrats and Republicans alike saw a possible political aspect to Kennedy's activities. Therefore, Senator Sam J. Ervin, Jr., of North Carolina, was chosen instead by the Democratic Policy Committee to make the major investigation.

I told my wife, Sara, about Arthur Miller's call and we talked it over. Sara was interested. "You have never been part of a congressional investigation." She enjoyed my undertaking new challenges, and we shared these experiences. Even though I didn't know Ervin and thought

I would have little contact with him, we agreed I should take on the assignment.

A few days later I called Miller back and told him I would be willing to talk to Senator Ervin about a consulting role. Miller was pleased and told me that he would call me again at an "appropriate time."

Three weeks passed before he called again. He asked if I could come to the Hill that afternoon to meet with Senator Ervin and Rufus Edmisten, chief counsel of the Separation of Powers Subcommittee which Ervin chaired. It was February 2, only three days after the Watergate trial had ended with the conviction of G. Gordon Liddy and James McCord. The other five defendants—Howard Hunt, Bernard L. Barker, Frank A. Sturgis, Eugenio R. Martinez and Virgilio R. Gonzales—had earlier pleaded guilty. The day after the trial ended, the Washington *Post* printed an analysis headed: "Still Secret: Who Hired Spies and Why." It was written by Bob Woodward and Carl Bernstein, the two reporters who had kept the story of Watergate alive from the time of the break-in. In their lead paragraph, they highlighted the problem: "The Watergate bugging trial was marked by questions not asked the witnesses, answers not given, witnesses not called to testify and some lapses of memory by those testifying under oath."

During the trial, U.S. District Judge John J. Sirica pushed for answers. "Who hired you to go in there? Where did this money come from? Who was the money man? Who did the paying off?" He repeatedly told the chief prosecutor, Assistant U.S. Attorney Earl Silbert, that he was not satisfied with the investigation and that other witnesses should be questioned and called to testify. Although the suspicion of cover-up had not yet permeated public opinion, Judge Sirica's questions and remarks made many people throughout the country wonder.

The morning Professor Miller called me to meet with Ervin, Sirica said in an open court hearing on bail for McCord and Liddy:

> Everybody knows there is going to be a Congressional investigation in this case. I would hope frankly—not only as a judge, but as a citizen of a great country and one of millions of Americans who are looking for certain answers—I would hope that the Senate committee is granted power by Congress by a broad enough resolution to get to the bottom of what happened in this case.

It was this resolution Ervin wanted to talk to me about that afternoon. A big man with a ruddy, jovial face, Senator Ervin was seated behind his sizable desk waiting for Miller, Edmisten and me when we arrived. His office was spacious, but warm-looking and comfortable; there was a marble fireplace, crammed bookshelves and a large overstuffed sofa facing Ervin's desk. Soft leather armchairs were spaced throughout the room.

Ervin put me at ease. "I know all about you, Professor Dash. I recently used your research on preventive detention in a speech I made on the floor. And I have been following your work in the American Bar Association."

I returned his warm greeting and told him that I was pleased my work had been of some use to him.

"I admire a man who will fight for criminal justice," Ervin said, holding up his right hand, fingers outstretched, as if to emphasize the point. "As a country lawyer and judge in North Carolina, I knew what it meant to champion an accused's rights." His eyes began to twinkle, and with a broad smile he added, "You know, every prosecutor's criminal skunk is some defense lawyer's aggrieved client."

Ervin chuckled at his own quip; then his face quickly took on a serious look. "This Watergate investigation is a mighty important assignment. It has to be the most thorough and objective inquiry ever made by the Senate. It must be broad enough to cover everything that needs to be looked into, and the committee must be given all the powers necessary for such a broad investigation. I have drafted a resolution which I plan to introduce on the floor in the next couple days, which I hope is adequate for this purpose. I'd be happy if you would glance at it and give me your opinion." Senator Ervin gave me a copy of the resolution. He also gave copies to Edmisten and Miller. I read it through slowly, and was impressed with the exhaustiveness of its coverage. It restricted the investigation itself to the presidential campaign of 1972, but within that area of investigation it authorized an inquiry into every form of illegal, unethical or improper conduct. It was very specific in referring to the break-in of the Democratic National Committee headquarters in the Watergate and to dirty tricks, campaign practices and illegal campaign financing.

I suggested some language to make it clear that acts in combination with others constituting conspiracies would be included in the investigation as well as individual acts. Also, I suggested that the resolution contain a specific authorization to the new committee to exercise the immunity powers granted to congressional investigations by the Organized Crime Control Act of 1970. Senator Ervin agreed and made note of the suggestions.

Ervin then turned to another subject. "I'm looking for an able non-partisan lawyer to be chief counsel of the committee," he said. "I have a number of lawyers, some judges, who have applied for the job. Do you have any names to suggest?" I told Senator Ervin that I would want to give the matter more thought and would give Edmisten some suggestions in the next day or two.

Miller drove me the short distance to the Georgetown University Law Center. "Sam, this can be a great opportunity for you," he said as I left the car. "Senator Ervin's a wonderful man to work with."

"I'm sure that's true, but the real working relationship will be with the chief counsel," I said a little dryly. I believed that the post of chief counsel to a congressional committee was a political appointment. "Who do you think the senator will pick?" I asked Miller.

"Gee, Sam, it's a can of worms," Miller replied, indicating that the competition extended far beyond staff people on the Hill.

"I suppose it can mean a lot to the lawyer who becomes chief counsel," I said.

"Would you like the job?" Miller asked me.

The question stunned me. The idea had never entered my mind. Not that I wouldn't like such a challenging position, but I didn't think it was possible. I had not been active politically and had no real contacts on the Hill. "I suppose," I told Miller, "any red-blooded trial lawyer would be thrilled to have that job—me included." I didn't know whether he had any say in the decision. Miller stared seriously at me for a moment and then said, "Ervin knows that the person has to be nonpartisan. Although a lot of people are pushing him, he can be very stubborn and independent when he wants to be. You'd be a natural with your background as district attorney of Philadelphia and having been both the national president of Criminal Defense Lawyers and chairman of the Criminal Law Section of the American Bar Association. Just don't tell anybody about your meeting with Ervin today and keep your hat on." He smiled at me, shook my hand warmly and drove off.

Bewildered, I stood for a moment outside the Law Center. I had seen Senator Ervin merely to explore the possibility of my providing certain consultant services to help him get started on his Watergate investigation. Now Miller had been talking to me about the position of chief counsel of the new Senate Select Committee. This was absurd. I told myself not to think about it, but it was hard not to.

That night I shared my experience with Sara. "Don't get excited, it will never happen," Sara said matter-of-factly. "You're not political and I'm sure the sharks have already moved in."

I thought Sara was right and I decided to stop speculating.

The next day I called Edmisten and gave him the names of three lawyers who I knew had excellent criminal trial experience and good national reputations at the bar. Any one of them would make a good chief counsel. After listening to me, Edmisten said tersely, "Arthur told me about his talk with you yesterday. Just sit tight and stay the hell away from this place." I started to protest that I wasn't a candidate, but he shot back, "Let the senator make that decision. God only knows what will happen. So just don't do anything." With that, Edmisten hung up.

The telephone call left me uneasy. What were Edmisten and Miller up to? Miller had certainly lost no time in telling Edmisten about our brief discussion. I knew one thing—I would do exactly as I had been advised: nothing.

On February 5, Senator Ervin introduced his resolution to create the Senate Select Committee on Presidential Campaign Activities. At the request of Minority Leader Hugh Scott, the voting on the resolution was put off until the following day. The resolution called for a five-member committee, three Democrats and two Republicans, which would have the broadest powers to subpoena White House aides and probe fully into the Watergate bugging, its funding, planning, purpose and sponsorship. The resolution was approved by the Senate on February 7 by a vote of 77 to zero. It had been amended, however, to enlarge the committee to seven members, four Democrats and three Republicans, and to authorize the hiring of a minority counsel and staff to serve the minority members of the committee. Most congressional committees provided for minority counsel and staff. However, the amendment went further and specified that the minority would have the right to spend funds up to one-third of the total budget of the committee.

The Washington *Post* reported on February 8 that Republican sources had said that some of the unsuccessful efforts by Republican senators to amend the resolution had been orchestrated from the White House by H.R. Haldeman, the President's number one assistant. The committee's investigation would later prove in greater detail the truth of the *Post* story. I sent one of my research assistants to get a copy of the Congressional Record for February 6 and February 7 so that I could read the floor debate. When he returned and I had read the printed record, I saw how organized the Republican effort had been to cripple the investigation that Senator Ervin was to undertake.

The two principal Republican amendments that had failed would have opened the investigation to include presidential elections prior to the 1972 election and reconstituted the committee so that there would be six members equally divided between Republicans and Democrats. The first of the amendments would have given the committee an impossible task and diverted the investigation from the alleged wrongdoings in the Nixon reelection campaign to the probing of every misdeed charged to Democrats in years past. The second would have guaranteed a stalemate.

The Congressional Record revealed another interesting item. Senator Ervin had previously announced that his investigation would look into the job done by the FBI and the U.S. attorney's office in the Watergate prosecution. In short, he would be investigating the investigators. Although on February 7 the resolution was not amended to prevent such an investigation, Senator Ervin bowed to the strong urging of Senate Republicans that the investigation not probe the adequacy of the Watergate prosecution by the Department of Justice. Ervin promised that the investigation would not cover this area, although he warned that an inquiry into wrongdoing during the presidential campaign of 1972 might indirectly reflect on the Justice Department investigation.

The Senate lost no time in appointing the new committee members. The Democratic leadership named Senator Ervin as chairman and Herman E. Talmadge of Georgia, Daniel K. Inouye of Hawaii and Joseph M. Montoya of New Mexico as majority members of the committee. The Republican leadership named Howard H. Baker of Tennessee as ranking minority member and Edward J. Gurney of Florida and Lowell P. Weicker, Jr., of Connecticut as minority members.

With the exception of Ervin, and perhaps Talmadge, it seemed a lackluster committee. Inouye, Montoya, Baker, Gurney and Weicker were little known nationally and were not leaders in the Senate. At first it appeared strange that what was being called the most important investigation ever to be undertaken by the Senate was being entrusted largely to senators with little national reputation or influence. I was to learn later from Senator Ervin that this was no accident, but was part of his strategy for the committee which was shared by Senator Mike Mansfield, the majority leader.

Mansfield and Ervin wanted the investigation to be an objective, bipartisan one that would have the confidence of the public. Ervin was picked because of his nonpartisan reputation and the fact that he was clearly not a potential presidential candidate. The three other Democrats were chosen with the same standard in mind; they were low-key and were not considered likely presidential candidates.

None of the three Republican members was a possible contender for the presidency, either. Only one—Senator Gurney—was a known partisan. Senator Weicker was a freshman senator and an unknown quantity. Senator Baker, the ranking minority member of the committee, gave the impression initially that he would not play a partisan role; he told reporters on his appointment that he favored "a full, thorough, and fair investigation with no holds barred, let the chips fall where they will." Baker said he expected full cooperation of the White House, the Justice Department and other federal departments and agencies.

I didn't go to the law school on Tuesday, February 20. I had come home the evening before with a scratchy throat and felt a cold coming on. By late afternoon I was feeling better and started to read over some of the cases I was going to take up with my class the next day. Sara had been answering the telephone all day, and when it rang about 6:30 P.M. I hardly noticed. But a moment later I heard her calling me to say that Senator Ervin was on the telephone and wanted to speak to me.

When I picked up the phone, Ervin said, "Professor Dash, I'm calling to find out if you would be willing to accept the position of chief counsel for our Senate Watergate investigation." Ervin's abrupt question caught me unprepared, and I didn't say anything. But he wasn't waiting for me to speak. "I want you to know," he continued, "there have been many lawyers asking for this job. Some of them have even volunteered to quit their law firms and serve the committee without pay. But I've always been worried about people who are willing to work for nothing. Sometimes that's all you get from them, nothing. Also, I have no way of knowing what their motives are. This is too important for me to worry about motives, so I've made a decision that anyone seeking the job won't get it. Your name was given to me some time ago. Everything I hear about you makes me believe that you have the qualifications and the right temperament for this job. It is not a partisan position. You'll be responsible to the full committee. We're having a meeting of the committee tomorrow. May I submit your name for the committee's approval as our chief counsel?"

Senator Ervin stopped talking. I actually had hoped that he wouldn't, since I didn't know how to reply to him. I knew I wanted the job. It was a trial lawyer's dream. And I knew that the Senate's Watergate investigation had become the most significant public activity in the country. But I hadn't talked it over with Sara. It would have to change our lives. The responsibility was so great and complicated that I knew that it would take all of my time. Also, how could I break away from the law school? the research center? I was frightened, too. Was I good enough? My whole professional career seemed to have prepared me for this call from Senator Ervin, but I couldn't prevent the self-doubts, which began to give me a chill.

"Senator," I said, managing to keep my voice steady, "this is of course a great honor and I'm very flattered by your offer." However, I explained, I was busy at the law school with my teaching and the research center; I asked how soon he would need me to begin.

"Almost right away," Ervin said. "This thing has been dragging on too long in the country. We put off the investigation until the trial was over. Now the Senate and the public expect us to get right on with it. We've got to get to the bottom of this matter and find who were behind those people convicted at the trial. They were just the foot soldiers. Everybody suspects that. It's absolutely vital that we start digging right away and find out what really happened." Ervin's voice was urgent and filled with excitement. He was looking forward to getting started with this great mission that had been entrusted to him. "You shouldn't have any trouble getting the law school to give you a leave for this investigation. If you want me to talk to anybody over there, I will. I know they will want to let you make this contribution to your country."

"Let me talk to Dean Fisher myself, first," I told him. "I want to say yes to you, and probably will, but I'd like to talk with the people at the school. And also, of course, my wife."

Ervin asked me to call him by noon the next day. I promised to call him in the morning and hung up. Sara had been in the room and I didn't have to tell her what Senator Ervin had called about. We were both quiet for what seemed a long while.

"That's quite an offer, honey," I said to Sara.

"Do you really want it?" Sara asked. She looked at me with a partly worried, partly frightened look in her eyes. She had a good idea of the pressures that were involved in this kind of position.

"I don't know, I'm not sure. But I think I should want it very much." I paused. "But can I handle it?" Our voices were almost a whisper.

"What do you think?" asked Sara, throwing back the question to me.

"I think I can. I know I can," I said with a sense of exhilaration.

Sara gave me a long look and smiled warmly. "I don't know anyone who can do it better than you. But I'm worried. Will you be able to take the pressure?"

"I think I'll thrive on it," I said. "But you're the one who will have the worst of it. You know that I'll hardly ever be home."

Her response was that my present commitments often kept me away from home anyway. There was nothing more to talk about.

I called Dean Adrian Fisher at home, and when he heard my news he reacted with a burst of enthusiasm that was out of character.

"You accepted, of course!" he exclaimed.

"But what about my class, the institute . . ."

Fisher quickly said he would assign another faculty member to teach my class and suggested that my deputy director, Herbert S. Miller, could run the criminal law institute. "If I were you, I'd call Sam Ervin right back before he changes his mind."

He was right. I shouldn't wait for tomorrow to call Senator Ervin. I told Sara what Fisher had said and then looked at her expectantly. "Well?" It was more a conclusion than a question.

"Of course you've got to do it," she said reassuringly.

Senator Ervin was still in his office when I called. I accepted his offer of the chief counsel's position and told him how honored I was at his choosing me. "That's fine," Senator Ervin replied. His voice was very warm. "I can't tell you how happy I am to have you working with me on this investigation. It's going to be a tough job, but a very, very important one to the country."

The following day, February 21, 1973, the new Select Committee held its first meeting and unanimously approved my appointment as chief counsel.

Before I did anything with the committee, however, I wanted to meet with Senator Ervin to clarify my role as chief counsel. The next morning I went to Ervin's office. I came right to the point: "Senator, I know I will have no problem in working with you, but there is the rest of the committee, the Senate and other agencies. I think it is important that we agree on some definition of my role."

"What do you have in mind?" Ervin asked.

"Well, if I'm going to be able to run this investigation the way I think it should be run—and, of course, under your supervision—I think it has to be understood that I can select my own staff, that I will be given independence in the conduct of the investigation—of course, again under your supervision—and that I will be allowed to follow the trail of the facts as far as it takes me, no matter what it reveals."

Ervin gave me a steady look. His blue eyes were shining, his eyebrows arched. "That's the only way I'd expect you to run this investigation," he said firmly. "You wouldn't be any good for this committee if you didn't insist on such conditions. Do you want them in writing?"

I hesitated. Ervin was so sincere, I didn't want to create the impression that I didn't trust him. But I had worked with committees before and I knew how important it was to clarify from the beginning the strong role I had to play in the conduct of the investigation. "Without meaning to offend you, yes, I would like to have these conditions spelled out in a letter from you."

"No offense at all," Ervin said with a smile. "And if I ever go back on you on any of them, I want you to come into my office and throw the letter right in my face."

"I don't expect I'll ever have to do that, Senator."

I recalled another important matter: office space. "That's going to be a tough problem," Ervin said, shaking his head. "The Senate office buildings are just about filled up. I've talked to the chairman of the Rules Committee and he has promised to let me know what space is available here. And I've asked Rufus to look around. I think I may have an answer soon."

Ervin chuckled. "You know, senators hoard office space around here like misers, and it may almost take dynamite to blow some of it free for us."

At that point the only place I had to work was a conference table in Edmisten's office. But I thought that the high priority set by the Senate for the Watergate investigation surely would enable us to obtain adequate space in the Senate office buildings. I was wrong. I had no idea I would have to spend the first full month as chief counsel with only a table in another person's office, and that Ervin would have to join me in threatening drastic measures before the space problem was solved—though never satisfactorily.

Before I left Ervin's office, I told him I was thinking of appointing Rufus Edmisten as my deputy chief counsel. I was following the recommendation of Arthur Miller, who told me that Edmisten knew his way around the Hill and would not undercut me.

Ervin smiled, "Rufus is one of the best politicians on the Hill, although I have to slap him down once in a while because he is still young and makes some mistakes. But he is a bright young man and is very loyal to me and I think you'd be smart in doing just what you said you're planning to do. I'll ask him to put his Subcommittee on Separation of Powers in low gear and devote most of his time to you for our Select Committee. He could also let you use some of his staff people he has over at Separation of Powers. A lot of our work will overlap, especially in the area of executive privilege. I think this will be a good move, Sam."

Later that day, when I told Rufus I wanted him to be my deputy chief counsel, he beamed and said he would be delighted to serve in that role. "Sam," Rufus stated, "we both have one goal and that is to see that this will be the best goddamn investigation ever made up here. So long as what you're doing is good for Senator Ervin, you'll have me squarely behind you."

That week I met my class for the last time. By a remarkable coincidence I reached the materials in the casebook dealing with wiretapping and bugging. For the past six years, when I reached this point in the course, I had given a two-hour lecture on the background, practices and technology of electronic eavesdropping based on my book, *The Eavesdroppers,* which I had written after making a nationwide investigation of wiretapping.

The word quickly spread throughout the school that I was going to give this lecture again. Many more students joined my regular class, cramming into the large lecture hall. Someone had told the press about the lecture and a number of reporters came to the classroom to find out what the new Watergate prober had to say about wiretapping. The lecture I gave was very much the same as my earlier ones, only updated to include some recent cases and events. However, the atmosphere in the lecture hall was singularly different because of Watergate and the role I was about to play in the Senate investigation.

2

No Room at the Hill

SHORTLY AFTER MY APPOINTMENT AS CHIEF COUNSEL, SENATOR Baker announced the appointment of Fred Thompson as minority counsel. Thompson, a young lawyer from Nashville, had been Baker's campaign manager. He had criminal trial experience as a former assistant U.S. attorney in Nashville. I was eager to meet him and get off to a cooperative start. I called Thompson and invited him to lunch.

Thompson came over just before noon. Physically he seemed to dominate the room—he was tall, big-boned and husky. He had a broad, handsome face and a full head of thick brown hair that curled down the back of his neck.

"So this is where the Democrats are hanging out?" he quipped. "You'll have to take it easy on a poor backwoods lawyer just come up to the big city." Fred spoke with a drawl and a wide smile. He was easy to like immediately.

We walked to the Monocle Restaurant on D Street, just one block from the Senate office building. After we had given our order, I explained our space problem to Thompson and urged him to ask Senator Baker to do what he could with the Republican leadership to free some space for us. At least, I told Thompson, he should be able to get an office for himself and the staff with whom he would be working.

"Sam, I don't think that's going to be a problem." Fred had the same illusions I'd had. "First, I have to rent a room before I use up my salary in hotel bills."

I knew from the newspaper announcement that Fred was married and had children. "Are you moving your family up to Washington?" I asked.

"I can't do that. The kids are in school, so my wife and the kids are going to have to stay in Nashville while I become a weekend Daddy. That's going to be expensive. I don't suppose I can get reimbursed from our budget for my trips back and forth to Nashville."

"I'm afraid the answer is no, unless you can find some witnesses in Nashville that should be interviewed."

Fred laughed. "Now, that's an idea. But I'm afraid Senator Baker wouldn't be too pleased with that. Besides, it's not going to be so bad. I'll only be up here a few months. Senator Baker said we'd be through by June."

I was startled. "June!" I almost shouted. Heads turned toward our table. I lowered my voice and said, "You must be joking. Have you read the resolution? We've got so much to do that we'll be lucky if we're able to file a report by February 28, 1974, as required by the resolution."

Fred looked surprised. "I'm not joking with you, Sam," he explained seriously. "I only took the job for a few months, since Baker said we would be through by then. I have a law practice in Nashville, and my partner and I thought I could manage being away for a short while. I know the resolution gives us up till February 28, 1974. But Senator Baker says the public wants to get this thing over with as quickly as possible and we're not going to need a year or anything like a year."

My instinct told me to drop the subject. I knew of Senator Ervin's plans for the investigation which included a thorough fact-finding process and full public hearings. Baker's views seemed to be completely foreign to Senator Ervin's concept of our investigation as well as with the explicit mandate of Senate Resolution 60. I thought at the time that either Fred had misunderstood Senator Baker or that Baker was intending to use Fred only for the beginning of our work.

"Well, we'll get a better idea of timing when we get into this investigation and learn just what it entails," I said.

"This investigation can be successful only if we have the confidence of the public that we are doing our job objectively and not politically," Thompson said. "Senator Baker and I want to work with you and Senator Ervin with only one main goal, and that is to get at the truth. Hell, I don't know what happened. Whether anybody in the White House or in the hierarchy of the Committee to Re-Elect the President was involved in this mess. But if they were, then, damn it, let it all come out. Sam, I don't see my job as trying to protect Republicans any more than I'm sure you don't see yours as protecting Democrats." I told him that I was not involved in party politics and that my understanding with Senator Ervin was that I could carry this investigation to wherever it led me. I had been warned by old-timers on the Hill to be wary of the minority counsel, but my first meeting with Fred Thompson led me to believe I had gained an ally.

During the first few days of March, I began making courtesy calls to introduce myself to the six other senators on the committee. I met with Senator Inouye in his dimly lit, beautifully furnished office, which conveyed the atmosphere of his native state, Hawaii. As in the case of each of the other senators I met, he began by telling me that he had not asked to be a member of the committee, and was only serving, with some regret, because he thought the investigation was a vital one for the country. He was coming up for reelection in 1974 and at this early stage of the committee's existence could not predict what impact his work on the committee could have on his election. Senators Ervin, Talmadge and Gurney also had to run for reelection in 1974. This struck me as odd, that with all the care that the Senate majority and minority leaders were supposed to have used in selecting this committee, they had taken the risk of choosing four senators, the majority of the committee, to participate in a controversial investigation in a year that was politically sensitive for them. Rufus had told me that Ervin, Talmadge and Inouye had solid positions in their states, and short of an unlikely catastrophe, were assured reelection. Even so, smart public officeholders run scared and avoid unnecessary risks in a reelection year.

With Senator Gurney it was a different matter. Gurney had tough opposition in his state of Florida. But his service on the committee could bring him the support of the Nixon administration if he played the strong partisan role that he had already projected at the time of his appointment.

When I mentioned our office-space problem to Inouye, he asked me to come with him immediately to walk through the halls of the two Senate office buildings to see if we could identify unoccupied offices. At the end of about an hour of looking through the halls, Inouye found that there were at least six offices, three of which were connected, that were unoccupied. We returned to his office and he told me he would call me as soon as he got a report back from the Rules Committee as to these offices. When he did call me back he said with wonderment in his voice, "There must be a number of ghosts around this building. I'd swear those offices we saw today were empty, but the Rules Committee reports that the senators who have claims to the rooms insist that they are occupied every day by members of their staff. Well, now, Sam, maybe our committee ought to investigate that mystery." He added, "No senator wants to give up any space he has acquired, and the Rules Committee is not going to push any senator out of any office."

Senator Talmadge invited two of his staff aides to sit in on our meeting. He spoke in a dry, no-nonsense drawl between puffs on a cigar. "I think you should get a good competent staff of lawyers and investigators and do a thorough investigation before we have any public hearings. You've got to dispel the belief of some people that this is going to be a witch hunt. I know you agree with me that this must be an independent and objective investigation and we want the people to support us." Though Senator Talmadge impressed me as being sincere, the gist of his admonition was so self-evident—and at least publicly subscribed to by every member of the committee—that it sounded like a slogan.

Talmadge stressed two themes that he was to continue to emphasize throughout the existence of the committee. "We should deal only with facts, Sam, and stay away from rumors and only hearsay. We don't have to prove anything, and we shouldn't try unless we've got the evidence. And let's not drag this investigation too long. I want us to be able to make our investigation, hold our public hearings and file our final report even before, if possible, the termination date of the resolution."

The briefest meeting was with Senator Montoya. He told me that he would give me whatever help I needed to make the investigation successful. He said that he strongly supported Chairman Ervin and that I could count on him to demonstrate this whenever needed.

Senator Weicker, from Connecticut—a huge man, about six foot six, two hundred and fifty pounds—was a freshman senator on the committee. He was breezy in his style, and our meeting was brief. He told me he was going to devote most of his time to the committee's work. In fact, he said he was planning to develop his own staff investigation. But he promised to coordinate his work with me to run "the finest investigation this Senate ever had."

I looked forward to meeting with Senator Baker. As vice chairman of the committee he would have more to do with me than any other member except Senator Ervin. A short, youngish-looking man, he smiled frequently as he spoke to me. He immediately made me feel at home by reminding me of the time, seven years earlier, when he brought his daughter, Cynthia, to my house to play with my younger daughter, Rachel. He repeated the pledge he had made to Senator Ervin that he would do everything as vice chairman of the committee to ensure that the committee would operate in an objective and bipartisan manner. He told me to come to him any time I needed his support and that he would give it to me. "Sam," he added, "I especially urge you to get together with Fred Thompson and work as a team. As I have said over and over again, this is not an investigation that is going to be made by Democrats and Republicans. We are going to operate as a group of senators and staff members having one goal, and that is getting all the facts that we can uncover no matter what they show. Hell, I might be committing political suicide, but I don't think so. Although I don't hesitate to acknowledge my loyalty to the President and the Republican party, I feel my first obligation in this position is to the American people. You have my word on that." Baker gave me a firm handshake, patted me on the back and told me he expected to see much of me.

Senator Edward Gurney, a tall, distinguished-looking man, spoke as though he were projecting his words to an audience larger than just myself. Like the others, he protested that he hadn't wanted to serve on the committee but was willing to do his job and help get straight to the bottom of Watergate. He fixed his eyes on me and said, "You know, this thing has scarred all of us in public life. Why, a senator like me, who thinks he's honest and is trying to serve the people, finds many people point at him and think he's a crook. We just have to show that there is decency and integrity in public service, or it's just going to be impossible to get good men to run for office. I know that I'm not sure whether I'll want this position anymore if it means I've got to put up with the slanders that we get every day."

Senator Gurney wished me luck and promised me his cooperation in the conduct of the investigation. He was an impressive figure, and persuaded me at this first meeting that he meant what he said. It wasn't long before I learned differently.

Life was becoming hectic in Rufus' office. There was a constant flow of reporters who wanted appointments to get material to write a profile on me or an analysis of our investigation. I was trying to conduct job interviews and study applications. The phone rang constantly. People kept walking in and out. We had become desperate for office space.

For a brief period I thought we had a partial solution. The Rules Committee tentatively assigned to the Senate Select Committee space which had been donated to the television, radio and newspaper reporters who regularly covered the Senate. Taking the space would have meant evicting the newsmen, which, for obvious reasons, we were hesitant to do. However, the problem of our incurring the wrath of the press became academic when the press lobbied the Rules Committee, which quickly withdrew its offer of this space to us.

We even considered a little frame building midway up C Street adjacent to the new Senate office building annex. It was a narrow three-story Civil War–vintage house next to an open Senate parking lot, so that it gave the impression it was the parking-lot office.

We rejected the building for practical reasons: the obvious ease with which it could be broken into and the information supplied by a Capitol policeman that the second and third floors weren't strong enough to support any heavy safes or files.

My personal and pressing need for private office space was met when Rufus finally had to surrender to me the suite of two rooms he used as chief counsel of the Separation of Powers Subcommittee. He moved to the frame house on C Street which we had rejected for the Select Committee. That solved my immediate problem, but not the long-range one of finding sufficient space for a large committee staff.

I decided to see Senator Ervin. When he asked how the work was going, I explained that without space we were really at a standstill. I had refused to accept any important document or other evidentiary material that had to be kept in a secure place. And I could not hire any lawyers or investigators without offices for them. I urged Ervin to tell the Senate leadership that our investigation could not go forward until we were given the facilities we needed.

Ervin agreed. He said he was trying to persuade the Rules Committee to give us the Senate auditorium, which could be converted into partitioned staff offices. He had a back-up plan to introduce drastic legislation to allow the committee to rent office space in downtown Washington—which would set aside a rule of the Senate prohibiting such rentals. However, he was ready to offer the legislation if I thought it was necessary, since he did not expect the senators to willingly give up their favorite auditorium where they entertained their constituents. "Senator," I said, "I don't know of anything more necessary for the success of this investigation." I was ready to fight with anybody at this point and didn't give a damn what the Rules Committee thought.

The following day Ervin introduced the bill to allow us to rent outside space and got unanimous consent of the Senate to have it taken up for a vote without referral to a committee. It was to come up for a vote the next day, Friday, March 9. Late that afternoon I received an urgent call from Bill Cochrane of the Rules Committee. "Senator Ervin has to withdraw that bill from the Senate," he urged.

"Why?" I asked. "We need that bill desperately. Otherwise this Select Committee might just have to go out of business."

"But don't you understand?" Cochrane asked. "You're going to create a terrible precedent that will cost the Senate a tremendous amount of money. Most committees up here don't have enough space and will want to take advantage of an opportunity to rent office space downtown. Can't we make a compromise to satisfy your needs?"

"What do you have in mind?" I asked.

"Well, I understand that Senator Ervin had asked about the Senate auditorium. I think I can get that for you now if Ervin will withdraw his bill."

Of course, we really wanted to stay inside the Senate office building. The auditorium was on the floor below and close to the suite of offices I was now occupying, whereas offices in downtown Washington would be very inconvenient for our investigation. "I'll talk to Senator Ervin and see what he thinks," I said.

"Do it right away, Sam," Cochrane pleaded. "We can make the deal this afternoon."

When I told Ervin about Cochrane's call, he chuckled and said, "That's what I expected would happen. I never thought we would have to push this bill through. The auditorium is much better for us than moving out of the building. Tell Cochrane you persuaded me to give up the bill and we'll take the auditorium."

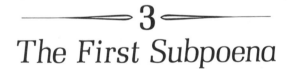

3

The First Subpoena

I WAS IMPATIENT TO GET MY KEY STAFF TO WORK. I HAD SETTLED on a general format for the investigation and on a concept of how it would be staffed. The committee's resolution identified three primary areas of investigation. The first was the Watergate break-in and the cover-up. The second was political espionage and campaign dirty tricks. And the third was illegal campaign-financing practices. I wanted three assistant chief counsel, each assigned to one of the principal areas of investigation. Under each assistant chief counsel I would build a staff of younger lawyers, investigators and research assistants, so that there would be three task forces each with a responsibility to investigate thoroughly the assigned area, collect the evidence and identify the witnesses for the public hearings that would be held in that area.

I had received a huge pile of applications from lawyers. However, most of them were recent law school graduates with little or no trial experience. For two weeks I had made calls all over the country talking to trial lawyers and prosecutors seeking recommendations for the three positions of assistant chief counsel. I especially wanted the advice of Robert M. Morgenthau, former U.S. attorney for the Southern District of New York. Two names that Morgenthau gave me were David M. Dorsen and Terry F. Lenzner. Both had handled major cases for him in his office when he was U.S. attorney. Dorsen was at the time deputy chief of investigations for the City of New York. This office had been set up more than a hundred years ago, after the Boss Tweed scandal, to investigate official corruption in New York City. Specializing in bribery and fraud cases, it had been responsible for numerous important prosecutions in recent years.

Dorsen, in his late thirties, looked older because of his thinning hair, lined forehead and conservative dress. He had just separated from his wife and found in my offer a respectable excuse to leave New York. He agreed to be one of my top aides. He was enthusiastic about tackling the work of the committee, and I felt lucky to get him.

Terry Lenzner had worked for the Justice Department's Civil Rights Division and had been in charge of the legal services program for the Office of Economic Opportunity. In the OEO position he had had a major dispute with the Nixon administration on the issue of adequate legal defense for the poor. Lenzner claimed that the administration was short-changing the poor and was consequently fired.

Terry, of medium height, was built square and muscular. He had been a star football player for Harvard. He combed his straight dark-brown hair to one side, but it usually strayed, unruly, over the front of his forehead. His language was curt and gruff. He had recently participated as a member of the defense team for the Berrigan brothers. I had also had a brief working relationship with him when I served on the American Bar Association's Crime Prevention and Control Committee. Terry was on the staff of the committee to investigate the problem of narcotics control. I wanted him to join me. And he wanted to, especially after hearing about my plans. The only caution one of his former employers gave me was that Terry required close supervision, since he was very independent and preferred to go his own way for his own advantage. My interviews with Terry did not reveal this attitude;

on the contrary, he pledged to work closely with me and the rest of the staff.

Dave Dorsen and Terry Lenzner, like myself, were Harvard Law School graduates. For my third assistant counsel, I hired James Hamilton, a Yale Law graduate, and a native of South Carolina. Jim had been a trial lawyer with the prestigious Washington firm of Covington and Burling. Unlike Terry and Dave, he did not have criminal trial experience, but had worked on complicated anti-trust trials which provided the same kind of experience in dealing with many witnesses and a large quantity of documentary evidence. A little younger than Dave and Terry, Jim was a slim, handsome bachelor with thick, well-groomed sandy hair and pale blue eyes.

I decided to let each of my assistant chief counsel question some of the witnesses at the public hearings. This was unusual if not unprecedented. But I thought the promise of participating in the public hearings could serve as an added incentive to my top assistants to make the investigation as thorough as possible and thus guarantee excellent public hearings.

To make sure we had a tight working team, I planned to have my assistant chief counsel participate with me in selecting the young lawyers and investigators for the staff. When I had interviewed Terry, Dave and Jim, I explained my strategy of a three-pronged investigation and asked each of them to tell me which phase of the investigation he wanted to run. Terry quickly identified with the political espionage and dirty tricks phase. Dave Dorsen said he was interested in the campaign financing investigation. This left the Watergate break-in and cover-up phase for Jim Hamilton, which he indicated was his preference, anyway.

Senator Ervin suggested that we persuade Carmine Bellino to become our chief investigator. In his late sixties, heavyset and bald, he wore thick-lensed glasses and was hard of hearing. Carmine had been working for Senator Kennedy on the preliminary investigation of the Watergate break-in and was thinking of retiring. I was convinced he would be invaluable, and he agreed to hold off his retirement until the completion of the Senate Watergate investigation. Actually, Carmine was an investigative accountant and would not have much to do with the general field investigation. His expertise involved reconstructing financial records from scratch. In a number of major congressional investigations Carmine was noted for having been able to trace every dollar and penny no matter how complicated the transaction or how clever the efforts at concealment—and even if many of the original documents and records had been destroyed.

Though by the middle of March I had picked my top aides, I would have to wait awhile before they could aid me in the investigation. Terry and Jim could not free themselves to join me until the end of the month. Dave required even more time to settle his affairs in New York; he could not come down to Washington until the middle of April. Rufus Edmisten still had to complete some hearings and a report as chief counsel of Senator Ervin's Subcommittee on Separation of Powers. But even when he was finished with that task, Rufus would be of little help to me in the investigative or legal work of the Senate Select Committee. I counted on him principally to solve nuts-and-bolts administrative problems.

However, I could pursue the investigation with the aid of whatever temporary help I was able to commandeer. At Senator Ervin's request, a veteran investigator for the Senate Permanent Investigations Committee, LaVerne Duffy, collected all material on Watergate relevant to our Senate resolution that had appeared publicly. He developed a chronology of facts and gave me some investigative advice.

I also met with Bob Woodward of the Washington *Post* to propose an unusual arrangement in which he would provide tips to the committee without receiving any information from us in return. I did not ask for his sources—just investigative leads. Bob agreed to help me, and I told him I would assign a staff member to be his contact. This relationship never proved productive. The few names Woodward gave me at our first meeting turned up quickly in my staff's own routine investigation, and it wasn't long before our knowledge of the facts far exceeded Woodward's. Since Bob and his partner, Carl Bernstein, had been supportive of the committee and willing to assist me in the beginning, I was sorry to have to express a firm "No comment" when they began to call me regularly to confirm a story. But I had made it clear from the start that even if they helped me, I could not return the favor and become a news "leak."

Duffy, from the Permanent Investigations Committee, had advised against our initially tackling the Watergate burglary, since the trial had just ended and the newspapers had been filled with the story of the prosecution. He thought the burglary and suspected cover-up were currently too hot to produce new information or witnesses and recommended that the committee open up some fresh new hearings on political dirty tricks centered on Donald Segretti as the key witness. He said he had collected some good information about Segretti and thought we would be able to put enough evidence together in a short time to support a few days of interesting hearings.

Coincidentally, I received the same advice from James Flug, chief counsel of Senator Kennedy's Administrative Practices Committee. Flug had conducted a preliminary investigation of Watergate when Kennedy thought his committee would be assigned the major Senate Watergate probe and had interviewed Segretti sometime in November 1972. He endorsed Duffy's view that our investigation and hearings should begin with Segretti and political dirty tricks, and urged me to have my staff meet with him for a background briefing before we conducted our own interrogation of Segretti.

This advice to start out with Segretti rather than the Watergate break-in surprised me. The major reason for the creation of the committee was the widespread belief that the Justice Department had done a poor job in the Watergate prosecution in not uncovering the real higher-ups behind the burglary. But Duffy and Flug had experience with Senate investigations and had been working with the material they had collected. I was starting from scratch. Until I knew more, I thought it would be wise for me to be guided by their judgment.

Flug urged haste because he feared that Segretti, who had been hounded by the press when he was first exposed, might go into hiding. A San Francisco private detective, Harold Lipset, with whom I had worked in the past, agreed to help the committee on a temporary basis until my top aides joined me. I asked him to find Segretti in Los Angeles and serve him with a subpoena requiring his appearance in Washington in ten days. It was the committee's first subpoena, and when Ervin signed it he had been enthusiastic that our investigation was being launched. But the launching was inauspicious. Lipset found that Segretti had disappeared, and settled for serving the subpoena on a Los Angeles lawyer who represented Segretti and agreed to accept it. Even though this constituted legal service of the subpoena, we still didn't know whether we could get any information from Segretti. My guess at the time was that he would take the Fifth Amendment.

LaVerne Duffy claimed we didn't need Segretti's cooperation for the committee to present two or three days of public hearings on political dirty tricks. Months earlier the newspapers had carried the stories that Dwight Chapin, Nixon's appointments secretary, had selected Segretti for the dirty tricks job and that Herbert Kalmbach, Nixon's personal attorney, had paid Segretti's salary. There was also the Los Angeles *Times* exposé of what Segretti supposedly confided to a close lawyer "friend" about his espionage activities.

But to present these matters at a public hearing would be rehashing old news, a function that did not require the efforts of a Senate select committee. I believed there was a larger and more significant political espionage program in which Segretti was involved and that it would take the investigative digging of committee staff members to uncover it. We would just have to wait until Terry Lenzner, who would head up this part of our probe, could get to work with a team of lawyers and investigators we would recruit together.

The Segretti investigation in the air, I turned my attention to the problem of how to begin developing some cracks in the wall of silence which the Watergate burglars had constructed and maintained. I had no doubt that our investigation was confronting a major cover-up conspiracy. It seemed obvious we would need the help of an insider—an informer to successfully expose this conspiracy. Some extraordinary tactic had to be employed to induce one or more of the burglars to start talking.

Soon, on March 23, the convicted Watergate defendants would appear before Judge Sirica for sentencing. This would be the most opportune time for Judge Sirica himself to assist in undermining the cover-up he had previously asserted he believed existed. Other judges had used the sentencing power as a carrot-and-stick strategy to provide an incentive for a convicted defendant to turn informer.

I had personally observed this practice in both my former roles as prosecutor and defense counsel. In fact, only recently as defense counsel for Speaker John McCormack's former administrative assistant, Martin Sweig, I had opposed such sentencing procedures before the U. S. Court of Appeals for the Second Circuit in New York. I argued that the trial judge had acted improperly when he imposed a substantial prison sentence on Sweig and then promised to be receptive to a request to reduce the sentence if Sweig gave information to the prosecutor the judge believed he withheld at the trial. But I had lost. Although I still believed the practice was wrong, the Sweig case was a legal precedent that a trial judge could use the sentence as a pressure tactic on the defendant.

As chief counsel of the Senate committee, I had no standing in the criminal case before Judge Sirica. But I had a committee reason to meet with him prior to the sentencing date. Senator Ervin had earlier requested Sirica to let the committee inspect the grand jury minutes of the Watergate case. On further review of the law I had concluded that Sirica could not legally grant this request. Ervin concurred with my opinion and had asked me to withdraw his request. This could have been accomplished by letter, but it gave me the opportunity to talk to Judge Sirica in his chambers. Sirica and I had been friends for years as faculty colleagues at Georgetown University Law Center.

When I met with Sirica I was careful to emphasize I was not recommending anything regarding his sentencing of the Watergate defendants, but I expressed the hope that one of them might give us information about the cover-up and I referred him to the Sweig case. Judge Sirica responded that he understood the committee was not making any request of him, as it had no right to do, and that he would study all the law and would sentence as he determined the interests of justice required.

A few days later, on Wednesday, March 21, my secretary buzzed me and told me Judge Sirica was on the line. "Sam, you know I'm sentencing the Watergate defendants this Friday, the twenty-third," Sirica's heavy, deliberate voice announced as I picked up the phone. "I think you should be present in the courtroom when I sentence them. What I plan to do should be of special interest to you and the committee. That's all I can say, you understand." I told Sirica I would be in his courtroom early enough to get a seat on Friday morning.

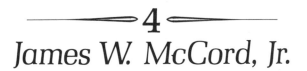

4

James W. McCord, Jr.

IT WAS A DAY TO REMEMBER. FRIDAY, MARCH 23, 1973. THE SEVEN convicted Watergate defendants were scheduled to be sentenced at 10 A.M. Chief Judge John J. Sirica's courtroom was unusually crowded that morning. I managed to get a front-row seat in the public section of the courtroom instead of the lawyer's section because I had no official reason to be in the courtroom.

The jury box was filled to capacity with reporters. The defendants, with their lawyers, sat at one long table and the prosecutors sat at another. As the hands of the large clock on the paneled wall behind the judge's bench approached ten, the din of many conversations throughout the room faded into an expectant silence.

A door opened, a gavel banged and Judge Sirica entered. We all stood to the ceremonial cry of the bailiff. When we were seated after Judge Sirica took his place at the bench, he announced, "Prior to the beginning of the sentencing scheduled for this morning, I wish to put a certain important matter on record in open court. On Tuesday, March 20, of this week, a letter addressed to me from one of the defendants, James McCord, was delivered to me by a probation officer. After reading the letter I had it sealed in the presence of my court clerk and placed it in his custody. Mr. Clerk, would you please unseal the letter and hand it to me at the bench."

The clerk stood up with an envelope in his hand, opened it, took out a folded paper from the envelope and gave it to Judge Sirica. The room was silent. Slowly, Judge Sirica unfolded the letter. He paused for a moment and looked up at all present in the courtroom. The suspense was great. Then, in a clear, deep voice, Judge Sirica read aloud James McCord's letter:

To: Judge Sirica

Certain questions have been posed to me from Your Honor through the probation officer, dealing with details of the case, motivations, intent and mitigation circumstances.

In endeavoring to respond to these questions, I am whipsawed in a variety of legalities. First, I may be called before a Senate Committee investigating this matter. Secondly, I may be involved in a civil suit, and thirdly there may be a new trial at some future date. Fourthly, the probation officer may be called before the Senate Committee to present testimony regarding what may otherwise be a privileged communication between defendant and Judge, as I understand it; if I answered certain questions to the probation officer, it is possible such answers could become a matter of record in the Senate and therefore available for use in the other proceedings just described. My answers would, it would seem to me, violate my Fifth Amendment rights, and possibly my Sixth Amendment right to counsel and possibly other rights.

On the other hand, to fail to answer your questions may appear to be non-cooperation, and I can therefore expect a much more severe sentence.

There are further considerations which are not to be lightly taken.

Several members of my family have expressed fear for my life if I disclose knowledge of the facts of this matter, either publicly or to any government representative. Whereas I do not share their concerns to the same degree, nevertheless, I do believe that retaliatory measures will be taken against me, my family, and my friends should I disclose such facts. Such retaliation could destroy careers, income, and reputations of persons who are innocent of any guilt whatever.

Be that as it may, in the interests of justice, and in the interests of restoring faith in the criminal justice system, which faith has been severely damaged in this case, I will state the following to you at this time which I hope may be of help to you in meting out justice in this case:

1. There was political pressure applied to the defendants to plead guilty and remain silent.

2. Perjury occurred during the trial in matters highly material to the very structure, orientation, and impact of the government's case, and to the motivation and intent of the defendants.

3. Others involved in the Watergate operation were not identified during the trial, when they could have been by those testifying.

4. The Watergate operation was not a CIA operation. The Cubans may have been misled by others into believing that it was a CIA operation. I know for a fact that it was not.

5. Some statements were unfortunately made by a witness which left the Court with the impression that he was stating untruths, or withholding facts of his knowledge, when in fact only honest errors of memory were involved.

6. My motivations were different than those of the others involved, but were not limited to, or simply those offered in my defense during the trial. This is no fault of my attorneys, but of the circumstances under which we had to prepare my defense.

Following sentence, I would appreciate the opportunity to talk with you privately in chambers. Since I cannot feel confident in talking with an FBI agent, in testifying before a Grand Jury whose U.S. Attorneys work for the Department of Justice, or in talking with other government representatives, such a discussion with you would be of assistance to me.

I have not discussed the above with my attorneys as a matter of protection for them.

I give this statement freely and voluntarily, fully realizing that I may be prosecuted for giving a false statement to a Judicial Official, if the statements herein are knowingly untrue. The statements are true and correct to the best of my knowledge and belief.

James W. McCord, Jr.

When Judge Sirica finished reading the letter, the courtroom exploded with excitement and reporters ran to the rear entrance to phone their newspapers. The bailiff kept banging for silence. It was a stunning development, exactly what I had been waiting for. Perjury at the trial. The involvement of others. It looked as if Watergate was about to break wide open.

The courtroom quieted. Judge Sirica announced that he would take McCord's letter under advisement and put off McCord's sentencing for a later date. Sirica proceeded to sentence the other defendants.

As to G. Gordon Liddy, who had pleaded not guilty and had been convicted by a jury, he imposed a final sentence of imprisonment for at least six years and eight months and a fine in the amount of $40,000. The other defendants—E. Howard Hunt, Bernard L. Barker, Eugenio R. Martinez, Frank A. Sturgis and Virgilio R. Gonzalez—had pleaded guilty. In their cases he utilized a special provision of the Federal Criminal Code, which imposes the maximum possible sentence to permit the Bureau of Prisons to conduct complete clinical studies and report back to the judge, at which time the judge could reexamine his sentence and impose any new sentence he believed appropriate.

This was a heavy blow to the defendants. But Sirica added a significant warning to them which clarified the reason he wanted me to be in the courtroom. Looking directly at the defendants, he said, "I recommend your full cooperation with the grand jury and the Senate Select Committee. You must understand that I hold out no promises or hopes of any kind to you in this matter, but I do say that should you decide to speak freely, I would have to weigh that factor in appraising what sentences will be finally imposed in each case. Other facts will, of course, be considered but I mention this one because it is one over which you have control." Sirica cited *United States* v. *Sweig,* the case I had referred to him as authority for his making this statement at time of sentence.

He had really turned the screw on the defendants. I had mixed feelings about Sirica's use of the sentencing power to induce confessions, even though I had hinted to Sirica that such a strategy would help the committee and the grand jury. I still thought, as I had argued in the Sweig case, it was an abuse of the sentencing function. But now my perspective was different. As chief counsel of the Senate committee I was a beneficiary of Sirica's tactic. Candidly, I had to admit to myself that one's view of such issues often depended, as in the old adage, on "whose ox was being gored."

The events of the morning had left me in a state of tension and confusion. Dramatic new disclosures about the Watergate break-in appeared to be imminent when my staff was not even assembled and at work. Also, McCord's accusations in his letter to Sirica must suddenly now change our priorities.

When I returned to my office, after stopping briefly in the Senate cafeteria for a sandwich and coffee, there was a message on my desk —McCord had called. It had only been an hour since Judge Sirica had left the bench.

I dialed the number and reached Bernard Fensterwald's law office. I knew Fensterwald from the days when he had been chief counsel for a committee of Senator Long's. More recently, I thought of him as an eccentric wealthy lawyer, who spent a large part of his time and considerable sums of money seeking to establish a sinister conspiracy linking together the assasinations of John Kennedy, Robert Kennedy and Martin Luther King.

"I have James McCord in my office and he is ready to meet with you," Fensterwald said. "How soon can you get over?"

"Right away," I said.

Fensterwald's office was on 16th Street near Pennsylvania Avenue, a short distance from the White House. Fensterwald was waiting when Hal Lipset, my only investigative assistant, who had just returned from California, and I came into the reception area of his suite of law offices. He greeted Lipset with a handshake and a slap on the back. They had known each other for several years.

"I told you I would bring McCord to you," Fensterwald said to me triumphantly.

He was right. Shortly after my appointment as chief counsel, Fensterwald had dropped in on me. It was a strange meeting. Fensterwald said that he had just met with James McCord at the District of Columbia jail, and that McCord was resentful and thought he had been abandoned. Fensterwald said he would be able to raise the money needed to release McCord on bail, and that if he did, he was confident he could produce McCord for me as a witness. I had been skeptical.

As we entered the conference room and library of Fensterwald's office, James McCord rose to greet us. I introduced Lipset as one of my investigators. I was too embarrassed to let McCord or Fensterwald know that I did not have any other investigators at the time.

I was impressed immediately with McCord's straightforward and friendly manner. I had expected to find him hard and devious, but his appearance belied the movie version of the secret agent. Rather, he looked like a middle-aged businessman with a determined expression on his face. Even during our brief introduction, he appeared to be trying to communicate his earnestness.

It is an investigator's dream to have a participant in a major conspiracy talk to him. The excitement over the realization of this dream was enhanced in McCord's case. He had become a mystery figure who had sealed his lips since the break-in on June 17, 1972. His letter to Judge Sirica suggested he was ready to reveal evidence that would implicate others in Watergate who were higher up than Liddy.

This first meeting, however, was disappointing. I was eager to get McCord's explanation behind his letter, but Fensterwald interceded: "Sam, I don't think it's a good idea for Jim to go into that now. I wanted you to meet with him and establish a relationship. But he wants to be very careful that anything he says to you is accurate, and he is somewhat handicapped by not having access to the transcript of the Watergate trial. Can you make a copy available to us?"

I told Fensterwald that I could. We agreed to let McCord work on the transcript in Fensterwald's office that evening and the following day until the late afternoon, when we would meet again to obtain McCord's information. There was much more, of course, that I wanted to learn from McCord which was not related to the trial transcript—his knowledge of the planning of the Watergate break-in and of any other participants—but for the time being I thought it best to let McCord disclose information at his own speed.

When we met the next day, I asked McCord to explain his statement in his letter to Sirica about his not trusting the grand jury, the FBI, and the Justice Department. McCord said it was only based on inferences he had drawn from the way the investigation had been handled and the trial conducted.

He explained that a number of false stories concerning the break-in had appeared in the newspapers prior to the trial and that he suspected these stories had been leaked by the prosecutor's office. One of the stories, he claimed, was planted to make it appear as though he had recruited the Cubans and that the break-in was a McCord operation. He said this was an effort to try to put the responsibility of the break-in below Liddy or Hunt, since they had White House ties, and to place it down at the level of the Committee to Re-Elect the President, thereby divorcing the entire activity from the White House.

McCord said that he let it be known through his counsel that he would not be silent if this defense theory was used. As a result, that idea was dropped and stories were next leaked to the newspapers that the break-in was a CIA operation. McCord said he reacted very strongly against any attempt to falsely blame the CIA. Just how strongly he reacted we were to learn later from a copy of a letter we uncovered written by McCord to Jack Caulfield, a White House aide, on December 28, 1972. It read:

Dear Jack

I'm sorry to have to write you this letter, but felt you had to know.
If Helms goes and the Watergate operation is laid at CIA's feet, where it does not belong, every tree in the forest will fall.
It will be a scorched desert. The whole matter is at the precipe now.
Just pass the message that if they want it to blow, they are on exactly the right course.
I'm sorry that you will get hurt in the fallout.

When I pressed McCord as to why he was suspicious of the U.S. attorney's office, he said he believed that the prosecutors seemed to accept too readily the false stories that were given to them. The Watergate grand jury had been reconvened and Assistant U.S. Attorney Earl Silbert was planning to start presenting witnesses before it in only two days. I asked McCord whether he thought this would be harmful to the exposure of the real story behind Watergate.

McCord's craggy face tensed. His eyes showed resentment. He replied tersely and quietly, "I think the very fact that since both agencies, the U.S. attorney's office and the FBI, are in the chain of command to the White House, a reasonable man would assume that whatever is told to the FBI would get to the White House within a matter of hours. My assumption is exactly the same in terms of testimony before the grand jury. Anything I might say before a grand jury would be to the White House in a matter of hours, perhaps a matter of minutes. The integrity of the system would not be preserved."

I made a note to alert Judge Sirica about McCord's fears concerning the grand jury. Then I asked McCord to tell me about the perjury he claimed had occurred at the Watergate trial. But Fensterwald again prevented a reply. "Can I just interpose one statement, Sam? Mr. McCord has indicated to me that because of the gravity, complexity and political ramifications of this, he prefers to debrief himself to the committee in written memoranda which he will give you and about which he will be willing to answer any questions. He is aware of the time frame in which you are operating, but he thinks it's an extremely touchy area and he wants to be absolutely sure he's correct, and he thinks he can do that easier in written form than in just answering questions off the top of his head."

This appeared to me to be a clumsy way of communicating with McCord. However, since I had not yet received any substantive information from McCord, I decided not to object initially to the plan Fensterwald had set out. There would be time enough later to call a halt once McCord was revealing information and it became apparent that we would have to proceed in a more direct method of interrogation. I told Fensterwald I was satisfied.

On the basis of his review of the Watergate trial transcripts I had given him the previous day, McCord had prepared a brief memorandum to support the perjury charge he had made in his letter to Judge Sirica. He also had a cover statement for the Senate committee. He handed them to me. The contents of the papers were characteristic of McCord's cryptic manner of communication. The cover statement simply said:

I, in addition to my own sworn testimony, am prepared to give the Senate Watergate Committee sufficient supportive information and/or leads to convince them beyond reasonable doubt that the statements I have made in the attached memorandum are true and correct.

The memorandum itself read:

1. A witness who testified who committed perjury was Jeb Magruder. Specifically, perjured testimony was given by Mr. Magruder in the afternoon session of Tuesday, January 23, 1973 as follows:

Mr. Silbert: Question: "Did you know anything about these activities and prior to the arrest at the Watergate on June 17, 1972?"

Answer: "No, Sir."

The subject matter under discussion immediately prior to the above question was the bugging and photography operation of the Watergate team.

2. Mr. Magruder knows the names of others knowledgeable of and involved in the Watergate operation sequence. One of such persons was John Dean of the White House staff. Had Magruder answered truthfully the question propounded above at page 1422 of the transcript and made

full disclosure of the names of others involved, he would have named Dean.

3. Mr. Magruder was, himself, knowledgeable of and involved in the Watergate operational sequence prior to June 17, 1972.

The memorandum was signed, "James W. McCord, Jr."

I was struck by the impact of the abrupt naked assertions in the poorly typed memorandum. I assumed McCord must have typed it himself. Though the memorandum provided no corroborative facts, it permitted the Senate committee now to act on information, rather than suspicion, that G. Gordon Liddy was only a subordinate in the Watergate burglary. Furthermore it accused Jeb Magruder of having lied at the trial. He was involved in the break-in. Magruder had been second to John Mitchell in command in the President's reelection campaign! And John Dean, counsel to President Nixon, was also involved! Clearly McCord's revelations propelled our investigation in one distinct direction—the Watergate break-in and cover-up. The Segretti matter would have to be shelved for the present. I would notify Segretti's lawyer that the hearing date on the subpoena had been postponed and would be rescheduled later.

I asked McCord for supporting details of his charges. But he said he preferred to prepare another memorandum, setting forth the details as accurately as he could recall them. Again I was annoyed at the delay, but did not protest.

The question of whether to keep my meeting with McCord secret— usually the best investigative strategy—or release it to the press, in the hope others would come forward, resulted in my first crisis as chief counsel.

I sought to reassure McCord that I would do everything I could to maintain the integrity of our relationship and the confidentiality of the material he was giving me until we were ready to use it in public hearing. But Fensterwald surprised me: "Jim has no objection whatever to your making public, through whatever means you want to, the fact that you have had several meetings and that he is supplying information."

I suggested it might be better to keep our meetings a tight secret, but McCord said, "The problem is that, in fairness, you ought to know that obviously in a number of areas I may have very limited knowledge. I may have firsthand knowledge pertaining to some things and secondhand knowledge as to others and in some cases my information is based on piecing different things together. In short, I've got one slice of it. I think Mr. Hunt has the other slice you want, the biggest slice."

"Will Hunt talk to us?" I asked.

McCord replied, "Well, I think that depends on a lot of things in the next few days. What he's thinking about, what he reads in the paper, what he sees. I suspect that will affect him very greatly."

Fensterwald added that it was important to McCord that the other defendants knew that McCord had come forward and was talking to the committee. It was important, he said, that Magruder and Dean knew this. And he added that it was, of course, important that Judge Sirica knew of McCord's cooperation.

When we left Fensterwald's office and were on 16th Street again, Lipset observed, "You know, Fensterwald might be right. The whole cover-up depended on a wall of silence and McCord is now cracking that wall. If we let it out that McCord is talking, there are going to be some pretty scared characters around town who may be able to make some bigger cracks in the wall, and it might all come down."

Senator Ervin had driven to Raleigh, North Carolina, to attend the Jefferson-Jackson fund-raising dinner, so I called him there on Sunday morning. When I had given him a complete report of the meetings with Fensterwald and McCord, he exclaimed, "That's wonderful, Sam. That's a real break in the case. We have to pursue this thoroughly now and get all the facts from McCord and follow up on all the leads he gives us. But just think of it! Jeb Magruder and John Dean! This is the damnedest thing I ever heard of. I never believed Liddy was the top man behind it all. But it's still amazing to find out that this outrageous conduct involved the President's counsel and the President's top man running his committee for reelection."

I told Ervin about Fensterwald's and McCord's request that the committee make public the fact that McCord had come forward and had been talking with the committee. I suggested that I could release a statement to the press that day, which would be limited to the fact of McCord's cooperation and which would not reveal what McCord had told us. Ervin thought that a limited press release was a good idea and authorized me to prepare the release and get it out to the press on Sunday afternoon.

I then called Fred Thompson, who also had taken the weekend off and was at his home in Nashville, and told him what we were doing. Since Ervin had approved the press release, Thompson saw no reason why it shouldn't be made. He said he would call Senator Baker and tell him of our plans.

I called my secretary and asked her to meet me at the office in an hour. I wrote out a short release to the press on a yellow pad. It revealed only that McCord had met with me on Friday and Saturday and had begun giving information to the committee, including the names of other persons involved in the Watergate break-in. The release mentioned no names or any other information McCord had given us.

I was not familiar with Senate procedures for news releases. This was the kind of problem I would have given Rufus Edmisten to handle, but he, too, was out of town. My secretary suggested that she could call the major newspapers, the wire services and the television networks and ask if they would each send a representative to our office to pick up the release.

I could have left and let my secretary distribute the release when the reporters arrived. However, this was the first public action of the committee involving the investigation, and I thought it was important for me to be there to answer questions so that no misleading inferences could be drawn from the release.

It didn't take long for me to realize what I had exposed myself to. By three-thirty, reporters started to stream into the office. The first to come began asking questions about why the press conference had been called. I found myself repeating that this was not a press conference, that I would simply be releasing a statement from the committee and I would be willing to answer questions only on that statement. Then the television crews arrived and set up their cameras and lights. By four o'clock the room was jammed. It did not occur to me to inquire whether all of the major newspapers, wire services and networks were present. From the size of the crowd, I thought everybody had to be there. I called for order and announced that the purpose of the meeting was to give out a press release on behalf of the committee which concerned a recent, significant development in the committee's investigation. I then read the news release to them.

Immediately there was an explosion of questions. I could hardly see the questioners because of the bright lights from the cameras. "Who did McCord name?" "Who did McCord say committed perjury at the trial?" "Why does McCord think that he and his family are in danger?" "Why did McCord come forward?" "Why did McCord talk to you instead of Judge Sirica?"

I parried all these questions by repeating that the chairman of the committee had authorized only the release of the facts that McCord had come forward, was giving us information and was naming names. I would not comment on the information McCord had given us or reveal the names that McCord had provided.

"But do you believe that McCord is telling you the truth—can you trust him?" one of the reporters asked.

I decided to answer the question. "I was impressed with McCord's sincerity and earnestness. From my experience in questioning witnesses in other situations in the past, I believe that McCord is trying to tell us the truth."

I should not have made that statement. Although I did believe McCord was sincere, I had not talked to him enough to form a real judgment. Besides, it was premature for me to characterize the information given by a witness or to comment on his credibility. I rationalized later that it was important not to have given the impression that I had doubts about McCord's story if I wanted to encourage other witnesses to come forward.

When it became clear that I was not going to add to my statement, the reporters picked up copies of the release and left. But a woman, who had been holding out a microphone in my direction while I had been speaking, approached me and asked, "Mr. Dash, would you just sit behind your desk and briefly repeat your statement for our CBS camera?" I hesitated. I did not think I should give a separate interview to one network, and told her that her camera and microphone must have picked up everything I had said while I was speaking to the whole group.

"I'm not sure," she said. "There was so much noise and a number of heads were in the way that we may not have gotten a good picture. It will only take a minute. Please." She was persuasive. I could not see what harm it would do for me to repeat the statement for CBS News —I had already exposed myself to the cameras and the other reporters. I agreed to do it but insisted that it had to be very short.

I sat behind my desk and a cameraman attached a small microphone by a string around my neck. She signaled the cameraman when she was ready and began speaking into her microphone. "This is Leslie Stahl, CBS News, in the office of Senate Watergate Committee Chief Counsel Sam Dash. Mr. Dash has just broken the news that Watergate convicted burglar James McCord has met with him on two occasions and has named names of higher-ups in the Watergate burglary. Mr. Dash, who did Mr. McCord tell you were also involved in the Watergate break-in?"

I was taken aback by what I considered a double-cross. I had not agreed to answer questions about what McCord had told me, but had thought I was only going to repeat the press release.

"I'm sorry," I said. "As I told all the reporters who have been here this afternoon, I am not at liberty to reveal what Mr. McCord told me. The purpose of this meeting with the press was simply to announce that Mr. McCord has come forward and is talking to the committee."

Leslie Stahl was not to be put off. "But surely, Mr. Dash, you have arrived at some conclusions after talking to Mr. McCord and a strategy for your investigation. What are your next steps?"

I replied that I did not think it was appropriate to reveal what the committee's investigative strategy was and refused to comment further. However, I did repeat, at her request, that I thought McCord was sincere and was telling the truth. She thanked me and left my office with her camera crew following her.

I stayed for a while. About a half hour later the phone began to ring. Editors from several newspapers were calling saying they had not been notified about the press release and had just learned the news from the wire services. Each wanted to send a reporter for a separate interview. I refused, expressing my regret that they had been overlooked.

Later that evening, I received a call at home from Carl Stern of NBC. He was angry that NBC had not been notified and that CBS had been given a special interview. He wanted to send a camera crew to my home for an interview. I said I was sorry that a mistake had been made, but that I was not going to be giving any more interviews with regard to the McCord story.

I soon learned that the newsmen who had been overlooked were not the only ones aroused. Senator Baker called me and told me he had just returned to Washington and had already received about ten calls from reporters. "Sam, what's all this McCord thing and press conference about?"

I told Baker about my meetings with McCord and Ervin's approval of a press release. But I did not inform him about McCord's new information and he did not ask. I expressed surprise that Fred Thompson had not reported this development to him after my call to Fred, since he had told me he would.

Baker was irritated. "Well, I don't like to learn about these things for the first time from newspaper reporters. I think we ought to meet in Senator Ervin's office tomorrow morning."

On Monday morning, I called Senator Ervin and explained how my meeting with the press got out of hand. He did not seem concerned. "You did exactly as I had asked you to do," Ervin said generously. "I think the news stories on TV, radio, and in the newspapers were very good. Senator Baker is a little upset, though, and wants us to have a meeting this morning. Can you come over about ten o'clock?"

Senator Baker entered Senator Ervin's reception room moments after I arrived, and we went into Ervin's office together. Rufus Edmisten was already there and Fred Thompson followed shortly afterward. Baker got right to the point.

"After I talked to Sam Dash last night, Fred told me all about his call from Sam on Sunday. I think it's great that James McCord has contacted the committee and is now talking to us. And I realize now that the chairman authorized the news release for Sunday. But Sam Dash held a press conference and didn't just issue a news release."

I insisted I only issued a release, but the Washington press corps made it look like a news conference. Senator Ervin backed me up: "Howard, I authorized Sam to make that statement to the press and I can't see that there was any harm in what he did."

"But I didn't know anything about it, Sam," Baker complained to Ervin. "It's embarrassing to first hear about such an important development from news reporters. I now know that Sam told Fred about it and, perhaps, that's all he could do. But I think we should have a rule on who is authorized to hold a press conference for this committee. I think it should be either you, as chairman, or me, as vice chairman, and not the staff without our authorization." Then he added with a conciliatory smile, "Okay, that's all settled. Let's get back to the more important business of McCord. I think Fred and Sam should follow that matter up right away and talk to McCord together. Perhaps this afternoon."

I agreed to call Fensterwald to set up an afternoon meeting, but I expected that McCord would object to talking in Fred's presence, since he was fearful of a leak.

When I returned to my office a dozen telephone messages were on my desk, all from the press wanting me to call back. I started with Carl Bernstein, of the Washington *Post*. "The L.A. *Times* reported this morning that McCord named Magruder and Dean to you as having advance knowledge of the Watergate bugging," Bernstein said. "Did McCord make that statement to you or was the L.A. *Times* just guessing?" The tone of Bernstein's voice implied he had a right to have me answer his question. For a moment I was speechless, stunned. How the hell did the Los Angeles *Times* learn that?

"I'm sorry, but I have no comment on that story," I told Bernstein after a pause. Then, realizing my statement might have created an inference, I added, "When I say 'No comment' you cannot take that to suggest that the story is true or untrue. I'm simply not going to reveal what McCord told us."

"Somebody's leaking it," Bernstein persisted. "Why not confirm it, at least for background and not for attribution?"

"I still have no comment," I said firmly.

The next two calls I returned brought the same questions about the L.A. *Times* story. I decided not to call any of the other reporters and told my secretary to reply to any news inquiries about the L.A. *Times* story that I would have no comment. I felt lousy. I had promised McCord that the information he gave me would be kept confidential for only the committee's use. How did it leak?

On Sunday night, when the L.A. *Times* story had gone to press, only four persons knew that McCord had divulged the names of Magruder and Dean during his Saturday meeting mith me—McCord, Fensterwald, Senator Ervin and I. Although Lipset had been in the room, McCord had never spoken the names; he had mentioned them only in the memorandum that he gave me. I had not shown Lipset the memorandum or told him of its contents—not because I did not trust Lipset, but because I felt instinctively that such an important revelation should be known initially only by Senator Ervin and me.

At our meeting the next morning in Senator Ervin's office I had repeated McCord's disclosure at Ervin's request in the presence of Senator Baker, Fred Thompson and Rufus Edmisten. But by then the L.A. *Times* story was already out.

I called Fensterwald to set up a meeting for later that day. Before I could mention the meeting, Fensterwald exploded: "Who's shooting his mouth off? I've been getting calls all morning about that lousy leak to the L.A. *Times.* McCord is damn angry. He thinks he's been double-crossed."

"I'm just as upset as you are," I said almost apologetically. "I can't explain how the L.A. *Times* got the story. What about that young lawyer in your office who sat in at our meeting?"

"He doesn't know anything. He never saw McCord's memo."

"Well, it can't be Lipset," I said, anticipating Fensterwald's obvious next question. "He didn't see the memo, either. It's a real mystery. Could McCord have wanted to get this out?"

"Shit! Of course not. Why the hell do you think he didn't want to talk with the FBI or the grand jury? Don't try to pin this on McCord." Fensterwald's voice was loud and angry.

I then told Fensterwald that Ervin and Baker wanted Fred Thompson and me to meet with McCord that afternoon to get more detailed information from McCord. "Fred Thompson!" Fensterwald exclaimed. "Do you think McCord will want to talk to the lawyer for the Republicans?"

"I understand the problem," I said, "but I can't exclude the minority counsel from these interviews. Senator Baker insisted that Fred Thompson be present and he has a right to make the demand. Sooner or later McCord is going to have to come before the full committee anyway."

"Can I call you back about this?"

"Of course, but I hope you can let me know before noon. Because of this damn news leak I think it's important that we get McCord's complete story as soon as possible."

Lipset had been sitting in the office. He had no other place to sit. Although he appeared to be busy proofreading the typed drafts of the summaries of his recent activities on the West Coast, he had obviously heard what I had been saying on the telephone.

"Fensterwald's giving you a snow job," Lipset said.

"What do you mean?" I asked.

"Believe me, Sam," Lipset said, "I know Bud much better than you do. Who wrote that L.A. *Times* story?"

"Bob Jackson."

"Then it's a cinch Fensterwald leaked the story. He's a very, very close buddy of Jackson. They have worked on a number of stories together." Lipset's triumphant smile was annoying.

"Why didn't you warn me?" I asked sharply, disturbed that Lipset had not fully briefed me on Fensterwald.

"What good would it have done? You had to deal with Fensterwald anyhow if you were going to get to McCord. Besides, I didn't want my personal feelings to prejudice your relationship with him."

"But why would Fensterwald leak the story?"

"Because he just loves publicity. Why do you think he latched on to McCord? He's got lots of dough and loves to be where the action is. This was natural for him to get into the limelight. Hell, he wasn't interested in your promises to McCord to keep everything secret. That wouldn't be good for Bud Fensterwald."

It struck me that with Fensterwald under suspicion as a leak, it would be unwise to have any further meetings with McCord in Fensterwald's office. It could be bugged.

When Fensterwald called back to tell me that McCord would meet with Fred Thompson and me in the afternoon, I suggested that we select a neutral place for the meeting, since I thought that his office and the Senate office building were both being watched by newsmen. I suggested my law school office. No reporter would think of staking out the law school. Fensterwald agreed and we set 6 P.M. as the time of the meeting.

Fred Thompson and I walked the six blocks to the Georgetown University Law Center for our meeting with McCord and Fensterwald. When they arrived, I introduced them to Fred, closed my office door and began to take my note pad from my brief case.

"You may not need that, Sam," Fensterwald interrupted me. "Jim has something he wants to say first."

McCord cleared his throat. His face was grim and very tired-looking. He gave the impression of a man with a heavy burden on his shoulders. He spoke in the same low, almost inaudible voice. "I feel I have been compromised," he said. "I entered into my relationship with you, Mr. Dash, with the greatest of trust. These news leaks right after our meeting are in violation of our understanding. I have discussed this with Mr. Fensterwald and have decided that I do not want to have these informal meetings. I prefer to give my information under oath to Senator Ervin or to the full Senate committee."

I was angry at the insinuation in McCord's statement. "It was you and your counsel who insisted that our committee make a press statement about your cooperation with us. And I did not say anything in that statement about the substance of the information you gave me. Are you suggesting that I leaked the story to the L.A. *Times?*"

Fensterwald interjected. "It is our position that it doesn't matter whether you did or didn't. The fact of the matter is that we met with you in good faith and after that meeting there was a leak to the newspapers that Jim had implicated Magruder and Dean. Now we're meeting again here with you and Fred Thompson, the minority counsel. This thing is being dragged out at the staff level and what Jim wants is to tell his story under oath to the committee."

I was becoming even angrier at what seemed to be a game Fensterwald and McCord were playing for some devious purpose. "How do I know that you or McCord didn't give the story out to the newspapers?"

McCord seemed indignant. "I haven't talked to any news reporters.* It is ridiculous to suggest that I have. I want to tell my story in a proper forum."

"What reason on earth would I have to leak the story?" Fensterwald asked. "Sam, I'm not accusing you personally. But we have no guarantee that if Jim gives you more information today, we won't read about it in the newspapers tomorrow."

"You can be almost sure of a story getting out if McCord talks to the full committee, even in executive session," I said to Fensterwald. "In any event, I don't like your attempting to dictate how this investigation will be conducted."

Fred Thompson remained silent listening to the discussion. He now spoke up. "The way it looks to me, Sam, the problems of leaks isn't what is bothering these gentlemen. I think McCord doesn't want to say anything now because of my presence. I take it he believes that I'm a pipeline to the White House. Isn't that your real problem, Mr. Fensterwald?"

"Well, that's part of it," Fensterwald replied.

"Then, what if I just leave the room and you talk to Sam Dash alone? Would you be willing to carry on the interview if I do that?"

McCord answered Fred's question. "No, that would not satisfy me. I have information that I want to give to the Senate committee. I think all the facts should come out. My life has been threatened, my family has been threatened. But I don't care. There has been too much perjury so far and I want the whole story to come out. But I want to testify before the senators under oath."

McCord's voice was stubborn, and it was clear that he was not going to change his mind. It occurred to me that McCord really wanted to get his story out publicly as well as tell it to important officials, such as the United States senators on our committee. He could accomplish both by a leak from a meeting with our full committee.

"All right," I told McCord, "I will tell Senator Ervin of your desire to appear before the committee. I will oppose such a session, but if the senators want to have one with you, we can set up a hearing very quickly. The committee meets tomorrow afternoon, and we probably

*In the book McCord later wrote about his Watergate experiences, he admitted he had leaked the story to Bob Jackson, of the L.A. *Times*.

can arrange for an executive session to take your testimony the following day."

Angry and frustrated over the turn of events, I walked back with Fred to the Senate office building. Fensterwald and McCord were screwing things up, I told myself. The walk in the brisk air had been refreshing, but it did not dispel my disappointment over the faulty start of my investigation.

McCord's tactics worked. The committee at its meeting on March 27 voted to hear McCord's testimony under oath at a special executive session of the full committee set for the following day. The senators were eager to take over the investigation. Some believed the limelight belonged to them and appeared to be responding to the instinct of the politician. They were sitting on the hottest committee in the Congress and a sensational witness like McCord was irresistible.

Senator Talmadge voiced a different concern. He took a long puff on the cigar he seemed always to be smoking. His lean face was weather-lined and appeared stern. This harsh appearance, I was to learn, masked a warm and generous personality and an incisive legal mind. "Seems to me we better get this McCord fella in executive session as quickly as possible," Talmadge said. "He's made some mighty serious charges against two high-placed officials. One of them is the President's counsel. We better see if he can substantiate them, because if he's making wild statements it's our duty to set the record straight. Otherwise we'll get the reputation of acting like the old McCarthy committee."

Actually, my plan for staff interrogation of McCord and follow-up investigation was better suited to achieve Talmadge's objective. Had Senator Ervin supported me at this very first meeting of the committee since its organizational meeting on February 21, Talmadge would have readily gone along with my recommendation. And Inouye and Montoya would have followed Ervin's and Talmadge's leadership.

But Senator Ervin was in no mood to offer leadership that morning. The day before, he had received a family telephone call informing him that his younger brother had died. They had been very close and the death was a deeply wounding loss for the senator. He had delayed his sad journey home to Morganton in order to preside at the committee meeting. He thought the meeting too important to miss because it was the first working session of the Committee and he believed McCord's disclosures made it unusually significant.

Although Ervin's mind was not on the discussion of how the committee should deal with McCord, he had caught its drift. He knew that most of the senators wanted to question McCord and were not satisfied to leave this dramatic turn of events to me. He wanted most of all to preserve harmony among the committee members before he left Washington. He was almost brusque when he expressed his support of a committee executive session hearing for McCord the following day. "I think this is an important opportunity for the committee," he said. "McCord is the first Watergate burglar to break his silence, and it's a tribute to the committee that he is willing to trust us with this information. I can't say that I blame him for not wanting to talk to the FBI or to the prosecutor. I have serious questions myself about the way the government investigated the Watergate matter."

I started to object, but bit my lip and remained silent. Without Ervin's backing, it would be no use anyway. I realized I would have to prepare better for future committee meetings by briefing Ervin in advance and obtaining his support on crucial questions.

Senator Baker, who had seated himself as close to Senator Ervin as the space by the side of Ervin's desk permitted, crossed his legs and said, "I've got a hunch that McCord is out to save his own skin. He's probably trying to reach out for some big names to get a break from Sirica. Sure, we should take his testimony, and especially take it under oath. But I think we should be very wary about what he tells us and we should get him to document chapter and verse. I'm not ready to share Dash's confidence in McCord's credibility." Baker paused, then said softly to Ervin, "I'm very sorry to hear about your brother's death, Sam. We could postpone McCord's hearing for a couple of days until you get back."

"No, I don't think we should put off getting McCord's evidence until I get back. You can all go ahead without me, although I would like to be there and hear what McCord has to say. But it's important that you have the hearing tomorrow. You can preside over it, Howard." Ervin suggested we use S-143, his other office in the Capitol. "It's the office I hide out in when I want to be alone," he said. "It will make a nice hearing room and will give you more privacy."

"But why do we need privacy?" Senator Weicker asked. "I completely disagree that we should hear McCord in secret executive session. The whole country now knows that McCord is talking to this committee and I think we should hold a public hearing to take his testimony. I think this committee will make a big mistake if it starts out doing its work behind closed doors."

Ervin was surprised by Weicker's recommendation of a public hearing. "But, Lowell, we haven't the slightest idea what McCord is going to tell us. He may have defamatory information about individuals we will want to further investigate before publicly airing it. From what Sam Dash says, a good deal of his information is hearsay and we will want to determine how much hearsay testimony, if any, we want to allow at our public hearings. I just think it's very unwise to put a witness right out there in the public before the staff or the committee knows what he's going to say."

Weicker stood up and walked over to lean against a section of Ervin's wall-length crammed bookshelves. "Mr. Chairman, I must respectfully disagree with you. I think what we are doing now, meeting privately in this office, while the press is crowded in the hallway on the other side of the door, is totally wrong. There has been too much secrecy and concealment in this Watergate mess. The most refreshing thing we can do is to open up the doors and let the press come in so that even our meetings would be public. The people want to know what we're doing. I think we should be careful not to create the appearance of covering up evidence, although I know damn well that this committee is not going to conceal anything. Please understand me, I have complete trust in you, Mr. Chairman, and the other members of the committee, but appearances are just as important as what we are in fact doing. Let McCord tell his story out there in public. The committee can rule on questions of hearsay and can announce that we are going to follow up any accusations McCord makes by a thorough investigation and that we will produce publicly the results of that investigation."

Talmadge spoke up firmly. "Putting McCord on at a public hearing would be the most dangerous and irresponsible thing this committee could do. The chairman's absolutely right. We can't put on public testimony until we do our homework and develop the facts which should be presented to the public. I move that the committee hold an executive session hearing tomorrow afternoon for the purpose of taking Mr. McCord's testimony under oath." The committee voted six to one in support of Talmadge's motion.

As we left Senator Ervin's office after the meeting the reporters who had camped outside in the hallway gathered around individual senators seeking to learn what had happened in the meeting. Some of the reporters ran after me asking if I would tell them what actions the committee had taken. I replied that I would not comment on what occurred in a private meeting of the committee. The reporters ran back to the senators. The largest crowd was around Senator Weicker. Newspapers that evening and the following morning carried the full details of our meeting, quoting "Senate sources." Highlighting the stories were Senator Weicker's call for the committee to do its business publicly and the committee's vote to hear McCord in secret session on Wednesday afternoon, March 28.

Rufus walked back with me to my office after the meeting. When I closed my office door, Rufus shook his head in astonishment. "In all the years that I've been up here on the Hill I have never seen a performance like the one Weicker put on at the meeting. Now, he's just a freshman senator, a low man on the totem pole on the committee. A senator in that position never speaks out and challenges the chairman of a committee the way Weicker did. Senator Ervin is just too nice a person. Another chairman would have quickly put Weicker in his place in no uncertain terms."

"Weicker worries me," I said. "Can he really want us to do all of our work out in the open or is he just trying to get some publicity for himself?"

Rufus was sure Weicker's motive was publicity. But it didn't really matter why he was playing to the news media—the same threat of leaks of committee strategy and evidence existed. I expressed surprise that the committee had not tried to restrain him.

Rufus said simply, "Nobody up here can stop a senator from doing anything he wants to do." I was to learn that he was right.

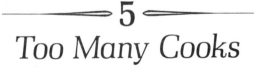

5

Too Many Cooks

MCCORD'S PRIVATE HEARING BEFORE THE FULL COMMITTEE WAS A disaster. The committee was not prepared to ask the right questions or to offer McCord the necessary protections of immunity to permit him to make full disclosures on his own. And McCord found himself at times unwillingly and disappointedly trapped into silence, when what he wanted was to reveal all he knew. He felt betrayed and the senators felt misled. I was angry at both for rejecting, for selfish reasons, my plan to obtain McCord's evidence informally.

McCord had prepared a new memorandum providing the details of his charges against Dean and Magruder. The memo identified the biggest name yet to be accused of Watergate involvement—former Attorney General John Mitchell.

But McCord had no firsthand knowledge about Mitchell, Magruder or Dean. He could only say what he had learned from his boss, G. Gordon Liddy: that Magruder supervised the intelligence plan at the Committee to Re-Elect the President; that Mitchell had to approve the plan; and that Mitchell, Dean, Magruder and Liddy were gathered in Mitchell's office in the Justice Department in February 1972 to hear Liddy present his wiretapping and bugging plans.

McCord expected to be embraced by the committee as a witness with inside information who had voluntarily come forward. Instead he found himself subjected to rather hostile cross-examination aimed at proving his information to be unreliable hearsay. McCord never claimed in his meetings with me or in his memoranda that his information about the involvement of higher officials in Watergate was based on anything more than hearsay. Yet he had believed Liddy's statements to him would be helpful to the committee as important leads for our investigation.

McCord even offered possible ways to corroborate his story. He told us that Sylvia Panarites, Liddy's first secretary at CRP, might have typed budget sheets of the bugging plan and that Sally Harmony, who later became Liddy's secretary, might have retyped information coming out of the Democratic National Committee headquarters. He also said that several large, elaborately prepared charts Liddy told him he was going to use at the meeting in Mitchell's office to illustrate political intelligence plans might still exist. Liddy claimed that he was not going to destroy them, despite an order from Dean, because they cost $7,000 to prepare and he wanted to keep them. McCord also provided the important information that Robert Reisner, then Magruder's appointments secretary, kept a log of Magruder's meetings. McCord even departed from his usual tendency to understate facts by saying he had an "impression" from something Hunt had said that Charles Colson, special counsel to the President, was involved in the planning of the political bugging.

Despite McCord's apparent earnestness in giving this information to the committee, the senators demonstrated that they were not impressed with McCord as a witness. Senator Talmadge snapped a series of short, sharp questions to McCord which reduced his testimony about Mitchell, Dean and Magruder to the bare hearsay that it was.

"Did you ever have any conversations with Mr. Mitchell regarding this Watergate incident?"

"No, sir."

"Did you ever have any conversations with Mr. Colson regarding this Watergate incident?"

"No, sir."

"Did you ever have any conversations with Mr. Dean regarding this Watergate incident?"

"No, sir."

"Did you ever have any conversations with Mr. Magruder regarding this Watergate incident?"

"No, sir."

"Did you ever see the charts?" Talmadge asked impatiently.

McCord explained that he had only seen them wrapped in brown wrapping paper.

Talmadge snapped, "To your own knowledge, you do not know what they contained?"

"Other than what Liddy said, no, sir."

Talmadge paused, gripped the table with both hands, leaned forward looking directly at McCord and asked with a tone of finality in his voice, "Do you have any information whatever except some statements of Gordon Liddy's that these individuals that you named were engaged in this operation?"

McCord replied hoarsely, "Only as I've described it previously concerning the joint conversation with Mr. Hunt."

"Mr. Hunt or Mr. Liddy?" Talmadge wanted the record clear.

"In the presence of Mr. Liddy, yes, sir."

Talmadge sat back in his chair and threw his concluding question at McCord. "Have Mr. Hunt and Mr. Liddy been indicted and convicted?"

"Yes, sir."

"I have no further questions at the present time." Talmadge looked away from McCord, picked up the long cigar he had placed on the ashtray when he began his questioning, and puffed at it slowly.

McCord was visibly frustrated and ill-at-ease. He became more cautious. There was much he could tell that was not hearsay—threats he had received and promises of hush money and executive clemency—but he held back, promising to prepare additional memoranda for the committee. And more important, he had hoped to receive immunity from the committee as a result of his revealing the possible involvement of Mitchell, Dean and Magruder. He indicated there were other activities involving Hunt, Liddy and CRP which he wanted to talk about freely to the committee, but thought that without immunity he might be vulnerable to further criminal prosecution.

However, at Baker's recommendation, the committee turned McCord down in his request for immunity for the time being. Baker told the committee in a brief executive session, with McCord and Fensterwald out of the room, that McCord had not provided sufficient solid information to justify the committee's giving him a blanket immunity for everything he might say in the future.

When McCord and Fensterwald were readmitted to the hearing room, Baker informed them of the committee's decision not to offer McCord immunity at that time. In the questions that followed, when the Senators strayed into areas not directly related to McCord's criminal conviction, McCord clammed up and took the protection of the Fifth Amendment—a stand he had not expected or wanted to take before the Senate committee.

More than ever now I was convinced that I had to get back control of the investigation. By working with McCord informally on a staff level I would be able to determine whether to recommend to Ervin that McCord be offered immunity by the committee. But late in the afternoon, the committee, at a standstill with McCord, scheduled another formal executive session hearing with McCord for the following week to allow him to prepare the memoranda he had promised. The committee adjourned and McCord left resentful and dejected. I was determined to persuade Ervin, when he returned to Washington, to cancel the new hearing.

Practically the entire executive session hearing was leaked to the press. McCord's naming of Mitchell became a sensational news story. The *Post*'s Woodward and Bernstein might just as well have been present in the hearing room, so precise were their details. Even worse, all the news stories emphasized that the evidence McCord gave the committee was only hearsay and that he had no corroborative proof to back up his accusations. My strategy for our investigation, based on McCord's cooperation, had been seriously damaged. For effective follow-up interrogation of other witnesses from the White House and from the Committee to Re-Elect the President it was important that the scope and details of McCord's evidence be kept secret.

In fact, I had hoped that we could create the impression, by keeping a tight lid on what McCord was telling us, that McCord was providing detailed and incriminating evidence about the complicity of others in the Watergate break-in. I was counting on the natural tendency of persons possessing important evidence or information to want to get their share of the credit by coming forward if they believed that the whole story was going to come out anyway. Also, reluctant witnesses who had to be subpoenaed might hesitate to withhold information or falsify the facts if they believed we had solid evidence from McCord.

Knowing the limits of McCord's story, President Nixon publicly denied that his counsel Dean had any involvement in Watergate. A spokesman for the Committee to Re-Elect the President issued a statement for Mitchell and Magruder denying they had any knowledge of Watergate and charging McCord with making wild statements to get a more lenient sentence from Sirica.

Who was responsible for these leaks? Fensterwald or McCord? I did not trust them since the first leak. But the news stories claimed Senate sources. Who the hell on our committee or staff was shooting his mouth off? My first suspect was Senator Weicker. He had wanted McCord's testimony to be given publicly in the first place. Also, Woodward and Bernstein reported in one of their stories that Weicker had confirmed the accuracy of the leaked information.

Whoever it was, he was seriously hampering the committee's ability to carry out its mandate. McCord's revelations had dramatically defined the complexity and gravity of our mission. If the former Attorney General, the President's counsel and the deputy director of the President's reelection campaign were indeed involved in the Watergate affair, then we were at the brink of a scandal that could dwarf Teapot Dome. The committee's chances for success at uncovering the facts of wrongdoing of such magnitude, where the stakes were so high, depended considerably on its ability to discipline itself to safeguard its evidence.

When they exploited the committee's leaks, Woodward and Bernstein were no longer engaged in investigative reporting, as they themselves have admitted. They had found an easy mark or two on the committee and were lazily rewriting the committee's investigative product. Their exposure of the committee's evidence was not for the purpose of preventing a cover-up, for they certainly knew Sam Ervin's committee would soon publicly and fully reveal this same evidence. Rather, it was their haste to produce "scoops" which led them to raid the committee's investigation—and imperil its continued access to witnesses and evidence. By employing this increasingly popular press tactic of hit-and-run reporting, they apparently forgot the initial purpose of their earlier effective investigative reporting, which had helped support the creation of our committee and its investigation.

When the first news stories were published following the executive session hearing, I was tempted to call Senator Ervin in Morganton, North Carolina, to vent my feeling of frustration. But I decided not to disturb him while he was with his family preparing for the funeral of his brother. However, the following morning, when I read the Washington *Post,* I was shocked to find that Woodward and Bernstein had been told that we had subpoenaed Sally Harmony, Sylvia Panarites and Robert Reisner. They not only reported that the subpoenas had been issued, but they provided a full explanation, based on McCord's testimony before us, of the information we expected to get from these witnesses.

"Goddamn it!" I found myself shouting in the kitchen as I read the paper. "We might as well conduct this investigation right in the middle of Pennsylvania Avenue with everybody looking on!" That was it. I had to talk to Senator Ervin right away. When Ervin answered the telephone at his home in North Carolina, I was sorry I had made the call. The exuberant voice I usually experienced in my talks with Ervin was gone. Rather, he spoke quietly, almost indifferently. I apologized for interrupting him during the sad occasion. But I pursued my reason for calling. "Senator, our investigation is falling apart and we might as well close it down, unless you insist on proper professional methods of procedure. I would like to meet with you as soon as you return to your office Monday to recommend what I think has to be done."

"I have been reading about these awful leaks down here. They have disturbed me terribly. Who do you think has been talking to the press?"

"I have my suspicions, Senator, but I would rather talk to you personally about this, and not on the telephone."

"All right, let's meet in my office Monday morning and talk about it." I went to Senator Ervin's office that Monday prepared to give an ultimatum: either I would be given control of the investigation, and the senators stay out of it until the staff was ready to present evidence before the committee, or I would quit.

I did not have to say it. Ervin was completely receptive to my statement of the crisis the committee was facing. "I don't believe the members of this committee have any business meddling in the investigation." Ervin said. "That's why we hired you. You have to run this investigation with an adequate staff. I see ourselves, the members of the committee, as judges receiving the evidence you will present to us. There just isn't any other way to do it, or we will surely fail and look like fools before the public."

I anticipated an explosive time the next day, when he assembled the committee to restore order to the investigation, because I did not think the senators would readily remove themselves from the investigation without a fight. I was wrong. It was not Ervin's style to assert his authority with his colleagues. He preferred to run the committee by gentle persuasion. I had not counted on the overriding rule of the Senate as a club—the rule of civility. Quietly Ervin expressed his concern over the black eye the committee was getting because of the leaks from McCord's testimony. He did not even suggest that any member of the committee or the committee staff was at fault. Rather, he said the leaks must have come from Fensterwald or McCord.

He then recommended that the best way to avoid future leaks and to permit a systematic and thorough investigation, was to place the control of the investigation in the hands of the chief counsel and the staff. The senators should remove themselves from the investigative process so that they could properly serve as objective judges of the evidence when public hearings were held. Without debate, Senator Talmadge moved that the chairman's recommendation be adopted. The motion was carried unanimously. My blood pressure deescalated rapidly and I sat back marveling at how easily a problem that had kept me annoyed and frustrated for days could be resolved in the serenity of S. 143 in the Capitol.

Ervin also gently suggested to the senators that they try not to make public statements about the committee's work, although he recognized their right to do so. Senator Baker added, "I think we should also direct Sam Dash and Fred Thompson to order the staff to not talk to reporters. And anybody violating that rule should not be given a second chance, but should be fired." I agreed to implement that directive immediately.

Then Baker surprised me by an effort to rush us into hearings even though we were not ready. "I think we should be in public hearings no later than two weeks from now," Baker said to Ervin. "This is the surest way to get our work done and get the evidence out to the public before everything is leaked out."

Senator Talmadge was more cautious. "Although I think that the public will get sick and tired of this committee if we drag things out, I don't want public hearings unless the staff can get solid evidence to corroborate what Mr. McCord has told this committee. That was nothing but pure hearsay, and we should not expose that to the public without corroboration. Otherwise we will be laughed at as damn fools."

I told the committee that I anticipated a difficult investigation and that I agreed with Senator Talmadge that we needed to obtain strong corroboration of McCord's testimony. I expressed concern over a two-week limitation on the investigation before public hearings, and couldn't promise we would be able to complete the investigation within that short time span.

Baker fixed his eyes on me sternly. "Well, you better do the best you can," he said. "We're not going to play around with this investigation, and the public doesn't want us to. Just you be ready for public hearings in about two weeks."

I started to reply to Baker, but Senator Ervin interrupted. "We can't put any fixed time limits on a complicated investigation like the one we're charged with under the Senate resolution," Ervin said. "Certainly, it would be wonderful if we could be ready to have public hearings in two weeks. But I suggest we just let the investigation go forward and wait to hear from our chief counsel when he's ready for public hearings. And we gently remind him that we don't expect to wait too long." Mildly chastised for his attempt to usurp the chairman's prerogative, Baker remained silent.

After the meeting, I told Terry Lenzner, Jim Hamilton and Hal Lipset about the committee's action. Terry and Jim had just joined the staff, and because of the leak, had already begun to worry about the reality of an independent staff investigation, which I had promised them. They were reassured by my report of the meeting. But I added a warning about the committee's agreement that the staff have control over the investigation. The responsibility to produce was ours, and we could not blame anybody else if something went wrong.

I could not imagine that Senator Weicker would still be making headlines in the papers and headaches for us after Ervin's warning. But the next day Weicker held a press conference and called for the resignation of Nixon's chief of staff, H.R. Haldeman, on the ground that Haldeman had to take responsibility for the broad campaign of political espionage that had been directed against Democrats in the 1972 presidential campaign. We had no evidence against Haldeman. I thought Weicker had now gone too far and exposed the committee to a valid charge that it was acting irresponsibly.

There was only one solution. The chairman and vice chairman would have to make a public statement announcing that the committee had no evidence implicating Haldeman with the Watergate break-in. Both Ervin and Baker agreed with my recommendation, and I prepared a press statement which Ervin released. It said in part: "In the interest of fairness and justice, the Committee wishes to state publicly that as of this time it has received no evidence of any nature connecting Mr. Haldeman to any illegal activities."

Weicker turned cool toward me for weeks, but my prime concern was not his feelings but moving forward with the investigation. We had little time, and I wanted to get back to questioning McCord. Fensterwald was not pleased when I told him of the committee's decision to require McCord to give his information to me before any further meetings with the committee.

Judge Sirica again postponed McCord's sentencing to allow him to complete his testimony to us and the grand jury, and suggested that McCord deal with us first. But Fensterwald went directly to U.S. Attorney Earl Silbert to seek immunity for McCord, since our committee had refused it to him. McCord desperately wanted to tell everything he knew to an official body without creating more legal difficulties for himself. Our committee had been his first choice (aside from Sirica), but we had failed to give him the immediate forum he wanted. So he turned to the grand jury and the U.S. attorney's office, despite his earlier claim of distrust of these agencies. He did not seem to care anymore about the White House learning about what he had to say. Sirica granted McCord immunity at Silbert's request, and McCord was lost to us for at least ten days while he appeared before the grand jury.

Shortly after McCord began testifying before the grand jury, most of the information he was giving to the prosecutors or the grand jury also began leaking to the press. Frankly, I gained some solace from the leaks. For a while, at least, another agency of government, with tighter security procedures than our Senate committee could maintain, was demonstrating that it could not control its blabbermouths. But the leaks were particularly disturbing because they contained information that

McCord had refused to give the committee. McCord was obviously telling the grand jury more because Silbert had obtained immunity for him and we had not. But the detailed release of his new information to the press was playing havoc with our investigation and morale.

Yet, while I was waiting for McCord to complete his grand jury testimony, my expanding staff made progress in their effort to corroborate McCord's hearsay account of the roles of Mitchell, Dean and Magruder in Liddy's political bugging plans. They pursued the recommendations McCord had made at the March 28 executive session hearing by calling in Magruder's former appointments secretary, Robert Reisner, and Liddy's former secretaries, Sylvia Panarites and Sally Harmony.

The most exciting find came early in these interviews. Reisner told us that Vicky Chern was responsible for setting up Magruder's meetings. She was then contacted and voluntarily appeared and told us she had kept a duplicate copy of Magruder's appointments in a green diary. She said she would look for the book, and would bring it to us if she could find it. Two days later, on April 4, she came back with the green diary and submitted to a second interview with Jim Hamilton, Hal Lipset and Don Sanders (a newly appointed minority staff member).

Hamilton examined the Magruder appointment book and suddenly stopped at an entry for February 4, 1972, at 4 P.M. Appearing next to that date were the initials A.G. and the names Gordon Liddy and John Dean. There it was—the February 1972 meeting attended by the attorney general, Magruder, Liddy and Dean which McCord had heard about from Liddy! Another entry on January 27 indicated a similar meeting.

Vicky Chern said that she had informed Magruder and Paul O'Brien, counsel for CRP, that she was coming to the committee and that she had found the green book containing Magruder's appointments, including the January 27 and the February 4 entries. Magruder began to fear that the cover-up would quickly unravel.

In June 1973 after our committee had obtained a grant of immunity for him, Magruder told me he knew everything would come out when he learned we had subpoenaed Reisner. *Neither Reisner nor Vicky Chern had been questioned by the FBI or called before the grand jury during the first Watergate investigation.*

Magruder also said that when his diary had been subpoenaed by the grand jury in August 1972 and he had been called to explain the reasons for the January 27 and February 4, 1972, meetings in the attorney general's office, Mitchell, Dean and he met and agreed on a false story for him to give to the grand jury. In this perjured testimony, Magruder explained that the first meeting, January 27, had been canceled and the second meeting, February 4, related only to a review of the legal problems involved in campaign financing. On March 29, the very day Magruder learned that our committee had served a subpoena on Reisner, Magruder met with Mitchell and Dean at the White House to obtain their assurance that they would stick to the false story about the meetings he had given to the grand jury in August if they were called as witnesses before our committee or the reconvened Watergate grand jury.

But Dean, who later told me about this March 29 meeting during a secret interrogation session, spurned Magruder's desperate plea to support his perjured testimony. He told Magruder that if he had to testify before the Senate committee or the grand jury, he would tell the truth about what had been discussed at both the January and February meetings in Mitchell's office. This clash of former conspirators, sparked by McCord's revelations and by our questioning of Reisner and Chern, formed a crucial part of the chain of irreversible events that led Dean and then Magruder to go to the grand jury and our committee and to finally expose the true story of the Watergate break-in and cover-up.

In addition to Vicky Chern's diary, we uncovered other pieces of McCord's jigsaw puzzle. A number of CRP secretaries and staff assistants remembered seeing Liddy, sometime in January 1972, awkwardly carrying a thin, large package, about four feet by four feet, and wrapped in brown paper, which they believed contained charts. Reisner also recalled Liddy asking him, just prior to a meeting in the attorney general's office, whether he knew if Mitchell had an easel. He thought this was sometime in February 1972. He called Mitchell's secretary in the Department of Justice and learned that she could not locate an easel. A hurried search in the CRP offices finally turned up an easel for Liddy.

Reisner told us he had a strange conversation with Magruder about the easel shortly before he came to his interview with us. Magruder had first reminded him that he should be careful about what he told us because "people's lives and futures are at stake." Then Magruder told him that the easel story Reisner had informed CRP lawyer Paul O'Brien he was going to reveal to us was incredible. "How come you remember an easel? There wasn't an easel," Magruder had complained to Reisner.

His grand jury testimony completed, McCord returned. Having received immunity from the federal prosecutors, he no longer requested it of our committee. Our earlier disagreements were forgotten. Also, McCord now did not insist on first preparing memoranda before answering questions. He was ready to speak openly and freely. In contrast with Fensterwald's earlier grandstanding and publicity ploys, McCord continued to communicate a sense of stoic dignity. My earlier interrogation sessions with McCord had convinced me of his sincerity and basic integrity. Now these qualities were even more evident as he quietly and thoroughly, with the exactness of a trained investigator, related to me and Fred Thompson what he knew about the Watergate break-in and cover-up conspiracy.

During the many hours we spent together in G-334, our interrogation room, I could not help wondering at the improbable paradox: McCord, the Watergate burglar, who was also McCord, the decorated and dedicated federal law enforcement and intelligence agent.

James McCord was born in 1924 in Waurika, Oklahoma. One could imagine his boyhood in that small Western town, where pride for the Stars and Stripes was still fundamental and was demonstrated more openly than in the big cities in the East. He must have thrilled at the exploits of G-men, told in the pulp magazines popular with boys growing up then.

At eighteen, McCord went to work for the Federal Bureau of Investigation in Washington, D.C. A year later, during World War II, he became an officer in the Army Air Corps. After the war, he returned to the FBI for three years as a special agent in San Diego and San Francisco. Then, in 1951, at the age of twenty-seven, he joined the Central Intelligence Agency and served as a security officer until 1970, when he retired, receiving the Distinguished Service Award for outstanding performance of duty with the CIA.

Two years later, McCord, at Liddy's direction, burglarized the headquarters of the Democratic National Committee at the Watergate and wiretapped the telephones of Lawrence O'Brien, the committee chairman, and Spencer Oliver, a committee official. Why?

During our many interviews of secretaries and staff members of the Committee to Re-Elect the President, I learned that McCord was the best-liked CRP official. They remembered him as being warm and considerate, always willing to take the time to discuss their problems and to respect them as individuals. This description differed markedly from the reports we consistently received of the rude, brusque and self-important behavior of most of the other CRP officials. McCord devoted a considerable part of his time to humanitarian causes, and especially to the problems of mentally retarded children. Having a child who was mentally retarded, he displayed a deep sensitivity to the concerns of other parents of handicapped children.

I developed a genuine affection for Jim McCord. He had the patriot's love for his country. His was not the flag-waving America-first brand of patriotism but a fierce and proud affection for his countrymen generally, and for the agencies of law enforcement especially, which he believed were the principal protectors of the country. McCord's testimony revealed, however, that his concept of his country did not include an appreciation of the constitutional processes that made it unique as a free republic. He simply had a blind love affair with America, and had spent his entire professional life as a federal agent trying to protect her. As we were to learn later, a similar view of the country was held by other Watergate figures. But the crucial difference was that McCord, unlike most of the others, gave his devotion unselfishly, without greedily seeking a *quid pro quo* in power or treasure.

It was his misguided respect for government superior officers that had led him to become a member of the burglary team that broke into the Democratic National Committee headquarters in the Watergate. He *believed* he was working for the attorney general of the United States and the White House. How indignantly he had answered "Never!" when I asked whether he would have agreed to participate in the break-in and wiretapping project if he had thought he was working only for G. Gordon Liddy.

His perception of himself as playing a familiar officially authorized role in the Watergate break-in was contradicted when the White House and John Mitchell sought to portray his actions as part of a cheap burglary. He felt totally betrayed by the false suggestions that Watergate was an operation of the CIA, to which he was almost fanatically devoted. It was his complete disillusionment that principally motivated him to break his silence and make the first deep crack in what had been a solid wall of cover-up.

When the long interrogation sessions ended and McCord was about to leave G-334, I walked to the door and put my hand on his shoulder.

"Jim," I faltered, "how the hell could *you* have . . ."

"Broken into Watergate?" he finished for me. McCord's dark eyes looked straight into mine. His voice was hoarse and it broke as he answered, "As I now see it for what it really was, it was an utterly stupid act, inconsistent with anything I have ever done before. Regardless of the punishment I will get from the court, I will regret what I did and pay for it for the rest of my life." He turned and walked down the ground-floor hall of the new Senate office building. I remained in the doorway for a while, feeling very sorry for Jim McCord and overcome by the realization of the madness we were investigating.

In early April an ugly incident occurred that briefly overshadowed our elation at uncovering new evidence. During an interrogation of a witness in my office one morning, Rufus took a phone call for me. I continued questioning the witness while Rufus whispered into the telephone, but I noticed that his face had reddened and he appeared to be deeply disturbed. As soon as he hung up, he motioned for me to join him in the hallway just outside my office. I excused myself from the interrogation and went out to talk with him.

"That was Senator Ervin on the phone." Rufus was speaking in a tense whisper. "He says we have to fire Terry Lenzner and wants to see us in his office right away."

"Fire Terry? Why?" I was jolted by his statement.

"He says it's something he's learned about Terry's background and that he'll tell us all about it in his office."

We rushed over to Ervin's office. Why was Ervin talking about firing one of my assistant chief counsel? I was becoming angry. Ervin had agreed that I would have the right to hire my own staff, and I had been delighted to be able to persuade Terry to join me. Already, he had proved to be a tough investigator and I did not want to lose him. Ervin's face was grim when we entered his office. It was obvious that he was uneasy.

When he did speak, he spoke rapidly and with determination. "Sam, Terry Lenzner will have to be removed from the staff. People, whose identities I prefer not to reveal, but who are part of the Democratic leadership and whose political advice I value greatly, have told me that Lenzner's continued presence on the staff will prove very embarrassing to the committee and to me personally!"

"But how could he embarrass you or the committee, Senator?" My throat had tightened, and my voice barely croaked the question. "He's one of the finest young lawyers in the country and he has a remarkable background."

Ervin shifted repeatedly in his chair and his hands shook noticeably on his desk. "I don't doubt that he's a good lawyer, and probably a fine young man, but unfortunately, he has a radical leftist background and has supported some causes which have been very harmful within the Democratic party."

"Terry a radical?" I exclaimed in disbelief. "He was one of the toughest federal prosecutors in the Southern District of New York."

"I am told he worked for the defense team in the Berrigan brothers case," Ervin said.

"But as a lawyer representing a defendant," I replied. That didn't seem reason enough to fire Terry. There had to be something behind Ervin's position that he didn't want to talk about.

"That was a very controversial case in the country," Ervin continued "and even though I personally feel a lawyer has a right to represent an unpopular client, people just won't understand why we have hired one of the Berrigan lawyers to work with us on this investigation which is bound to involve the Nixon administration. I tried to keep this committee from being partisan so that the public will have confidence in what we are doing."

"I can't believe that Terry will be considered a partisan just because he helped represent the Berrigans," I argued.

"Well," Ervin said, "I've been also told that Lenzner was fired by President Nixon from an OEO job because of some radical programs Lenzner was supporting."

I was familiar with the facts of that incident. "But, Senator, that was really an heroic episode in Terry's career. He was fighting the administration's effort to deprive the poor from obtaining effective legal services authorized under the OEO program. Terry had the support of the Bar Association in that fight."

"But don't you see, Sam, he was fired by the President. It doesn't matter how it happened. The fact is, he left the administration after a bitter dispute with the White House. Add to that his being in the Berrigan case, which was a major prosecution sponsored by the administration, and you can understand how people will think that we have a Nixon hater on our staff who cannot be objective. He will taint everything we do. People will have a suspicion that he is carrying out a vendetta against the administration. We will be fair game for that charge with Terry on the staff."

I was beginning to feel helpless. Ervin was unwilling to be persuaded by any argument that would support keeping Terry. This was the first time Ervin had interfered with me in an area in which he had given me independent responsibility. I had to think about how his decision would affect my ability to carry out my duties as chief counsel. Firing Terry would clearly have a serious impact on the morale of the rest of the staff and I wondered when the news got out whether I would be able to hire any really good, courageous young lawyers.

I made one last effort. "Will you do me a favor, Senator?" I asked. "Before you make a final decision on Terry, will you let me bring him up to your office this afternoon and have him hear from you why you think he must leave the staff, and let him have an opportunity to respond. You certainly owe him at least this procedure in all fairness."

"I don't see how it's going to make any difference. The decision has been made and I won't change my mind. But all right, bring Terry to my office at two o'clock." Ervin's face was still flushed as he closed our meeting. He had acquiesced reluctantly to my request for a confrontation between Terry and him. I left his office thinking Ervin resented my having put him in a position which could only be embarrassing for him.

I asked Jim Hamilton and Hal Lipset to join me in a meeting with Terry—this was a staff matter. Briefly, I recounted what Ervin had said in our meeting. The blood seemed to drain from Terry's face.

"But that's outrageous, so terribly unfair," he managed to say. "Me a left-wing radical! Why, I'm a member of the Board of Overseers of Harvard University. Does Ervin know that?"

I didn't know that myself. I already knew so much about Terry when I hired him that I didn't bother to read his résumé.

Terry continued, "I've given up everything I was planning to do and announced to the whole world that I was going to be one of your chief deputies in the Watergate investigation. What the hell do I tell people now? What have I done?" Terry added that he could not keep quiet when people asked why he was kicked off the committee. He said he had some good friends at *The New York Times.* "They'll blast the hell out of Ervin and the committee," he warned bitterly. I tried to calm him down, and explained to him that we still had a chance to persuade Ervin to change his mind.

"But what if he doesn't change his mind?" Terry asked.

"Then we will have time to decide what to do. Frankly, I can't see myself staying on as chief counsel if Ervin won't back down."

Rufus had been listening uncomfortably to the discussion. His loyalty to Senator Ervin weighed heavily on him and he urged us not to do anything that would hurt the senator.

"But what about me?" Terry burst out. "Is it fair that my guts are spilled all over the street?"

"Rufus, we can't look at this as a political matter," I said. "I didn't take this job to get Senator Ervin reelected. Ervin had to know he was exposing himself to political risks when he agreed to be chairman of this committee. We have to go back to Senator Ervin with Terry to convince him that what he wants to do is just plain wrong."

The meeting in Ervin's office was highly unpleasant. Ervin started by restating his position to Terry with a tone of finality. "I am sure you are a very fine young man, Mr. Lenzner. And an honorable and capable lawyer who could give great assistance to this committee. But we have a terribly difficult assignment given to us by a unanimous Senate, and we just can't take the chance of letting our enemies pull us off on some side road by attacking us for staffing the committee with partisan enemies of the President. No matter how unfair such accusations may be, if there is something in your background, as unfortunately there is, that will give them an opportunity to launch such an attack. We just can't take the chance of letting ourselves be open to it."

"On that basis, Senator, who on your staff or, for that matter, on the committee is not vulnerable?" Terry was deeply agitated and his voice was strained and hoarse.

"That may be true, but you have to admit that you got yourself involved in some mighty controversial matters that make you an obvious target. I don't disagree with the things you've done. They're the duties of a lawyer serving the interests and traditions of our profession. But this is not the time for us to champion your causes. Our investigation is far too important for us to allow it to be sidetracked."

Terry looked pained. "But don't you see, Senator, by asking me to leave the staff, you are condemning me just because I have acted in a professional way as a lawyer. I thought these were the principles you always defended and fought for and it seems incongruous that you think that an irresponsible attack on me would be embarrassing to the committee. I disagree with you. I think the public, the Congress and the legal profession would support you if there was in fact an attack on me and you faced up to it by asserting these principles."

Terry then tried to dispel the criticism against him that he was a left-wing radical. He reviewed for Ervin his entire professional biography, which demonstrated that he had primarily held governmental positions, most of which involved law enforcement activities. He ended by saying, "I'm a member of the Board of Overseers of Harvard University. Would anybody claim that's the kind of position a left-wing radical would hold?"

Ervin's eyes avoided meeting Terry's. He said slowly, "This is not an easy decision for me. But I must do what I think is necessary to protect our committee."

I wanted to prevent Ervin from making what now appeared to be a final judgment against Terry, so I asked him, since it was Friday, to let the matter rest until Monday.

Again I sensed that Ervin was impatient with me for not permitting him a quick and easy way out of his problem. "All right," he said, "I'll think about it over the weekend. But I don't promise to change my mind."

Although I had gained some time, I left the meeting depressed, believing that Ervin would not change his mind. Terry felt the same way and went home early. I, too, couldn't keep my mind on my work and decided to go home and wait out the weekend.

I told Sara what had happened that day. "You can't accept this, Sam," she said. "Otherwise you'll never be able to face the people you respect and who respect you." While I was in the middle of expressing my own doubts of continuing as chief counsel with the committee if Terry was fired, the phone rang. It was Senator Ervin.

"I tried to reach you in your office," Ervin said. "but you had already gone home. I wanted to talk with you as soon as I could. Sam, I want to ask you to forgive me for behaving in a way that I'm now thoroughly ashamed of. I owe you a great debt of gratitude for forcing me to reconsider the very unfair and unjust decision I had made. I'm so glad that you insisted on bringing Terry up to my office and letting me see him and talk to him. He's a very fine young lawyer and a credit to his profession. You chose wisely in hiring him and I know he will be a great help to you in our investigation. I was wrong to listen to attacks on his character, even though they came from people who have my own interest at heart and who have been good political advisers. Please call Terry for me right away and tell him that I admit I was wrong and I am proud to have him as a member of our staff."

Tears welled in my eyes. "Senator, I hoped you would come to this decision. I can only say that it takes a very big man to be able to so openly admit a mistake the way you have just done. I'm very proud to be working for you."

"Call Terry right away because I don't want him to suffer a moment longer than necessary."

I immediately dialed Terry's home number. When I told him about Ervin's call, he exclaimed, "My God! Is that right? That's really great! Ervin's a wonderful man, a really great man to bare himself to you that way. I'm almost speechless. I don't have to tell you what my wife and I have been living through these past hours. I really want to thank you, Sam, for going to bat for me."

Terry's voice had become emotional. We wished each other well and I hung up, feeling very happy.

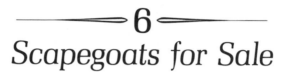

6
Scapegoats for Sale

SENATOR BAKER WAS PUSHING FOR PUBLIC HEARINGS. AT THE COMmittee meeting on April 16 he urged that a date be set. It was obvious that the other senators were also eager to bring the committee out in the open. I offered to try to be ready in a month, and the committee unanimously voted to announce the opening of public hearings on May 15.

Actually I was dismayed at the prospect. When the public hearing announcement was made, I was still concentrating on McCord's disclosures to the committee, which were mostly hearsay. Our independent investigation was producing enough corroborative evidence to meet Talmadge's initial objections to McCord as a hearsay witness and to justify producing McCord at a public hearing. But I believed our hearings would seem shallow and incomplete in contrast to initial public expectations and the sensational news stories of investigative reporters.

Baker's anxiety to have the committee set a date for public hearings occurred at the same time President Nixon indicated he would change his position and allow the appearance of White House witnesses before our committee. Earlier, in February and March, during the Senate Judiciary Committee's confirmation hearings on Patrick Gray for director of the FBI, Nixon had flatly announced, claiming executive privilege, that no White House aides would testify before a Senate committee. Senator Ervin was also a member of the Judiciary Committee and foresaw the implications of the President's position for the Senate Select Committee.

Ervin prided himself as an expert on constitutional law issues, especially those dealing with separation of powers and executive privilege. He was angry that Nixon was claiming an absolute power to withhold the appearance of White House witnesses from congressional committees. He was willing to concede that the President had an implied privilege to refuse disclosure of confidential communications with his aides for the purpose of assisting him to carry out his constitutional and legislative duties. However, Ervin repeatedly emphasized at committee meetings and at press conferences that executive privilege could not shield White House staff members from testifying about conversations in the furtherance of the commission or the cover-up of crimes.

Only two weeks before the President's turnabout and Baker's insistence that the Committee set a date for public hearings, Ervin told the committee at its April 2 meeting that he thought there was an increasing likelihood of a confrontation between the committee and the White House over the testimony of White House aides. His face reddening, he exclaimed, "Why, they have the gumption to suggest that White House witnesses should be permitted what they call informal cooperation—talking to us privately, off the cuff. Well I'm not going to let anybody come down in the night like Nicodemus, and whisper in my ear. For the life of me, I can't see why the White House aides shouldn't be required to give testimony under oath about the wrongdoings of another aide in the White House or in some other department of the executive branch. The President seems to extend executive privilege way out past the atmosphere. What he says is executive privilege is nothing but executive poppycock."

This had become Ervin's biggest issue in his role as chairman of the committee. He was not going to allow the President to assert a power not given to him by the Constitution or the Congress. "Frankly," Ervin said, "under the regular rules of evidence we have a right to draw negative inferences from the President's withholding of information. If the President won't let his aides testify under oath, I think the public can conclude that he is unwilling for the people to get the truth about Watergate."

"Now, Sam," Senator Baker said soothingly, "I don't think that's going to be a problem. I really believe the White House will be willing to negotiate that out with us. I'm sure we'll be able to persuade the

President to let Bob Haldeman, John Ehrlichman, Charles Colson, and a number of the others to come before this committee and testify under oath."

As Baker sought to reassure Ervin that the White House would cooperate with the committee, Ervin's eyebrows were in a state of unusual agitation. "Well, they better, Howard, or I'll insist on sending the sergeant at arms to arrest them and have them tried before the Senate."

"Sam, that just won't be necessary." Baker smiled at Ervin's threat. "I can't imagine the sergeant at arms of the Senate entering the White House and placing handcuffs on Bob Haldeman. They're not going to let it come to that. But there is some work we have to do to get the results we want."

Shortly after Baker made this statement, the White House agreed to negotiate with our committee. Baker and Ervin met with Ehrlichman, and Fred Thompson and I met with Leonard Garment, counsel to the President. Ervin told me that Ehrlichman had assured him that Garment had instructions to work up a draft of guidelines with Fred and me for the appearance of White House aides before our committee.

But when we met with Garment, he professed complete ignorance of such instructions. It was an unusual meeting. For its site, Garment selected the Taloe House, a reconstructed colonial town house facing on Lafayette Square. Supposedly, this was to preserve neutrality by avoiding a meeting either in the White House or in the Senate office building. But the Taloe House was owned by the government and used by the White House for meetings and social events.

Garment arrived late and spent most of the hour we were together trying to get me to state the committee's minimum conditions. For his part, he claimed that he had no idea what the President would accept and had not been informed by Ehrlichman about any White House position. He said he would report back to Ehrlichman my statement of the committee's position, which was simply that the White House aides would have to testify under oath in public session before the committee.

"Would the committee consider written answers by White House aides to written questions from the committee?" Garment probed.

Fred Thompson promptly replied that the procedure of written interrogatories was still an open matter in the committee. This was not true and I was surprised by Fred's statement. I did not like to argue with him in front of Garment, but I could not let Garment be misled. "I can assure you, Fred, that Senator Ervin will never accept written interrogatories," I said. "He has often said that he doesn't know how he can cross-examine a piece of paper with written answers on it. This is also the majority position of the committee, and Len Garment should not leave this meeting thinking it is still a bargaining point."

I was unhappy at the way the meeting ended. We had resolved nothing, and I had little to report to Senator Ervin. I surmised that this was another delaying tactic of the White House, and we had just wasted our time. I told Senator Ervin the next day about the meeting with Garment and expressed my doubts about the White House having any intention of cooperating with us. I suggested that instead of our getting involved in a series of useless meetings, it would be better for us to develop our own guidelines and confront the White House with them.

"I think you're right," Ervin replied. "I'm going to talk to Baker about this and tell him that I'm not going to put up with any dilatory tactics on the part of the White House. The Senate has the power to compel the attendance of White House aides."

Baker must have gotten Ervin's message back to the White House because shortly afterwards, Garment called me and suggested that we meet in his office to continue to discuss guidelines. I was willing to give it another try and went to Garment's office with Fred Thompson. Garment had a sumptuous corner office in the Executive Office Building, elegantly furnished in decorator colors. There was even soft piped-in music. Garment's principal concern was how the President's claim of executive privilege or national security should be asserted by a White House witness at our public hearings.

"Would this procedure be acceptable to you?" Garment asked. "When the White House witness is asked a question, which he believes is covered by executive privilege or national security, he would simply refuse to answer the question, and not specifically state to the committee that his refusal is based on the grounds of executive privilege or national security. But the committee will understand that is why he is refusing to answer the question."

I was startled at Garment's suggestion. It made no sense to me, but the manner in which he asked it intimated an unstated concern. "It seems like a very awkward and obscure way to present a constitutional question to our committee," I replied. "In fact, it could be quite misleading. How would we know why the witness is really refusing to answer? Maybe it's an embarrassing question that has nothing to do with executive privilege or national security, and he doesn't want to answer it. The committee would be completely in the dark."

Garment spoke candidly. "I think you know why I'm suggesting this procedure, Sam. Frankly, it's very awkward for the President to have his counsel assert executive privilege and prevent his assistants from answering questions from your committee on Watergate matters on live TV before the whole public. Many people don't understand the legal concept of executive privilege, and will assume that it is the same thing as asserting the Fifth Amendment right against self-incrimination. They will draw all kinds of terrible inferences against the President or the White House staff member."

"That's nonsense," I said. "The committee is not going to allow the White House to escape responsibility for publicly asserting executive privilege if the President believes that he has a right to make such a claim." I added that the issue of executive privilege would have to be fought out between the White House and the committee, and the courts might ultimately have to resolve the question. I said that we would not permit a procedure that would allow this important legal issue to be handled obscurely. If the President thought that his assertion of executive privilege would be interpreted by the public as similar to claiming the Fifth Amendment privilege against self-incrimination, that was a risk he had to take. But I assured Garment that Ervin could clearly explain the difference between the two privileges at the public hearings.

Garment had listened attentively, but he brushed aside what I had said by simply announcing, "Well, this is purely academic, since it's for the President alone to say what is covered by executive privilege."

I disagreed with Garment, but I did not think this was the appropriate time to continue the argument. Later events would expose to the scrutiny of the federal courts, including the Supreme Court, the fallacy of the President's position that he had the absolute unreviewable power to determine what information to withhold from Congress or the courts on the ground of executive privilege.

Once again we had not arrived at any guidelines or any agreements. It was clear that Garment was not authorized to present any positions on behalf of the President. Ervin now moved quickly on my earlier recommendation. We drafted our own guidelines for presentation to the committee. They were based on Ervin's concept of the doctrine of executive privilege as well as on the requirements of due process. They were predicated also on Ervin's unbending position that White House aides must appear publicly before the committee and testify under oath. With some clarifying amendments, they were approved unanimously by the committee at its meeting on April 16.

The following day President Nixon publicly announced his acceptance of these guidelines.

He reported in the same announcement that on Sunday, April 15,

Attorney General Richard Kleindienst and Assistant Attorney General Henry Petersen had met with him and disclosed major developments in the case. Although he declined to comment on the disclosures, he said, "If any person in the executive branch of the government is indicted by the grand jury, my policy will be to immediately suspend him. If convicted, he will, of course, be automatically discharged." The President also emphasized that he had expressed to the "appropriate authorities" his views that no individual holding a position of major importance in the administration in the past or present should be given immunity from prosecution. It occurred to me that this position on immunity might be calculated to protect top Nixon aides rather than to encourage an all-out prosecution effort, for knowledgeable informers were effectively cut off if they could not expect to be able to bargain for immunity.

When Nixon promptly agreed to our guidelines, I became worried that his agreement might be part of a shrewd maneuver to have Haldeman, Ehrlichman and Colson show up prematurely on our doorstep, demanding to give their testimony to the American people.

I talked to Ervin about this possible White House tactic. None of these White House aides, I stressed, had yet been implicated in Watergate by any evidence received by the committee. It would be foolish for our committee to provide a forum for their exculpatory statements when we were not prepared to cross-examine them or confront them with contradictory evidence. Ervin was quick to grasp the problem. He agreed that we should interrogate the President's top men privately, and only call them as public witnesses if they were willing to give substantive testimony, or were implicated by other witnesses or evidence.

During the third week in April investigative reporters revealed through leaks out of the prosecutor's office what Nixon had meant on April 17 when he said there were major developments in the case. They reported that Magruder and Dean were cooperating with the prosecutors and were seeking immunity in exchange for their testimony before the grand jury. This was the break I had been waiting for since March 26, when McCord's accusations against Dean and Magruder first became publicly known. I had expected that they would experience extraordinary pressures from the disclosures and might make a move to save themselves. Whatever they revealed secretly to the prosecutor they would have to tell our committee publicly, since we possessed the same subpoena, immunity and contempt power that were available to the grand jury.

But we were suddenly confronted with a dilemma. The flurry of activity in the grand jury and the U.S. attorney's office gave rise to strong rumors that major Watergate indictments were imminent. The prevailing view was that the U.S. attorney's office would have the grand jury return the indictments just prior to the scheduled opening of our public hearings on May 15. If this occurred, we would be confronted with the difficult question of the propriety of our holding public hearings on the same subject matter of the indictments.

My own staff was divided on this question. Dave Dorsen believed that the committee would be acting improperly if it went ahead with televised public hearings after new Watergate indictments had been returned by the grand jury. "How can you possibly expect the defendants to get a fair trial," he asked at a meeting in my office, "if we put out all the evidence against them on live TV?"

Terry Lenzner stared at Dave. "That's the damnedest cave-in talk I've heard! Even if Silbert gets indictments, so what? I wouldn't trust the investigation and prosecution to that U.S. attorney's office. They've got to be under the thumb of Justice, and therefore the White House. I thought that's why the Ervin committee was created—because Congress didn't want to trust the Watergate investigation to the Justice Department."

Jim Hamilton was ambivalent, but suspected a plot in the U.S. attorney's office to kill our hearings.

I was inclined to support Terry's position. Our hearings would not be criminal prosecutions. They served an entirely different purpose. The Senate committee had a constitutional duty to inform the public, and time would dissipate the prejudice to defendants. Even if Silbert got the grand jury to come down with indictments, the cases would not come to trial until the fall or later.

However, I concluded that we were not in a position fo fully analyze the impact of criminal indictments on the committee hearings. We had no idea what the grand jury was going to do and I thought it was time for us to find out. I called Senator Ervin and discussed the problem with him.

I told Ervin that I thought I should meet with Silbert and find out exactly what he was planning so that the committee would have some guidance. Ervin urged me to have the meeting immediately.

Fred Thompson readily agreed to join me, and Silbert said he would see Thompson and me right away. We took a cab to the United States Courthouse at 4th and John Marshall Place. Silbert was waiting for us in his office. He had asked Sy Glanzer and Don Campbell, his deputies in the Watergate investigation, to join him. After briefly explaining our predicament, I got right down to the business of our meeting: Will there be Watergate indictments before May 15? And if so, who will be indicated?

After some hemming and hawing, it became evident they would be of no help. Henry Petersen, chief of the Criminal Division of the Justice Department, supervised Silbert's work now that Attorney General Kleindienst had recused himself from the Watergate prosecution because of his close ties with John Mitchell, his former boss. Silbert admitted that Petersen was the only person who could answer my questions. In the taxi on the way back to the Senate office building, Fred chuckled. "Sam, didn't they look like three scared possums? Hell, they could have given us some hints. They just don't want to cooperate at all with us." I said that it was likely the federal prosecution didn't want competition from our committee and that I would call Petersen for the information when we got back to the office.

When I called, Petersen sounded friendly. We had known each other for a number of years. Petersen, who had spent his entire professional career as a prosecutor, believed I was too defense-oriented in my views on criminal justice matters. But he claimed he respected our honest differences of opinion. I repeated to him the same statement I had made earlier to Silbert. Petersen paused, then asked, "Couldn't Silbert help you?"

"No, he said he was not authorized to talk with me about the investigation. He said only you could do it."

"When do you have to have an answer on this?"

"Very soon, Hank, since the public hearings are only a month away."

Petersen promised to give me an answer within the next two days.

When a few days had gone by and I had not heard from Petersen, I called him. He told me that he could not give me any information. I replied that I would have to report to our committee that we could receive no cooperation from the Department of Justice and would have to operate on the assumption that there would be no indictments coming down. I told him our public hearings would go forward as planned.

However, I was far from sure. If Silbert did confront our committee with Watergate indictments before May 15, I could not predict the committee's reaction. Ervin himself was uncertain. And I had not decided what to recommend to the committee. I was not satisfied as to which position was more just and fair in the face of the Senate committee's duty to inform the public of wrongdoing in the executive branch of government.

I had told Silbert I could produce in public hearings the same evidence he had. But I was bluffing. From the newspaper reports, I knew he had Magruder and Dean. We did not, but we could get them when we wanted them. I was not yet ready for them; I wanted to accumulate as much background evidence as I could to permit productive cross-examination of Dean and Magruder when we did question them.

We were making good progress in this effort. In addition to McCord's information, we had received significant fragments of evidence tying Magruder to the bugging plan. McCord had told me that the Liddy covert political intelligence plan bore the code name Gemstone. On April 19, 1973, Reisner gave Terry Lenzner and Jim Hamilton damning evidence which established the existence of a Gemstone file kept by Magruder and Mitchell. At Magruder's request, on the same day the Watergate burglars were arrested, Reisner had actually taken the Gemstone file from a drawer in Magruder's desk and put it in CRP administrator Robert Odle's brief case for Odle to take home with him. Later Magruder told Reisner he had received the file from Odle and had destroyed it.

Reisner admitted he had seen the Gemstone file, before the Watergate break-in, on Magruder's desk and had opened it out of curiosity. He claimed he only glanced at the top material, which was typed on stationery with the letterhead "Gemstone" and which referred to a source by the code name Ruby. He also noticed that there were a number of glossy photographs at the bottom of the file, but closed it after a quick glance, fearing he might be caught snooping by Magruder. Reisner also remembered once being told by Magruder to put the Gemstone file in a Mitchell file that was being prepared for delivery to Mitchell.

If Magruder's Gemstone file indeed contained the typed logs recording the information received from the wiretapped phones in the Democratic National Committee headquarters, it seemed incredible that there would be *Gemstone stationery*. But there *was* Gemstone stationery! Sally Harmony, Liddy's secretary, informed Terry and Jim that she typed logs of telephone calls on Gemstone stationery that had been delivered to her by Herbert Post, a printer used by CRP. We subpoenaed Post and he produced a sample of the stationery. In large blue letters printed at the top was the code name Gemstone. Slightly below and to the right of the letterhead were the word "date" and a blank line, and on the left side, the word "source" and a blank line. Sally Harmony said three source code names were used—Ruby 1, Ruby 2 and Crystal.

But even more astounding was the brown envelope produced by the CRP printer which had been ordered by Liddy to serve as a container to store the Gemstone material. Printed at the top of the envelope in large one-inch-high red capital letters were the words SENSITIVE MATERIAL. In the center of the envelope in smaller red letters were the printed instructions "Handle as Code Word Material." At the bottom left-hand corner of the envelope were the abbreviations "Exdis" and "No Disem," which meant "executive distribution" and "no dissemination." Around the entire four sides of the envelope were bold red hash marks similar to the red lines on a barbershop pole.

Such garish announcements of secret material seemed to be an absurd burlesque of professional espionage practice. The only thing Liddy appeared to have omitted in this childish effort to proclaim his master spying were neon lights.

Then, on April 28, two witnesses three thousand miles apart gave us information that directly implicated Magruder and Dean and provided our first evidence tying Haldeman and Ehrlichman to the cover-up. I questioned Hugh Sloan, former CRP treasurer, in our interrogation room G-334 in Washington, and Terry Lenzner questioned Herbert Kalmbach, reputed to be Nixon's personal attorney, in his law office in Los Angeles.

Sloan's scheduled appearance at the Senate office building produced a flare-up by Silbert. When Silbert learned that Sloan was to be questioned by us, he immediately summoned Sloan before the grand jury on the same day he was scheduled to appear in room G-334. Sloan was caught in the middle. His attorney called me for help. Understandably, he was concerned about ignoring a grand jury demand for his client's appearance, even though our notice to Sloan predated Silbert's. This concern was heightened when Silbert angrily told Sloan's attorney that the grand jury had priority over our Senate committee and Sloan would be cited for contempt if he failed to appear.

I called Silbert and told him that his claim of priority was ridiculous. Silbert was adamant in asserting first right to Sloan, his voice sounding shrill and belligerent. I was tempted to fight him on the issue, but thought it would be unfair to Sloan, a voluntary and cooperating witness, to make him the target of a clash between the federal prosecutor and the Senate committee. I told Sloan to go to the grand jury and to come to us afterwards. Silbert's conduct betrayed his deepening annoyance with our investigation. It also revealed his special concern about Sloan's testimony, which we understood only after we completed our interrogation of Sloan.

When Sloan did appear for questioning by me and Jim Hamilton in G-334, Senator Baker's assistant Jim Jordan also showed up. I was surprised because Jordan was not a member of the committee's minority staff and, therefore, not authorized to sit in on witness interrogations. But Fred Thompson told me he was helpless to object, since Jordan had Baker's permission. I chose not to exclude him out of deference to the minority's right to the presence of a representative. Jordan's participation became even more disturbing when he openly admitted to being a friend of Sloan's and attempted to coach Sloan's answers. This produced angry exchanges between Jordan and me, and finally resulted in my accusing Jordan of interfering with the interrogation.

Despite Jordan's tactics, which appeared to be aimed at limiting the information Sloan was willing to give the committee, Sloan was an excellent witness. A slight, thin-faced man with a shock of premature gray hair, his eyes expressed a mixture of embarrassment and determination. As treasurer of CRP he had disbursed $199,000 to Liddy for what he believed were legitimate intelligence operations aimed at safeguarding the security of the Republican National Convention. He now knew this money had been used for burglary and wiretapping. He told us he first became suspicious of wrongdoing on Liddy's part when Liddy rushed by him at the CRP offices on the day of the Watergate break-in saying, "My boys got caught last night; I made a mistake; I used someone from here which I told them I would never do; I'm afraid I'm going to lose my job."

Shortly afterwards, Sloan learned that the FBI had traced the $100 bills in the possession of some of the Watergate burglars to Bernard Barker's Miami bank account, which was used to cash $89,000 in Mexican checks drawn to Manuel Ogarrio and a $25,000 Florida check drawn to Kenneth Dahlberg. Sloan knew that these checks had earlier been received by him for CRP and that he had given them to Liddy to cash. He also knew that the cash in $100 bills Liddy brought back to him was part of the cash stored in his safe from which he had made an extraordinary $83,000 disbursement to Liddy on the authorization of his CRP superiors.

Sloan said his fears worsened when Magruder on three separate occasions tried to pressure him to agree on a false story to tell the prosecutor and grand jury which would conceal the actual amount of cash Sloan had given Liddy.

When Sloan tried to warn Ehrlichman of the dangers he saw to the campaign from revelations about the money, Ehrlichman told Sloan he did not want to hear the details. Mitchell told Sloan cryptically when Sloan sought his advice, "When the going gets tough, the tough get going." Sloan did not know what Mitchell was talking about. When the lawyers for CRP heard from Sloan how much he had actually paid Liddy, Sloan was whisked out of Washington to California to keep him away from FBI investigators. Finally when Sloan returned, Fred La-Rue, a top CRP official and close friend of Mitchell's, told him he should think about pleading the Fifth Amendment.

Frightened and disenchanted by this behavior of his former colleagues, Sloan resigned from CRP, retained a lawyer and went to Earl Silbert in July 1972. He told Silbert and the grand jury about Magruder's efforts to have him commit perjury. He was bewildered when Magruder was not indicted but, instead, was used by Silbert as a principal prosecution witness and his own accusation against Magruder ignored. Ironically, at the first Watergate trial, it was Sloan who was berated by Judge Sirica for not telling the truth when Sloan claimed he did not know what Liddy had done with the cash Magruder had instructed him to give Liddy. Sloan told me that he had in fact objected to the first large request of $83,000 by Liddy, after Magruder had told him Liddy was authorized to spend a budget of $250,000 for security planning for the Republican convention. Sloan checked with Maurice Stans, chairman of the finance committee, to find out if Magruder could authorize so large a cash disbursement to Liddy. Stans told Sloan he would ask Mitchell, then returned and told Sloan that Mitchell said it was all right. According to Sloan, Stans added, "I don't want to know and you don't want to know."

Sloan also revealed a $350,000 cash transfer from CRP to Haldeman's control in the White House. This money would later be tied to some of the hush payments to the Watergate defendants. Sloan would make a good witness, I concluded, after our long hours of questioning him.

Terry Lenzner came back to Washington with even more exciting information after questioning Kalmbach. He had flown to California to learn more about Kalmbach's role in paying Donald Segretti for his political espionage work. But in the course of an intensive interrogation of Kalmbach concerning his cash transactions during the 1972 campaign, Kalmbach told Terry that he had been recruited by John Dean, shortly after the break-in, to raise funds to pay for legal expenses and family support of the arrested Watergate burglars. Kalmbach said he had checked out with Ehrlichman this assignment from Dean and Ehrlichman had approved it.

This was sensational evidence—the first we had received to support McCord's claim that the Watergate defendants had received cash payoffs. And it reached into the White House. Terry told me that he believed Kalmbach had held back important details and was sure that if I called his attorney, Jim O'Connor, of Phoenix, Arizona, and arranged for Kalmbach to come to Washington for further questioning, we could get additional valuable evidence.

I called O'Connor and set up an interrogation session with Kalmbach in Washington for May 2. Because of Kalmbach's reputed relationship with the President (we didn't know then that Kalmbach actually wasn't Nixon's personal lawyer) and to avoid any publicity, I scheduled the meeting at my office at the Georgetown University Law Center. I went to the meeting eagerly. Kalmbach was the highest ranking witness in the Nixon hierarchy we had questioned so far who had firsthand knowledge of cover-up facts.

Tall and impeccably dressed, his large face was almost expressionless except for a forlorn look in his wet eyes. Kalmbach's tale sounded like a combination of comic opera and the sinister activities of La Cosa Nostra. Kalmbach had been warned by Dean that his activities had to be conducted with extreme secrecy because they were dealing with political dynamite, which if publicly revealed, could cause the President to lose his reelection bid. Kalmbach was to be both the raiser of the funds and the intermediary "bagman" with the person who would actually make the payments to the defendants or their representatives. Kalmbach and Dean chose a former New York City policeman, Tony Ulasewicz, for that job. Ulasewicz had worked for Dean on White House assignments before.

Kalmbach told me that he and Ulasewicz developed an elaborate routine of code names and communications through telephone booths to identify the persons who were to receive money, the amounts to be given each Watergate defendant, and to arrange for transfer of the money from Kalmbach to Ulasewicz which was required for the clandestine operation. Kalmbach informed me that Fred LaRue played an important role in the plan. The conspiracy was widening and we now had another key witness to question, who probably could give us more information and additional names when he was confronted with Kalmbach's testimony.

Kalmbach told me that by July 1972 the undercover nature of the payments—the use of code names, telephone booths, secret drops—had become increasingly distasteful to him. He decided to check with Ehrlichman if the assignment was really necessary. (Kalmbach never altered his statement of this meeting—not when he talked to me privately, nor when he testified in public session before our committee, nor over a year later, when he was a witness in the Watergate criminal conspiracy trial prosecuted by the special prosecutor.) Kalmbach's voice was strained when he told me on May 2 that he had looked at Ehrlichman and said, "John, I am looking right into your eyes. I know Jeanne and your family, you know Barbara and my family. You know that my family and my reputation mean everything to me and it is absolutely necessary, John, that you tell me first that John Dean has the authority to direct me in this assignment and that I am to go forward on it." Ehrlichman, according to Kalmbach, confirmed Dean's authority and told Kalmbach he should go forward with the payoff plan. Kalmbach said that Ehrlichman emphasized the need for secrecy, stating that if the press were to learn of these activities, "they would have our heads in their laps."

When Ehrlichman later publicly testified before our committee, he denied that Kalmbach had made this personal request for assurance from him that his raising cash for the Watergate defendants was necessary and that he had told him it was. After Ehrlichman's testimony that day, Kalmbach called me from California. Actually sobbing on the phone, Kalmbach complained, "But, Mr. Dash, I did tell him I was looking in his eyes and depending on his telling me it was necessary—and he told me—*he did tell me* it was necessary. Why won't he admit it?"

Herbert Kalmbach was a sorry figure, stripped of the power and influence gained from his association with Nixon. Despite his activities in the cover-up, I could not help feeling sympathy for him. To retain the illusion of intimacy with the President, he had been a willing performer of dirty jobs for the White House, and like a moth attracted by a candle flame, he had been drawn to the bright light of Oval Office power and got terribly burned.

I was now ready to talk to Magruder. I asked my secretary to get Jim Bierbower, Magruder's lawyer, on the phone. I was pleased that fate had led Magruder to him. Bierbower was a colleague of mine at Georgetown, where he taught part time. We had also worked together on American Bar Association activities. He was cordial when he answered the telephone. "Hi, Sam. I've been expecting a call from you. What can I do for you?"

"You can bring in Magruder this afternoon."

"He's got a date with Silbert. We're spending a lot of our time over there now."

"I read about it in the newspapers. But I'm making the same investigation as Silbert, and I'm under pressure to get our public hearings started on May 15. You know, Jim, we could subpoena Magruder."

Bierbower apruptly changed from friend to defense lawyer. "Go ahead, but if you do, all you'll get from Magruder is the Fifth Amendment, unless you give him immunity."

"You must be kidding," I said, surprised that Bierbower was taking such an adversary position. "Your client has been talking to the United States attorney, incriminating himself all over the place. How the hell can he take the Fifth Amendment with us?"

"You're the criminal law expert, not me," Bierbower replied calmly. "You'll agree with me, I'm sure, that the scope of your investigation is much broader than Silbert's." He said the prosecutor's questioning would be limited to a specific subject—which would still leave Magruder a basis to plead the Fifth Amendment with our committee.

Bierbower was technically right, of course. But I didn't think that he believed that Magruder was in any real danger of exposing himself to additional criminal charges by appearing before our committee. For some reason Bierbower wanted to keep his client away from us. It occurred to me that maybe that was his arrangement with Silbert.

The only way I could ask the committee for immunity would be to be able to say Magruder was able to implicate people higher up the ladder than himself. But Bierbower said Magruder had no working relationship with Ehrlichman and could only give information regarding Gordon Strachan, Haldeman's assistant. When asked about Mitchell, Bierbower said, "Magruder's testimony would only give you the basis to draw a weak inference. He doesn't directly implicate Mitchell. He says that he came away from a third and final meeting with Mitchell in Key Biscayne on the Liddy intelligence plan with the belief that the plan was approved. But he can't say what he based this belief on. He does not recall any specific statement or action on Mitchell's part indicating Mitchell's approval of the plan. It's pretty weak, Sam."

"But the newspaper reports said that Magruder told Silbert that Mitchell approved the plan."

"He told Silbert exactly what I just told you. He had the impression that the plan was approved when he left Key Biscayne, but he doesn't go beyond that. He won't say that Mitchell approved the plan."

I told Bierbower that I would think about the question of immunity and hung up. Magruder's story seemed incredible. How could Magruder say he left a meeting with Mitchell in Key Biscayne believing that he had approval to implement the Liddy intelligence plan and, at the same time, claim that he couldn't recall any words or actions on Mitchell's part signaling an approval of the plan by Mitchell?

One explanation for Magruder's new story came to mind, and it was disturbing. I couldn't help suspecting that a new cover-up strategy was being fashioned. Not by Bierbower—I had complete trust in his integrity. He simply believed his client. Apparently, Magruder was now willing to take the blame for the approval of the Watergate bugging plan, thus providing the prosecution and the public with the prize they had suspected was there—the involvement of a CRP official who was superior to G. Gordon Liddy. The White House would be spared and so would former Attorney General John Mitchell.

If Magruder was still covering up, I asked myself, what about John Dean? According to news leaks, he was prepared to implicate Haldeman and Ehrlichman in the Watergate cover-up. If this was true, he would not be participating with Magruder in a new cover-up scheme. My best strategy now, I thought, was to contact Dean's lawyer and arrange a meeting with Dean.

Dean had initially turned for legal advice to his brother-in-law, Robert McCandless. But he and McCandless quickly realized that he needed an experienced criminal lawyer. When I called McCandless, he told me that Charles Shaffer had been retained to represent Dean. He said he would have Shaffer call me the next day.

When Shaffer got back to me in the late afternoon we made an appointment to meet in my office. He arrived twenty minutes later.

Tall and slim, with his hair swept back, Shaffer looked debonair. "I'm sure you don't know anything about me—just a little hick lawyer—but I've heard a lot about you." There was a matter-of-fact tone in his voice. True, I didn't know anything about Shaffer. But in a brief, unassuming way, he told me enough about himself to disprove that he was a "little hick lawyer." He spoke with a soft Southern accent. A native of Nashville, Tennessee, he had been a member of the elite team of assistant U.S. attorneys that had successfully prosecuted former Teamster boss Jimmy Hoffa.

Shaffer looked around the room. "Is it safe to talk here?" he asked.

"We've had the room 'swept' from time to time, but I suppose it is not really safe to talk anywhere."

"Well, okay, I see what you mean. I may be able to produce John Dean as a witness for you. The way he's thinking now, he'd like to testify before your committee without any immunity. You see, he'd be telling the whole story to the American people with no strings attached —no deals like immunity. As his lawyer, I'm not sure I should let him give up the protection of immunity, but we'll see."

"When can I talk to Dean, Mr. Shaffer?" I asked.

"Call me Charlie. You'll have to wait a little while. Maybe a couple of weeks. I am right in the middle of trying to work out something with Silbert, and I don't have to tell you how fucking mad he'd be if he knew John Dean was coming over here. I don't want to disturb anything for the moment. I'll call you in a week and let you know how things are coming."

"I understand, but we're working under more pressure than Silbert, and Dean might change everything for us."

"He will," Shaffer said simply. "But I'm sure you can put on plenty of witnesses before you'll need Dean. I don't know what I'm going to be able to work out with Silbert. Frankly, if I can swing a deal where Dean gets complete immunity and isn't prosecuted, then I may not be able to give him to you at all. Silbert might insist on it to keep his case from being loused up."

Shaffer's words stung me. I couldn't let Shaffer or Silbert determine Dean's availability to the committee. For all I knew, Dean was only looking for an escape route. Shaffer wasn't even disguising the fact that he was playing our committee off against the U.S. attorney's office.

"Look, Charlie, I know you have a client to represent. But I represent a United States Senate select committee. I don't have to jump through any hoops for you. I'm willing to wait a short while until you've clarified your position with Silbert. But don't talk to me about not producing Dean. I can get a subpoena for his testimony and compel him to come right down before our committee in executive session."

Shaffer brought up the Fifth Amendment and such objections as attorney-client privilege and executive privilege. But I didn't believe Dean would want to use any of them, since he was trying awfully hard to look as if he was cooperating with the Watergate investigations. Shaffer was still afraid of lousing things up with the prosecutor's office and offered to call me in a week's time.

When I reported to Ervin on my meeting with Shaffer, he was quite excited about the prospect of Dean as a witness. These meetings with Ervin were always cherished by me. At age seventy-seven, Ervin maintained a youthful and vibrant enthusiasm for the fundamental princi ples of constitutional government. He often blended poetry, the Bible and personal philosophy into his sometimes emotional expositions on his beliefs and hopes.

He was a fundamentalist on issues concerning the Bill of Rights and individual liberty. We were of one mind and heart on these matters. And our views blended together in a harmony that I believe sustained both of us in our committee work.

There were a number of areas, of course, where I disagreed with Ervin's positions. Happily, they did not relate to issues connected with our Watergate investigation. They primarily dealt with civil rights matters and such specific major issues as the genocide treaty and consumer protection, on which he took negative positions. But while I had the responsibility as chief counsel to the Senate Select Committee, I never discussed these matters with him, and especially refused to seek to alter his position in the Senate on such questions when requested to do so by organizations or individuals sharing my deep interest in them.

I knew I had an extremely difficult job to do which would require me to call constantly for Ervin's support to help me successfully perform that job. With regard to my responsibilities as chief counsel to the Watergate committee, I put no limit on my demand on Ervin's time. I expected no less than his complete support. To gain optimum access to his office and his attention, I believed I must present one, and only one, image to him—that of his chief counsel.

Despite a feeling of closeness to Ervin, I sensed an invisible barrier separating us. In fact, we were never completely relaxed with each other. We never abandoned ourselves to each other's inner self. Even our belly laughing at his stories fell short of complete emotional release. Perhaps, despite our common Harvard Law School background, we could not bridge two different worlds: Ervin, a descendant of Scotch-Irish Presbyterians who settled in South Carolina and North Carolina and fought against the English in the Revolution and against the North in the Civil War; and I, a first-generation son of immigrant Russian Jews, with my boyhood spent in the narrow streets of row houses in west Philadelphia. Whatever the reason, though professionally we were devoted friends and comrades, socially we were strangers.

At the end of April a crescendo of Watergate newspaper stories revealed shocking new facts. Pat Gray had burned documents contained in two manila envelopes, which Ehrlichman and Dean had given to him, with the admonition that the documents in the envelopes should "never see the light of day."

According to the Washington *Post,* the papers Gray destroyed included cables forged by Hunt to implicate President Kennedy in the assassination of President Diem of South Vietnam. We were to develop the story of the cables later, through Hunt's testimony. But here it was reported in a newspaper story, referring to sources from the prosecutor's office.

This story was followed by a release from Judge W. Matthew Byrne, Jr., who was presiding at the Daniel Ellsberg Pentagon Papers trial, stating that he had received a memorandum from the Justice Department revealing that Liddy and Hunt had burglarized the office of Ellsberg's psychiatrist, Dr. Lewis Fielding. This was shattering news. We were still struggling to uncover the facts of the Watergate burglary. Now there was proof of another political burglary by Liddy and Hunt. Were these burglaries related? What did it all mean?

Then Woodward and Bernstein reported in the *Post,* under a banner headline, that Dean was expected to implicate Haldeman and Ehrlichman in the cover-up when he testified before the grand jury. According to the *Post* story, citing White House sources, Dean would testify that he continually reported to Haldeman and Ehrlichman on the cover-up transactions and that he had written a report of his own version of the cover-up. Another *Post* story published a leak from the prosecutor's office that Magruder and Fred LaRue were telling the prosecutors that Colson had supported the Liddy bugging plan.

Gray resigned his position as acting director of the FBI on April 27, the same day the newspapers reported his destruction of papers given to him by Dean and Ehrlichman. And on April 30 the Watergate scandal erupted with the force of a volcanic explosion. President Nixon announced to the public on television that he had received the written resignations of Kleindienst, Haldeman and Ehrlichman, and had asked for and received the resignation of John Dean. American history had never before recorded such a devastating toll of a President's top staff caused by scandal.

On May 1, when the morning newspapers were headlining the resignations of the President's men, my staff gathered in my office with glum expressions on their faces. Most of them were thinking that our hearings could only be an anticlimax to such sensational news events.

"Shit, it's almost all over before we have put on our first witness!" Terry Lenzner expressed the general feeling of the staff.

Jim Hamilton was also frustrated. "Well, the newspaper reporters can look real good, writing all these stories. It's no great trick to get information from sources who know they will remain anonymous. We don't have that luxury. We have to dig up enough evidence to persuade a witness to stand up publicly and give his testimony under oath. Reporters don't have to do that. But they look like heroes, and we're going to look silly if we can't produce the same facts through sworn testimony."

"But you're missing the point," I admonished him. "Even though all these new facts have been in the press and Haldeman, Ehrlichman and Dean are out of the White House, nothing has been *proved* yet to the public." I pointed out that the resignations didn't establish any culpability. The President had gone out of his way to praise Haldeman and Ehrlichman and to emphasize that their resignations could not be taken by the people as an admission or indication of guilt. Perhaps the prosecutors and the grand jury were receiving provable facts. But they would not be presented publicly at a trial for a long, long time. There had not even been any indictments yet. In the meantime the public was confused and bewildered. They did not know what or whom to believe. "It's our job," I insisted, "to set the record straight—to put on the witnesses in public hearings to tell the Watergate story, not in the form of rumors or quotes from anonymous sources, but as participants and eyewitnesses to the facts."

Dave Dorsen looked skeptical. "That sounds great. But how are we going to be able to produce all these facts through sworn testimony?"

"We have a good part of it already," I replied. "But the real hard facts that have recently been in the newspapers are apparently coming from what Magruder and Dean are telling Silbert. If they are making these statements to the prosecutors or the grand jury, then they are going to have to tell us about them, especially if we give them immunity. I'm looking into that right now."

My assurance that Magruder and Dean would be public witnesses before our committee created a stir of enthusiasm in the room. The staff had been working day and night, seven days a week. They were tired, and then discouraged by the recent public disclosures. They needed to be given hope that their work was worth it all—that our public hearings would be really important to the country. By the time our meeting was over, my staff had agreed with me that only our public hearings at this time could fully inform the public about Watergate and that newspaper stories were no substitute for the public testimony of live eyewitnesses. They returned to their work with renewed zeal. Now I had to make good on Magruder and Dean.

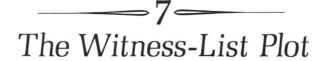

7

The Witness-List Plot

IT WAS SUDDENLY MAY, AND OUR PUBLIC HEARINGS WERE TO OPEN in two weeks. Though I needed no reminder of this fact, the reality of the nearness of the hearings brought inquiries from senators and news media representatives. Senator Baker asked me to produce a witness list. He displayed no specific interest in who might be on the list, but just asked that I reveal my recommendations to the committee for its early scrutiny.

Talmadge, however, wanted to know the name and purpose of each witness. He urged short hearings with a few key witnesses. This would not, he insisted, prevent the committee from exposing the essential facts of the Watergate scandal. As a candidate for reelection in 1974, he believed that prolonged public hearings could be damaging to him. Also he did not want the hearings to unduly interfere with his other senatorial duties, especially his chairmanship of the Agriculture Subcommittee. Inouye, too, was running for reelection in 1974, and was urging that we complete our public hearings in 1973.

The press was eager to dramatize the hearings and probed to discover who my "star witnesses" would be. At first this interest was not shared by the TV networks. On the contrary, I learned they had tentatively decided against providing live coverage of our hearings. I thought they were overreacting to the attacks made by Nixon administration spokesmen that their treatment of Nixon and his programs had been biased and unfair. At the time live TV coverage of our hearings was first considered, Haldeman, Ehrlichman and Colson were still Nixon's top aides and no revelations had yet been made to diminish the ability of the White House to be a formidable foe.

Public education TV and radio showed more courage. They decided that they would provide gavel-to-gavel replay coverage of the hearings in the evenings. But for live TV coverage they were dependent on the decision of the networks because they could not, alone, afford the high cost of such coverage.

I was disappointed with the initial decision of the networks. This was not because I yearned for TV publicity, as some columnists reported, but because live TV coverage was essential to my strategy for the hearings. I had planned to present our hearings to the public as a unique civics lesson in American democracy. Only the magic of television could permit all Americans to attend our hearings, no matter where they lived in the country. Newspaper reports of our hearings would be a very poor substitute, especially in such a politically controversial investigation. The people had to see and hear the witnesses for themselves.

The April 30 exodus of Kleindienst, Haldeman, Ehrlichman and Dean from Nixon's stronghold, along with the new guidelines of our committee which made it likely that these fallen and dramatic figures would be witnesses, changed the picture for the networks. Our hearings became irresistible to them. Now they and the rest of the news media pleaded with me for the names of my lead-off witnesses. The network TV reporters even had their own suggestions. They urged me to start out with a bang by calling big-name witnesses, such as Colson, Haldeman, Ehrlichman or Mitchell. These reporters seemed to consider themselves as packagers of entertainment and appeared to be concerned only about gaining the attention of their audience through sensational fare they hoped I would serve up.

My strategy was different. Though the hearings would inevitably be viewed as a show, they would have to be much more than a show. The narrative of the Watergate scandal would convey its own drama, but the gravity and meaning of that scandal had to be clearly communicated. Newspapers still reported that many persons were confused about the nature of the Watergate charges, or didn't believe Watergate was even a problem worth the attention it was receiving.

Therefore, it wasn't enough to merely win the public's attention. Some congressional investigating committees in the past had succeeded in doing that simply by producing a series of sensational show hearings. But they had accomplished little more than entertainment. Our hearings also had to create public understanding of the Watergate facts and produce a significant public response. Indeed the Supreme Court had recognized the public response role of congressional hearings as their most important function.

Through our hearings, I believed we could create an engrossing educational experience in homes throughout the country, and accomplish the goals of public understanding and response. But this would require organizing and structuring the hearings to impress on the millions of Americans watching the hearings that the people and events presented were real, that they were identifiable with themselves and their families, and that even their own freedoms had been threatened.

Some veteran Senate staffers and Capitol Hill reporters were skeptical of my goals for our hearings. "People are so damn complacent," one of them told me, "that no amount of exposure of public corruption can shake them." I disagreed. I did not believe that the people were complacent. Rather, I thought they felt powerless to affect governmental conduct—the kind of powerlessness that made people say, "You can't fight City Hall." Our hearings had to demonstrate that the people or their elected representatives could fight City Hall and that the public officials implicated by evidence of corruption and abuse of power, no matter how high their positions, could be made accountable to the people for breach of trust.

It was my plan to start out with little-known witnesses, who would provide the details necessary for the public to understand the background roles and activities of the major witnesses. Such a plan would call for a long witness list and a rejection of a "bombshell" opening. The use of innumerable witnesses would be opposed by some of the senators; the lack of instant drama would bring me the displeasure of the press. Nevertheless, I was committed to this plan. The witness list my staff and I developed was formidable. I estimated it would take the committee all summer to complete its public hearings on the Watergate break-in and cover-up phase. But as I and my staff contemplated this prospect we saw no acceptable shortcut.

A meeting of the committee was scheduled for May 8, during which the witness list would be discussed. Fred Thompson and I had agreed that prior to the meeting we would review proposals for a witness list together. When Fred saw my list, he said, "Goddamn it! Do you mean you want to call all these witnesses at the public hearings?"

"Of course," I replied.

Fred shook his head. "You want to produce 40 witnesses in the Watergate break-in phase, alone. Why, Sam, that would keep us in public hearings until September and we wouldn't have touched the dirty tricks phase or the campaign financing phase."

I asked, "What did you have in mind?" Fred said, "Well, Senator Baker and I have been talking. And he thinks that we might put on a brief set of hearings. We would have a few days of witnesses on Watergate, followed up by a few days of witnesses on dirty tricks and then a few days of witnesses on campaign financing, ending our public hearings sometime at the end of June or early July. We can then write our report over the summer and be finished."

"You must be kidding," I exploded, shocked by Fred's disclosure. "That would make our hearings a sham. We're dealing with the worst political scandal in our history. The committee has to fully expose all its relevant evidence to meet its responsibility to the public and to comply with the mandate of our Senate resolution."

Fred became defensive. "Hell, you don't have to put all these witnesses on to tell the story. Just a few witnesses are needed to testify to the facts. I know Senator Baker wants to have our public hearings finished by June because he thinks the public won't stand for the country being ripped apart by Watergate any longer than necessary."

"For God's sake, Fred," I said, "do you think you can just turn off the Watergate scandal in two months, and it will all go away?" I reminded him of the criminal trials that would follow our hearings and insisted that we had a responsibility to present a full disclosure of the facts.

Twenty minutes later Ervin and I met in his office. He was in an excellent mood and wanted me to hear a humorous story he had just shared with some of his colleagues in the Senate cloakroom. It was a very funny story, told only the way Sam Ervin could tell a story. But my inner turmoil must have been transparent. "What's the matter, Sam?" Ervin asked. I told him about Baker's strategy to truncate our hearings and my own plan for calling witnesses.

Ervin's face quickly took on a serious expression. His eyes spoke along with his voice. "Howard Baker's idea is preposterous," he said.

"We'd never get at the truth that way. I would never support it and I know the majority of the committee wouldn't, either. I wonder why Senator Baker is thinking this way."

"Can you persuade him to accept my plan?" I asked.

Ervin looked at me with arched eyebrows and opened his mouth as if to speak but did not. It was only a moment's pause, but it represented Ervin's way of giving thought to a question and not answering it too quickly.

"I'm not sure that I can," he finally said. "But that doesn't matter. I like your plan a whole lot. It makes sense to tell the facts to the public as a story in sequence. With our investigation, it's the only way to do it. We can't just jump into the middle. We've got to first explain how campaign cash in $100 bills from the Committee to Re-Elect the President was found in the pockets of the Watergate burglars when they were arrested and how this cash was paid out to Gordon Liddy by Hugh Sloan. Then we have to put on McCord and the witnesses who corroborate him."

Ervin paused dramatically after each sentence to punctuate his description of how the evidence would be presented. He moved his hands from one side of his desk to the other in accompaniment to his pauses. "And I like your idea, Sam," he added, "of having the former administrator of CRP and a White House staff aide explain how the Committee to Re-Elect the President was organized and how the White House functions. But these witnesses should be very brief, or they'll be too boring."

I alerted Ervin that there might be opposition to the witness list even from some of the Democratic senators. But he believed that all three Democrats would vote with him, giving us a majority. "And we might even have Weicker's vote," Ervin concluded with a smile.

Ervin's support was reassuring. But I worried about whether he had correctly assessed Talmadge's attitude. If Talmadge was firmly opposed to our hearings going through the summer, he might be able to persuade Ervin to reconsider his approval of my plan. And I was convinced that Baker would meet with Ervin privately to try to win Ervin over to his strategy. I could not put aside my sense of uneasiness about the committee meeting on May 8, only several days away.

In the meantime, however, my attention was absorbed by our continuing round-the-clock investigation, which was now focusing on President Nixon's former top aides, Bob Haldeman and John Ehrlichman.

Naturally, I anticipated the interrogation of Haldeman and Ehrlichman in my office on May 4 with some excitement. Earlier in the morning before the witnesses arrived, I had tensed myself for bitter combat. But the interrogation of Haldeman and Ehrlichman turned out to be a pleasant incident. Too pleasant, I thought. In contrast to the harsh image created by reputation, both were warm and friendly. They reacted good-naturedly to the interrogation and displayed a ready sense of humor. Even more surprising, they showed an almost fawning respect for me as well as for Jim Hamilton and Fred Thompson, who both joined me in the interrogation.

During a brief break Jim Hamilton came over to me and whispered, "You know, I like these fellows. Maybe they won't tell us everything they know, but they're certainly not the ogres they've been made out to be."

It was not, though, a productive interrogation session. These two friendly chieftains appeared to have never been around when any Watergate event occurred or was discussed. Ehrlichman, for example, claimed he was busy on domestic affairs for the country and knew nothing about the bugging plans or the aftermath cover-up.

Haldeman was even less informative than Ehrlichman. He recalled nothing about any of the major Watergate events. He had been too busy to be aware of such activities. His time had been spent with President Nixon on important international and national matters. John Dean was supposed to handle investigations and be the troubleshooter, and he thought that Dean had been doing his job well. He said Dean reported to him that there was no White House involvement in the Watergate break-in. He did not have the slightest idea that Dean or any other White House official or CRP official was engaged in any cover-up.

Through the questioning of earlier witnesses, we had heard some of the White House and CRP jargon that would later become familiar to the public listening to Watergate witnesses before our committee. Ehrlichman's language was peppered with these phrases. He seemed incapable of referring to any event without using the phrase "at this point in time." He was surprised when I asked for an explanation of his claim that Mitchell had "stonewalled" him. "Stonewall? That's easy. He just denied knowing anything. It was like talking to a stone wall. Understand?" I did understand.

When Haldeman, Ehrlichman and their counsel left, Jim and I briefly reviewed their interrogation. Although the pleasantness of the meeting lingered, we agreed that Haldeman and Ehrlichman had lied to us throughout the questioning. We were at a disadvantage, since we could not confront them with substantial contradicting evidence such as we might obtain from Dean, Magruder and other witnesses not yet questioned. This trial run proved the wisdom of not calling Haldeman and Ehrlichman as public witnesses unless we received evidence implicating them in Watergate.

Their testimony might have been more plausible if they had acknowledged awareness or participation in certain obvious events, such as a meeting immediately after the break-in to find out what had happened. But they were totally unbelievable when they sought to create the impression that they never saw, heard or questioned any of the Watergate activities that were being widely exposed in the press. Haldeman even refused to admit that after the Watergate break-in on June 17 he had met with or called anybody to talk about the burglary. Ehrlichman had been equally oblivious to Watergate events. From all accounts, Haldeman and Ehrlichman wielded almost absolute power in the White House and constantly demanded facts and accountability from White House staff and top CRP officials. It was therefore ridiculous that they took the posture of not knowing what was happening around them concerning a scandal that posed a threat to Nixon's reelection campaign.

"Jim," I said with a smile, "I have the feeling that we have been stonewalled."

Jim nodded. "I suppose you're right, but I still think they're not such bad guys, after all."

Senator Weicker had dropped in during the morning for part of the questioning of Ehrlichman, but had left after a short while. He returned to my office at the lunch break in a state of excitement. Motioning me to a corner of my office, he produced a typewritten report of three pages. Holding the face of the report close to his chest, he whispered, "Sam, this is a real breakthrough. I saw John Dean last night. He's told me a fantastic story. I dictated some notes of the meeting and had them typed up. I showed them to the chairman this morning. And now I want you to be the only other person to read them. You should follow up with Dean and get all the details and the rest of his story. But for God's sake, don't let this stuff get out."

He let me read the report of his meeting. It was sketchy, but sensational in what it revealed. It was written chronologically. There was Dean's version of the meetings in Mitchell's office when Liddy presented his covert political intelligence plan. Weicker wanted me to be sure to see that. According to Dean, the plan called for kidnapping, mugging squads, use of prostitutes and hugging. The so-called Dean Report which Nixon told the public in August 1972 found no White House involvement in Watergate had been a fake. Dean had made no report.

Haldeman and Ehrlichman had been involved in the cover-up and had directed Dean's efforts to obstruct justice. But the most shocking revelation in the report was Dean's account of a meeting he had with the President and Haldeman, after the first Watergate indictments had been returned, in which the President complimented Dean on the good job he had done keeping the prosecution away from the White House. This was the first real indication of the President's involvement in the Watergate cover-up.

Weicker took the report back from me after I had read it and again pledged me to secrecy. I was surprised at this new show of friendship and confidence in me. We had been having a chilly relationship because of my opposition to Weicker's efforts to open up all our interrogations and committee meetings to the press and the public, and also because of my authorship of the press release by Ervin and Baker indirectly slapping Weicker down for his unsupported public attack on Haldeman.

For a moment I was worried that this could be a setup. Weicker might leak the report of the Dean meeting, and then blame me, since I was the only staff person who saw it. But I discounted this fear. Weicker's enthusiasm was genuine. And he had made a special effort to persuade me that he had faith in my integrity and competence. Obviously, this pleased me, and I preferred to believe we were entering into a more pleasant and constructive relationship.

When I saw Ervin later that afternoon, he confirmed that Weicker had shown him the report. His eyes glistened as he expressed his amazement over the facts Dean had revealed. "Just think, Sam"—he almost bubbled—"this is only a small part of it. Dean told Lowell that he has many more facts to disclose to us. It will be your job to get them from him. It amazes me how this Watergate scandal becomes more outrageous and unbelievable all the time. Our hearings are going to stun the American people."

I wondered why Dean had been willing to meet with Weicker, when, only a few days earlier, Shaffer had asked me to wait until he called me. Perhaps, I speculated, Shaffer was trying to win over for me one of the Republican members of my committee to ensure that I could get the two-thirds vote required by the immunity statute. Weicker was the only

Republican member Shaffer could have approached for this purpose.

But only two days later, on May 6, I was dismayed to read in the Washington *Post* and *The New York Times* that *Newsweek* had announced that its next issue would contain a complete report of what John Dean was prepared to tell the grand jury about the White House involvement in Watergate. The advance excerpts of the *Newsweek* story, reported by the *Post,* covered many of the details contained in Weicker's typewritten notes of his meeting with Dean—even some of the same quotes!

Either Weicker had done what I had first suspected he might do— leaked his notes—or Dean was playing games. Shaffer had given me his office and home telephone numbers. I could not reach him at either place but left urgent messages for him to return my call. He finally called me back at my home Monday evening, May 7. He was irritated. "Look, Sam, I told you I'd call you. And when I say I'll call you, that means I will. If you can't trust me, then the whole fucking thing is no good!"

"What the hell are you talking about?" I almost shouted in the telephone. "I've been waiting all this time, and then I learn that Dean has talked to Weicker. But the biggest kick in the pants was yesterday's stories about the *Newsweek* report on Dean's Watergate testimony. Come on, Charlie, who's double-dealing?"

Shaffer's voice suddenly sounded very tired. He claimed Dean had nothing to do with the *Newsweek* leak, but he had his suspicions, which he'd tell me about later. As far as Weicker was concerned, he admitted it was a shot at getting Dean immunity. Anyway, what he had told Weicker was only a small part of the story.

I promised nothing until I talked to Dean myself, and it had to be no later than this week.

"Can your committee grant him complete transactional immunity, which will prevent him from being prosecuted?" Shaffer asked.

"No, the Organized Crime Control Act of 1970, which gave congressional committees the right to grant immunity to witnesses for the first time, only provides for use immunity. As you know, Charlie, this kind of immunity would only prevent a prosecutor from directly or indirectly using the specific testimony Dean gave us. If the prosecutors had independent evidence to support a prosecution, they could still indict and try him."

"Well, we'll have to take whatever kind of immunity your committee can give us," Shaffer said. "You know, he would be willing to talk to you and your committee without any immunity at all. But I've got the job of watching out for his ass, and I'm not going to let him take any chances."

When I hung up, it suddenly occurred to me how careless I had been —either of our phones could have been wiretapped. Sara found it laughable. "You're supposed to be the country's biggest expert on wiretapping," she scoffed. "And from what you've told me, Dean's lawyer has been a federal prosecutor and a trial lawyer. Yet you both blabbed away on the telephone. You've got to know that our phone must be tapped."

Initially, I was disturbed over my lack of caution. But then I shrugged it off. I had just proved the truth of part of my law school lecture on wiretapping—that no matter how knowledgeable a person may be about wiretapping, the need to use the telephone, coupled with a normal sense of optimism, will lead him to talk on the telephone about confidential matters—even incriminating matters.

The committee meeting on May 8 was crucial and I was nervous about it. I anticipated a battle with Senator Baker. I was puzzled about Baker. He had pledged to cooperate with Ervin in conducting a "full, thorough and fair investigation with no holds barred, let the chips fall where they will." Yet his actions implied that he might have a contrary purpose. His boyish grin and friendly attitude toward me were disarming. When we met frequently, outside the committee sessions, he made obvious efforts to show sincerity and commitment to nonpartisan cooperation with Ervin. I wanted very much to like and trust Baker.

Although senators are by definition politically ambitious, Baker was excessively so. And he wanted to move fast. Leaning on the power base built by his father-in-law, the late Senator Everett Dirksen, Baker in his first term as a senator unsuccessfully challenged Senator Hugh Scott twice for the minority leadership as the candidate of Senate conservatives. Judged by his background and alliances in the Senate, he had to be a strong and loyal supporter of Richard Nixon. How sound, therefore, I wondered, was his claim of independence on our committee?

Besides the witness list, another issue I anticipated would create trouble for me at the meeting was immunity for John Dean. I had briefed Senator Ervin earlier on this problem when I told him about my conversation with Dean's lawyer. Ervin had reacted favorably to my recommendation that the committee should apply to Judge Sirica for an immunity order for Dean, but that it should withhold its decision on whether to implement the order until I had a chance to interrogate Dean. Even if the committee obtained an immunity order for Dean, it did not have to use the order if it decided that Dean's testimony did not deserve a grant of use immunity. Ervin also agreed with my suggestion that the committee be asked to authorize a subpoena for Dean's testimony which I could use if I ran into any more delay from Shaffer.

Sooner than I was supposed to, I learned of Baker's strategy to scuttle my plan for public hearings. I had gone to Thompson's office shortly before the committee meeting to find out if he was going to oppose my witness list. Fred was obviously ill-at-ease. He hesitantly told me that Baker had directed him to prepare a substitute witness list to submit to the committee that morning. I grew angry at this information. Baker had planned to produce his substitute list at the committee meeting without prior notice or disclosure to me. This was underhanded tactics —even more inexcusable because I had disclosed my witness list to Fred, days before the meeting, and had been waiting for a response from Fred. Instead, Baker and Fred had planned a booby trap.

"Let me see your list," I demanded sharply.

Under the circumstances, Fred could find no way to refuse me. Basically a decent person, Fred was clumsy and ill-suited for a dirty tricks conspiracy. He handed me the list. I was astounded at what I saw. The list was outrageously inadequate and unbalanced.

After allowing for six days of testimony from the arresting police sergeant and the Watergate burglars, with the significant omission of Jim McCord, Baker's strategy called for producing first the principal witnesses who were the targets of the investigation—such as Mitchell, Colson, Ehrlichman and Haldeman—and offering as the last witness the potentially most powerful accuser, John Dean. It was topsy-turvy. The accused would testify before the accuser was heard. The only exception was Jeb Magruder, who was located on the list before John Mitchell for the obvious purpose of testifying against Mitchell. But we knew Magruder would provide no incriminating evidence against Ehrlichman and Haldeman.

I tried to get to Ervin's office to alert him before he left, but found that he had already gone to the meeting. When I arrived at S-143, the senators were taking their seats and Ervin was about to start. I managed to get to his chair, kneel beside him and rapidly whisper in his ear what I had just learned about Baker's plan. The noise in the room distracted Ervin, and I could tell that he had not understood my warning. He mumbled back to me that Senator Baker had the right to present his views on the witness list.

Baker, having been informed by Fred that I knew, interrupted my impromptu conference with Ervin. He engaged Ervin in a conversation, and I lost my opportunity for any further private discussion with Ervin prior to the opening of the meeting. I thought of asking Ervin to postpone the meeting briefly and leave the room with me. But before I could get his attention again, he looked at the clock and opened the meeting, commenting that some of the members had requested that the meeting be completed as quickly as possible because of important commitments they had elsewhere. I took my seat near Ervin and waited.

At the outset of the meeting, I recommended that the committee put off its public hearings one week until May 22, to give the staff more time to prepare. Senator Baker immediately objected. He said that he and Senator Ervin had both publicly stated that hearings would open on May 15 and that it would prove embarrassing to delay the opening a full week. Although the committee, out of deference to my recommendation, postponed the opening of the hearings two days—to May 17—Baker's objection prevailed.

I next raised the question of immunity for John Dean. I was asking the committee to vote only a tentative position favoring immunity. The committee could reserve its decision as to whether Dean should actually be given immunity until it received a staff report on the value of Dean's information.

Senator Baker rose to his feet and spoke vehemently against any immunity consideration for Dean. "I acknowledge that John Dean can be a key witness before this committee," Baker snapped, his face looking unusually severe. "But I believe he is probably the most culpable and dangerous person in the Watergate affair, and frankly, I don't want to let him get off the hook. This committee will run a grave risk of public criticism if it offers Dean immunity when the U.S. attorney's office has refused to give him immunity."

As I had anticipated, Weicker came to my support. He said that Dean could probably answer a lot of his questions and he wanted to encourage him to come forward to the committee and the staff. He urged the committee to vote in favor of immunity for Dean. Baker's face flushed when he heard Weicker's position. He responded heatedly that he wanted to give immunity to those who needed it and not John

Dean. He said he felt that Howard Hunt should be the one to get immunity.

Ervin said quietly, "Howard, I think John Dean is a mighty important witness, and we should accept our chief counsel's advice. We have to act now, since it is most likely that the Department of Justice will not waive the thirty days they are permitted by the statute, prior to the court's issuing of an order. I, therefore, move that the committee approve that a subpoena be issued to John W. Dean, III, and that the committee agree to grant Dean use immunity only if it appears (1) that he can testify to facts material to the committee's inquiry, and (2) that such testimony cannot be otherwise obtained."

With Senator Ervin making the motion and with the support of Weicker, a minority member of the committee, it was clear that immunity for Dean would be approved by the required two-thirds vote. Realizing this, and without the support of Senator Gurney, who was absent, Baker stated that if the committee was in favor of immunity for Dean, he would vote with the committee. He explained that committee unanimity would result in greater public confidence in the committee's work, but he said that he wanted the record to show that he had grave concern about asking for immunity for Dean at this time.

Baker was not fooling anyone. After the meeting, a horde of reporters and cameramen were waiting in the main hallway of the Capitol for the report of the committee's actions. It was known that Baker desired the public image of a nonpartisan in the Watergate investigation. Certainly, in Dean's case, he did not want to be revealed as the only committee member voting to repress the potentially most serious evidence against the White House.

Senator Ervin asked me to report on the witness list. Before I could respond, Senator Baker interrupted. "If the chairman will let me, I would like to say something about the witness list. I've asked Fred Thompson to prepare a list of witnesses which I think will do the job adequately on the Watergate phase and permit us to avoid lengthy hearings." I started to object to a consideration of an alternative witness list before my recommendations to the committee were presented, but Ervin waved me down, saying, "Let Fred distribute his list and we'll take a look at it."

I was annoyed with Ervin. He should have supported me by insisting on an orderly review of staff proposals to the committee. My worst fears appeared to be coming true. Baker had jumped the gun and Ervin was behaving in a gentlemanly and considerate way to his colleague.

As Fred's list was being handed out to the senators, Baker presented a rationale for his witness list which made it sound like the most effective and efficient plan to present the full facts of the Watergate scandal to the public. Looking at Talmadge, he stressed the fact that with his witness list, the entire public hearings would take only twenty days. "Even that is too long," Baker said, still looking at Talmadge. "We could probably slice off some of the witnesses. I swear that from what I'm hearing, the public is not going to treat this committee kindly if we drag our hearings out. People want this matter to come to an end."

I watched the senators study the list—especially Ervin. They appeared to be responding favorably to Baker's reasoning, and on the surface the list appeared adequate. The issue seemed to be lost. It was happening so fast. My head began to ache from tension, frustration and anger. I was ready to stand up and expose the Baker list for the deception that it was. Damn the civility of the Club!

But I noticed a telltale gesture by Ervin. His right hand was cupped at his lips and his brow was furrowed in deep thought. He looked up for a moment, his eyes showing disturbance and his eyebrows arching. His gaze returned to the list. I had watched Ervin read material often enough to know that these were signals of displeasure.

"Howard," Ervin finally said in a troubled voice, "I don't think this witness list is good for our public hearings. It omits important witnesses. You don't have James McCord here, and he's important. But what concerns me most is that you have Mitchell, Colson, Ehrlichman and Haldeman all testifying before John Dean is called, when John Dean is the witness who will probably give the most incriminating evidence against them. I frankly don't believe we should call any witness unless he is implicated in Watergate by testimony or other evidence we receive or he is willing to admit to his own involvement. Our resolution doesn't call for us to permit witnesses to use our hearings to make exonerating statements when no one has accused them of any wrongdoing before our committee."

Weicker emphasized Ervin's point about Dean. "Gee, all I can say is, and I'm quite disturbed about it, if we followed this list, Dean would be hanged, drawn and quartered before he got a chance to testify."

Talmadge frowned. "I see what you mean, Mr. Chairman, and I agree with you. But can't we take care of the problem by moving John Dean up on the list?"

"That's only part of it—" I started to say, but Ervin interrupted. "Herman, there are other witnesses we have to call that are not on this list," he said. "Sam Dash is preparing a witness list that I'm satisfied will permit us to develop the evidence on the Watergate break-in and cover-up part of our hearings fully and completely."

Baker could see his maneuver had failed. He retreated gracefully. "I'm not committed to any one special witness list," he said. "I only asked Fred to come up with a suggestion. If Dash has got a list that the chairman thinks is good, then let him get it to us right away, so we can see it and release it to the press."

Talmadge suggested that the chairman and the vice chairman should review my list, and if they approved it, they should be authorized to release it without the need for the committee to act on it. This suggestion was agreed to informally, and I promised to have my list ready for release the following day.

The crisis was over. I felt weak but immensely relieved. Ervin had been great, and I was ashamed that I had been afraid he might be taken in by Baker's "game plan."

The meeting appeared to be over, and Senator Talmadge stood up and started to go toward the door. Baker said, "Herman, could you stay a moment? There is one more matter having to do with the conduct of our hearings that needs decision. I hesitate to bring this matter up. But I think it's important that I do. I'm referring to the questioning of the witnesses at the public hearings. Now, I don't wish to denigrate in any way the courtroom abilities of our chief counsel, Sam Dash, or for that matter, Fred Thompson. But the Senate did not appoint Sam Dash or Fred Thompson to present these hearings before the American people. The public expects that United States senators will run these hearings and question the witnesses. I don't want to sound like a prima donna, but I've been a trial lawyer myself, and I think I'm a damn good cross-examiner. I'm sure the same is true about all of you. I recommend, Mr. Chairman, that the senators on the committee, following the usual rotation method, question the witnesses first. Then when the senators have completed their questioning, our counsel, Sam Dash and Fred Thompson, can ask what remaining questions they may have."

Baker's proposal took me by surprise, of course, but I quickly realized how harmful it would be to our hearings. My blood pressure went up again and I became furious. Baker was either on an ego trip, fearful that I would upstage him at the public hearings, or he was simply determined to wreck the hearings. Surely, he had to know that only my staff and I would be thoroughly prepared on the testimony we expected from each of the witnesses. Also, we would know, much better than the senators, the relevance of each piece of documentary evidence and would be able to challenge testimony from a witness that was contrary to the evidence in our possession. Therefore it was essential that I or one of my chief assistants open up with a witness to assure that all the essential facts were presented in an orderly manner.

The senators would of course have the opportunity to question a witness after the basic facts were developed by the initial questioning, and to perform this function properly they needed investigative material and documents from the staff. To meet this need, I planned to distribute summary fact sheets to the senators which would provide a brief statement of all the facts about which each witness could be expected to testify and a reference to relevant documentary evidence in the possession of the committee.

Before anyone else could respond to Baker's proposal, I protested against it, my voice cracking from the emotion of the long, tense meeting. I urged the committee to follow the experience of other major Senate investigating hearings in which committee counsel open up the questioning.

"What makes you think you can open up with the witnesses any better than I can?" Baker asked. "And for that matter, any better than the other members of the committee, who are all lawyers?"

"Simply because I've conducted this investigation, with my staff, and am more prepared. I'm not suggesting that I'm a better lawyer than you are, Senator."

Ervin cleared his throat. "Howard, I can't help but agree with Sam Dash on the matter of questioning the witnesses," he said. "Every important investigating committee I have ever sat on has always conducted its public hearings the way he recommends. It's the chief counsel's job to initially bring out the facts, and it's the job of the committee to then give them a particular emphasis or to sum them up. Frankly, I like to come in at the end and sum up with the witness."

Ervin had to notice that there was tension still in the room. None of the other senators had spoken on the subject, and Baker was obviously displeased with Ervin's opposition to his suggestion. Ervin suddenly chuckled. He cocked his head, and with an angelic smile on his face, said in a playful manner, "Well, my daddy used to say that if you hire a lawyer, you should either take his advice or fire him. Since we're not planning to fire Sam Dash, I suggest we take his advice."

Ervin's light touch dramatically released the tension. His comment produced smiles on the faces of everybody in the room, including

Senator Baker. The matter was settled. I would begin the questioning of each of the witnesses.

But the meeting convinced me that Baker was working against our investigation and public hearings. Senator Gurney was an obvious partisan and, therefore, had no more influence on the committee than his one vote. When he opposed committee actions or made recommendations, his motives were transparent and he was not taken seriously. But Baker was different. His strategy to publicly create a bipartisan image for the committee made him much more persuasive and credible—and less predictable. Perhaps Baker was trying to protect Nixon, and I wondered whether he was acting on orders from the Republican leadership, or on his own initiative. On the other hand, perhaps he was just an ambitious politician caught in a hurricane, seeking safe harbors. If this was true, and I hoped it was, Ervin had a chance to persuade Baker that the safest political role was that of supporter of full and open exposure of wrongdoing, no matter who the offenders might be.

But in any event I knew I had to watch Baker carefully and to anticipate his moves. To the extent he acted through Fred Thompson, I would have little trouble discerning Baker's strategy. To his credit, Fred lacked duplicity. He followed Baker's instructions loyally, but he could not conceal them from me when I questioned him directly. However, after this May 8 meeting, I decided I could no longer confide in Fred Thompson or allow him or his staff access to sensitive areas of our investigation.

I called Shaffer the next morning. Just a half-hour earlier he had been served with a subpoena for Dean to appear before the committee on Thursday. He was angry and wanted to see me in my office right away.

When Shaffer arrived, he seemed out of breath and irritated. It was essential that Dean deal only with me in the beginning and he urged me to call off Thursday's session. "Dean's public appearance won't be worth a damn," Shaffer said, "if what he tells you, in preparation for the hearings, is pipelined back to the White House. Those bastards don't know what the fuck Dean remembers or what fucking documents Dean has taken out of the White House. Do you understand? If they find out before he testifies, they'll do everything to screw him to the wall. They will have time to launch a public campaign to destroy Dean, as well as an opportunity to alter and fabricate documents and stories. Dean would be discredited before he gets a chance to open his mouth before your committee at the public hearings." Shaffer paused, then continued, keeping his eyes fixed on mine. "Now, I'm going to give it to you straight. From what Dean tells me, Howard Baker and Fred Thompson are working for the President. They are in regular contact with the White House, and as soon as they know what Dean has got, the White House will have it only moments later."

Shaffer's statement shook me. For a couple of minutes I just looked at him, unable to say anything. I wasn't surprised to hear it confirmed that Baker was a strong Republican partisan. I had come to that conclusion from his actions at our meetings. And I knew Fred was in Baker's pocket. He had been Baker's campaign manager in Nashville and had even admitted to me that he would have to take a partisan position if he was so instructed by Baker. But the accusation by Dean's lawyer that Baker and Thompson were tied to the Nixon White House was astounding indeed. Certainly, John Dean ought to know. This information explained many of Baker's actions which had left me wondering about his motives.

But I knew Dean was also talking to the federal prosecutors, who were under the control of the Justice Department, a source of leaks to the White House. "How do you know that the Justice Department people are not keeping the White House informed about what Dean is telling Silbert?"

"We know they are. But Dean hasn't told Silbert that much yet. They don't have his full story or his documentary proof. He hasn't told them anything about the President. Frankly, I would like to have him tell his story completely on television at your public hearings—even before he testifies before the grand jury."

"Okay, Charlie," I said, "You can forget about the subpoena. I'll tell Ervin about it. It will just be Dean and me. We'll have to meet outside the Senate office building. I'll come to any hideaway place you suggest."

Shaffer still was not satisfied. What would be the status of my meetings with Dean? If they were to be official interrogations, even if conducted by me alone, the committee would be entitled to have a report on what Dean was telling me. Also, the committee had not finally agreed to give Dean immunity. Dean would be taking the risk of talking to me without the assurance that I would not be a witness against him at some future time to reveal his admissions.

As Shaffer was defining the problem, I formulated a solution. "We will have to use a subterfuge—a subterfuge for a good purpose. I will treat my meetings with Dean as non-interviews. It will be as though I weren't there. Dean should feel free to tell me everything, and since I won't be officially interviewing him, I will keep what he says to myself.

I will not tell my staff or any member of the committee what I learn. The only exception will be Ervin, since I need his authorization to do this, and he can be completely trusted."

Shaffer seemed amused. "But how do your 'non-interviews' get Dean immunity?"

"I'll work it like this. If Dean's statements to me do not, in my opinion, justify my recommending immunity for him to the committee, then I'll treat our meetings as though they never occurred. I'll just walk away and not reveal what he tells me to anyone but Ervin. There will be no immunity and Dean will have to testify before the committee or plead the Fifth Amendment."

"And if you think his information is worth immunity?" Shaffer asked.

"Then I will recommend to the committee that they vote Dean immunity, without telling six members of the committee the factual basis to support their vote. They will have to act on my recommendation alone, with confidence in me that I would not make the recommendation if the facts did not merit it. I would really be counting on enough committee members having confidence in Ervin and Ervin having confidence in me."

"What if your prima donna senators turn you down?"

"Then, again, it will be as if Dean and I had not met, and I will not disclose anything he tells me. If Dean is willing to trust me, he has nothing to lose."

"That's no problem," Shaffer said, "He already trusts you. But you have to get Ervin's okay."

"I'll do that right away and call you."

As soon as Shaffer left, I met with Ervin and reported to him everything Shaffer had told me and the unorthodox plan I was recommending for my meetings with Dean. His face clouded when he heard me explain Shaffer's reasons for distrusting Baker and Thompson. But his only comment was, "I guess the White House is putting a lot of pressure on Howard. It's a pity."

Ervin conceded that my plan was tactically necessary and authorized me to meet with Dean under its terms. "I don't like holding back important information from my colleagues on the committee," he said, "but John Dean must have vital evidence and we have to use any strategy we can to secure it for our public hearings. We may be on the brink of learning the full Watergate story from him. And yet, we can't say at this time whether Dean is going to tell us the truth. I count on you, Sam, to challenge everything he tells you, and to thoroughly cross-examine him, so that you can report to me whether he is worth supporting as a witness."

I called Shaffer and told him of Ervin's approval. He said he would set up a meeting with Dean for the weekend and would call Saturday morning.

After I hung up, I contemplated my projected meeting with Dean. I was suspicious of Dean's motives, and knew I had to be careful. I had met John Dean about two years earlier, when he was working as a staff lawyer for the President's Commission for the Reform of the Federal Criminal Law, chaired by former Governor Edmund (Pat) Brown of California. I was told then by other staff lawyers on the commission to watch John Dean, since he was expected to go far politically. They correctly predicted his meteoric rise, which took him, at the age of thirty, from the Justice Department to the office of counsel to the President in the White House. Dean was to ruefully explain later that his White House post was big in title only, which, together with his large office, masked the fact that he had become only a glorified messenger boy for Bob Haldeman and John Ehrlichman.

Dean had been an ambitious, main-chance operator, who was skillful at working the angles to place himself close to the seat of power. His success story was a WASP version of *What Makes Sammy Run*. Caught now in a squeeze play between his former White House bosses and the prosecutors at the U.S. attorney's office, Dean could be capable of trying to protect himself by fashioning a story to make himself appealing to us and the prosecutors.

While cautioning myself to be wary, I could not help reflecting on an amazing paradox. Dean was now seeking complete immunity from prosecution from both the U.S. attorney's office and our committee. The irony of it could not be more striking. Dean had substantially contributed to his own inability to receive such immunity.

Since 1892 the Supreme Court had followed the rule that a witness had to be given complete immunity from prosecution for any crime related to the transaction under inquiry—called transactional immunity—if the government wanted to compel him to testify and deprive him of his Fifth Amendment right against self-incrimination. But in 1969 Dean, together with a small group of fellow government lawyers, sought to make it easier to convict criminal defendants. They proposed, among other things, in the Organized Crime Control Bill that a witness's claim of his Fifth Amendment protection could be overriden by giving him immunity only from the use of his testimony against him. With this new form of immunity—called use immunity—the witness could still be prosecuted for crimes relating to the same subjects of his compelled testimony if the government showed that its evidence was obtained independently of this testimony.

As the American Bar Association's incoming chairman of the Section of Criminal Law, I had attacked Dean's use immunity provision as an unconstitutional effort to dilute the Fifth Amendment. But the Congress, responding to its constituents' fear of crime in the streets, followed the recommendations of Dean and his group and passed the Organized Crime Control Act of 1970 containing the use immunity provision. President Nixon signed the new law, and later the Supreme Court, dominated by Nixon appointees, upheld the constitutionality of the use immunity provision.

Now the tables were turned: Dean, the suspect, was seeking the legal protection of the transactional immunity that Dean, the lawyer, had helped destroy; and I, the interrogator, could only offer him use immunity, which I had once so strongly opposed.

8
Secret Meetings

ON SATURDAY MORNING SHAFFER CALLED ME AT HOME TO TELL ME that I could meet with Dean at five o'clock that afternoon at his law office in Rockville, Maryland. Shaffer, McCandless and Dean were waiting for me when I arrived at the handsome and comfortable law office Shaffer had set up inside a row of town houses.

Despite his quickly emerging center-stage role as a Watergate figure, Dean was essentially an unremarkable person. He was short and slight, with an oval-shaped, intelligent-looking face—a look highlighted by his thin horn-rimmed glasses. Dean greeted me pleasantly, but with obvious nervousness. Later he confided to me that he had been worried about my opinion of him. He wanted me to trust and respect him, even to like him.

At the time of our meeting, he saw himself as a young lawyer who had pulled himself out of a powerful conspiracy and was expiating the wrongs he had committed by his willingness to expose them to the public and to testify to facts that only he was able and willing to reveal. He thought his informer role displayed courage which merited the friendship and good will of those who were investigating the conduct in which he was so enmeshed. Indeed, as he talked to me that evening, he spoke in a cold, matter-of-fact way, as though he was describing someone else's conduct, and not his own.

I viewed Dean differently. He was much the same as his colleagues in the Watergate conspiracy—Magruder, Mitchell, Haldeman and Ehrlichman. Although Dean had turned informer, I thought he had done so in an effort to save his own skin. By now he knew he was cornered. Magruder's and Kalmbach's testimony would be enough to convict him. His only means of escape was to trade off the incriminating evidence he had against larger game. Yet the longer I spent with Dean on his inside story of Watergate, the more appealing he became. Whatever his motives, he appeared to be committed to the exceedingly difficult role, for him, of exposing the full truth to the public—even the truth about the President of the United States. More than anyone else, Dean realized how weak an accuser he was against such powerful figures and how vulnerable a target for destruction he was making of himself.

Now as I came face-to-face with Dean, Shaffer leaned back in his tall judge's chair and announced matter-of-factly, "Here's John Dean, like I promised you. He wants to be a completely cooperative witness and tell you everything he knows. But as his lawyer, I have had to advise him that there are some restrictions on what he can tell you, at least initially."

"What restrictions?" I asked, surprised. "I thought these informal talks were to be wide open." I looked at Dean, who sat quietly in a leather chair beside Shaffer's desk.

"I'm not saying they won't be, eventually," Shaffer said. "But the purpose of your questioning is to prepare Dean for public testimony, and for the time being there are certain things I don't want him to tell you because he has problems with them—problems I'm sure you and I will be able to solve."

"What problems?" I asked, trying to keep my voice from showing the disappointment and annoyance I was beginning to feel.

"The President has ordered Dean not to disclose any matters relating to national security on pain of criminal prosecution. That's one problem. Also, Dean's position was counsel to the President, and he may be prohibited from disclosing presidential conversations to which he was a party by reason of attorney-client privilege or executive privilege."

Having received this kind of double-talk from Len Garment in my negotiations to obtain the testimony of White House aides, I was irritated at hearing it from Shaffer in what now appeared to me to be a stalling tactic on Dean's part. "Come off it!" I said, turning to Dean, my voice filled with exasperation. "You don't really believe that any information you have to give me about Watergate involves national security or any special privilege?"

Dean looked directly at me. His voice was clear and firm. "No, I can't honestly say I do," he replied.

"Neither can I," Shaffer snapped. "But that doesn't mean a fucking thing." Shaffer got up, walked around to the front of his desk, and bracing himself with his hands, half sat, half leaned against the edge of the desk. "My client hasn't made any serious mistakes yet since he decided to talk against his former bosses. But you can be goddamned sure that White House gang is watching every move he makes to catch him tripping up just once. They've spread out the word that he's an unscrupulous, back-knifing rat. And if they catch him breaking just one little rule, they'll pounce on him and try to crush him."

"But you both said you didn't believe he would be breaking any rules if he told his story without any restrictions," I argued.

"But I also said, Brother Dash, that right now that doesn't mean shit. They can make it look like he's doing something wrong and that's all they need." Shaffer paused, his eyes fixed on mine, and then continued. "When John Dean testifies before your committee and gets to any questionable area where a claim of privilege or national security may possibly be raised, I want him to be an honorable and patriotic young lawyer, who still obeys the instructions of the President. He's going to respectfully decline to answer those questions. Then I want your committee to hear his explanation in executive session, decide that there is no national security or privilege ground for his refusal to answer the questions and order him to answer. And then he'll answer, but he won't be a reckless volunteer. He will be reluctantly complying, under compulsion, with the order of a Senate committee, knowing that he would be jailed for contempt of Congress if he didn't answer." Shaffer's voice had gradually thickened into a Tennessee drawl as he spelled out his scheme to protect his client from adverse public opinion and White House vengeance.

I still wasn't satisfied, however, that this strategy had any relevance to my informal discussions with Dean. When I made this point, Shaffer sidetracked it by asking me to have a little patience. "This is only our first meeting, Sam," he said. "Let's live a little with each other."

Of course, he was right. Shaffer and Dean were as uneasy about me as I was about them. In my eagerness to milk Dean dry of everything he knew about Watergate I had ignored the reality of our relationship. Shaffer was proving to be an extremely able and cautious lawyer. His client's position was so sensitive that guiding him along a safe course of action was like moving in a treacherous mine field. Shaffer was taking his chances inch by inch. In the days ahead, as I continued to meet with Dean, when Shaffer became convinced that I could be completely trusted, barriers were removed and Dean was permitted to talk freely to me, without any restriction.

Neither Weicker's notes of his brief meeting with Dean nor the media stories on what Dean was expected to reveal had prepared me for the amazing disclosures that Dean then began to make even within the limitations set by Shaffer. My first jolt came when I asked him to tell me about the planning of the break-in.

"Sam, that is not the beginning," Dean said with an impatient look on his face. "You are making the mistake of concentrating on the break-in of the Democratic National Committee headquarters. Frankly, that was not very significant when viewed in its total context. You cannot understand the Watergate burglary without knowing its background."

"What background?" I asked, surprised. I did not understand what Dean was saying.

"The burglary at the Watergate was just the last of a series of similar acts over a period of years sponsored by the White House. It was really not unusual, in light of what had been going on. When I've told you everything, you will see that a way of life had developed in the White House which made a burglary or an illegal wiretap acceptable and almost normal behavior."

Dean's statement produced the amazed expression on my face that he expected.

"It's worse than anything you would ever guess at." Dean's face was grim "You have part of the beginning of it in the material I turned over to Judge Sirica in the safe-deposit box."

"Sirica hasn't let us have that material yet, although we have filed a motion for it. We expect to get it."

"Well, when you do get it, you will see that it is a plan for implementing police-state practices in this country approved by the President."

"Police state!" I repeated incredulously.

"That might be covered by a national security objection," Shaffer interjected. "The President has ordered Dean not to discuss these matters. That's why, under my advice, Dean put the documents relating to this subject in a safe-deposit box and gave the key to Judge Sirica. It was the only way I could figure out to protect Dean from violating the President's order, and still have the material in the hands of a proper legal authority for further disposition."

"They presently bear the highest national security classification possible," Dean explained. "But I don't think they have anything to do with national security. Your committee should be able to easily conclude that a plan, approved by the President, to engage in burglaries, wiretaps, and mail covers to destroy protests in this country is not a national security program."

"Why don't you go on and tell me what you know in your own way," I suggested.

Dean began to meticulously relate his insider's account of conspiracy, lawlessness and deceit in the White House and at the CRP. Although under Shaffer's ground rules for the first meeting, Dean withheld facts about President Nixon, he forged chain upon chain of incriminating evidence against Haldeman, Ehrlichman and Mitchell.

Dean talked on in a dry monotone. I took pages of notes on a yellow pad, interrupting frequently for clarification or to probe an apparent inconsistency. I received not only full explanations but additional facts that Dean recalled as a result of my questioning. His ability to spontaneously remember facts and events in sharp detail when challenged, as well as the fact that these recollections were consistent with facts he had earlier related, made Dean very credible.

"You have to understand, Sam," Dean explained at one point, "that I still haven't reconstructed all the facts. I did not keep a diary and I've had to use a number of memos and other documents that I took with me from the White House. Most of my records are still in the White House. I have been spending a lot of time trying to recollect all of the events that are important. Therefore, I won't be able to give you all of the facts at this meeting or even the next one. It's going to take some time for me to refresh my memory and to put most of the facts in order." I told Dean that I understood this and that I would do the best I could to help him refresh his memory by my questioning.

Dinner time had passed and McCandless went out to an all-night restaurant and brought back sandwiches. Dean continued to talk while I questioned and took notes. I had lost all sense of time. When I did look at my watch, I was startled to see that it was two o'clock in the morning. Dean and I had been working intensely for nearly nine hours.

Shaffer had fallen asleep in his chair. McCandless was stretched out on the couch and was finding it difficult to keep his eyes open. I suddenly thought Sara would be panicking over what might have happened to me. I interrupted Dean's narrative and told him that I wanted to call my wife.

My home phone had hardly completed a full ring when Sara's anguished voice asked where I was. I tried to calm her by telling her that I was fine and that I was still working at Shaffer's office questioning John Dean.

"But why didn't you call me? I have been going out of my mind. You have no idea what I thought could have happened to you! I was ready to call the police. But I didn't even know where you were meeting. When are you coming home?"

"I'll be leaving here in about a half-hour. Don't worry, honey, everything is all right. Why don't you go to sleep."

Sara said she was too worried and would wait up for me. Dean and I decided to get some rest and we made arrangements to meet again Sunday evening at seven.

As I drove home through the silent, empty streets at three in the morning, I thought of what Dean had told me. It seemed unreal. Dean had been wise to take the memos and documents from the White House to support his story. He would need them, since, as Dean feared, the White House would surely launch an attack to discredit him.

I started out again for Shaffer's office in the early evening of that same day. This time I told Sara where I was going and gave her Shaffer's office telephone number. She said she didn't like my going alone because I could be in danger. But I kissed her and told her there was nothing to worry about.

Dean was more relaxed with me this second meeting. Once again he began methodically to lift the curtain on the Watergate drama. Initially, he focused on a February 1973 meeting at La Costa, California, in which he, Haldeman and Ehrlichman devised various schemes to derail our Senate investigation. One plan, Dean said, was aimed at locating the soft belly of the Senate committee that had just been appointed. The obvious choice would be an influential Republican member. Their first try was to persuade the ranking minority member of the committee, Senator Howard Baker, to accept their guidance in appointing the minority counsel. But Baker declined their help and appointed his campaign manager in Nashville, Fred Thompson.

However, Dean said, Baker redeemed himself at the White House shortly afterwards when he requested a private, off-the-record meeting with Nixon. Nixon interpreted Baker's overture as an indication that Baker wanted to help him with the committee. Dean was asked to prepare agenda and briefing papers to guide the President on the points he wanted to make to Baker concerning the best way the Senate committee's activities could be restricted to protect the White House. The President felt the meeting went very well, Dean said, and believed that Baker would work for him inside the committee.

Dean showed me a copy of the agenda and briefing papers for the President's meeting with Baker which he had taken with him from the White House. Dean's agenda paper dealt with a number of other Watergate topics, but the Baker meeting was the first item listed. This subject was outlined for the President as follows:

AGENDA

Matters to be discussed and resolved:

(1) *Baker meeting with President:*
—Baker requested secret meeting re Watergate hearings.
—Baker told Timmons he wants guidance, but to maintain his purity in the Senate he doesn't want anyone to know of meeting with the President.
—Timmons believes that Baker wants to help.
—Timmons does not feel Baker would object if there was staff present during meeting, so long as fact of meeting never gets out.
—Meeting would be excellent chance to find out what Baker plans to do and set up channel to work with him.

The briefing paper, in scriptlike fashion, provided a more detailed "scenario" for Nixon's secret meeting with Baker:

Potential Matters for Discussion with Sen. Baker
Meeting to be totally off the record
Time: 30–45 Min.
~~Staff: Timmons and Dean~~

General

—Take Baker's pulse and find out how much he wants to help keep this from becoming a political circus.

—Baker can be assured that no one in the White House had any knowledge that there was going to be a break-in and bugging of the DNC.

—If Baker appears to be truly desirous of cooperating—and the fact he is seeking guidance may so indicate—he might be told that there are matters unrelated to the bugging incident per se (e.g., Segretti, Kalmbach) that could be embarrassing and tarnish good people whose motives were the highest. Surely he can appreciate that things which occur at the White House have a degree of sensitivity that occur nowhere else in government.

1968 Bugging

—Tell Baker that J. Edgar Hoover personally informed the President shortly after taking office that his campaign had been bugged. Presently seeking to obtain documentation and evidence of the 1968 incidents.

Appearances of White House Staff Members before Senate Committee

—Statement coming out shortly on the matter of Executive privilege. (Draft attached)

—Cannot state at this time if such witnesses will be provided to Committee. Must wait to determine how the issue develops.

—A possible resolution of the problem may be that when the Committee believes a White House staff member is essential as a witness, we can compromise and agree upon a sworn written interrogation.

General Guidance

—Seek to get hearings over as quickly as possible because they really are a potential witch hunt. The President can note that hearings of this type damage all government officials and the institutions of government. The public wants to believe the worst about all politicians and hearings of this type are going to damage all elected officials.

—Committee procedures should protect the rights of minority members to information, calling its own witnesses, notice of meetings, etc.

—Minority Counsel should be tough, aware of the way things operate in Washington, and able to handle a fellow like Sam Dash who has been selected as Majority Counsel. Dash is a partisan.

Communication with White House
—Wally Johnson should be initial contact point, but if Baker feels he
wants to raise something that he chooses not to discuss with Wally,
then arrangements can be made to meet with Dean. (NOTE: Frankly,
the naming of Dean as the man who deals with the President on such
matters preserves our posture on Executive privilege should Dean be
called as a witness.)

According to Dean, Baker told the President that he did not want
his contacts to be directly with the White House, and preferred to deal
through Attorney General Richard Kleindienst as an intermediary. As
recently as the latter part of April, according to Dean, a Baker staff
assistant had been in constant touch with the White House, and had
even complained to Ehrlichman that his efforts at maintaining contact
with the White House had been unsatisfactory. Dean said that when
Nixon learned of this complaint, he told Ehrlichman to direct Kleindienst to call Baker, so that Baker would not be unhappy.

The details related by Dean presented a much more damning case of
double-dealing by Baker than Shaffer had earlier disclosed to me. How
was I to work with Baker and Thompson now? What would Ervin's
reaction be? Should we expose Baker publicly when we had not even
opened our public hearings? Wouldn't it destroy the committee? Although these questions rushed through my mind, I put them aside for
the time being.

Dean continued to speak rapidly from the notes he had prepared. He
wandered from one event to another, telling a story of White House
hysteria over public dissent and the illegal repressive actions to counter
dissent that were taken or authorized by the President's top men and
agents during a period spanning from 1969 to the date he was fired,
April 30, 1973. From time to time he would name persons he thought
should be interrogated and suggested key questions to be asked of them.
Also, he identified various types of White House papers that he said
were important to our investigation and should be subpoenaed by the
committee.

The President's news summaries were especially important, Dean
said. The White House position had been that the President paid little
attention to his political campaign because he was too busy with foreign
affairs and important domestic matters. Dean said that was not true.
The President spent most of his time with political details and was
engrossed in the Watergate scandal. Dean said this could be proved if

we could get copies of the news summaries that daily went to the President. Nixon would mark up these summaries with directions for action, most often with obscene comments. Dean predicted that the President's notes on the news summaries would primarily deal with Watergate-related matters, rather than with foreign or domestic affairs.

When I asked him to tell me about his conversations with the President concerning Watergate, Dean hesitated and looked at Shaffer. Shaffer nodded to him. Dean's voice became almost inaudible. "The President was involved in the cover-up," he said quietly and unemotionally. "I will give you all the details of my meetings with the President. But I prefer to postpone that until I have thoroughly reviewed my notes and refreshed my recollection of these meetings. I want to try to be as accurate as possible when I talk about the meetings I had with the President."

However, to satisfy me that there was a basis for his accusation, he offered two examples. One occurred in March and the other in April of 1973. Dean said that in March, after Hunt had threatened to expose "the seamy things" involving the White House if he didn't get paid, Nixon coldly told him that he would be able to raise one million dollars if necessary to pay off Hunt to remain silent. Nixon's only question was about how the payment would be made, and he seemed satisfied when Dean explained the money would be "laundered" to keep it from being traced to the White House. In April, Dean said, the President admitted to him that he had told Colson prior to the opening of the first Watergate trial, in January 1973, that Hunt could be assured he would receive a pardon if he pleaded guilty and kept silent. However, Dean told me that Nixon was worried about this meeting with Colson, and after telling him about it, he added nervously, "I suppose I shouldn't have talked to Colson. I was a fool."

The manner of Dean's presentation lent credibility to it. He spoke reluctantly, almost apologetically and without animosity. Another factor was persuasive of its reliability. In the course of his statement, John Dean had told me he could not lie to the President. It would be unlikely, then, for him to lie about the President. Though opportunistic and desperate, this young lawyer, who had known the spell of the Oval Office and was now at the mercy of the government, would hardly dare accuse the President falsely.

The impact of Dean's facts left me silent for a while. It was now imperative that Dean's testimony before our committee be extremely clear and well organized, and whenever possible, supported by documents. I told Dean that although I was impressed with the information he was giving me, it was still very unorganized and required as much documentation as he could give. Dean told me that he needed time to work with the numerous papers he had taken from the White House and to put his facts in an orderly and topical form.

"That's what I've been trying to get him to do," Shaffer said. "When he's finished that job, he will have a statement that I want him to read to the committee before he answers questions. It will be a complete narrative." I told Shaffer that I wanted to continue to meet with Dean as he was preparing his statement.

"My God!" I exclaimed as I looked at my watch. "It's two-thirty A.M.!" I had been so absorbed in Dean's story that I had once again not noticed the hours flying by. I decided it was too late to call home, since Sara must have gone to sleep. I suggested that instead of meeting the next day, Dean should take the time to go over his materials and be prepared to give me the details about his meetings with the President. We arranged to meet again on Tuesday evening at seven. Since Dean would be working with his papers at home, in Alexandria, he thought it would be better to meet there, and gave me directions for driving to 100 Quay Street.

Once again I took the lonely drive from Rockville back to my home in Chevy Chase.

When I arrived home, Sara was standing in the open doorway, her face wet with tears. "But I was perfectly safe," I said, trying to calm her fears. "How do you really know?" Sara cried, and threw herself, sobbing, into my arms.

Monday morning, I reported to Ervin on my weekend meetings with Dean. He listened to me hungrily. "Is he a believable witness?" Ervin asked when I had finished.

"I couldn't break his story," I replied, "and he provides enough supporting details that naturally fit together to persuade me he's telling the truth."

Ervin's face reddened, his brow became deeply furrowed and his eyes darted about. "If Dean is telling the truth, then we've come mighty close to losing the Constitution we've cherished and the kind of country it has nurtured. Why, the thinking of those men in the White House is not much different than the thinking of the Nazis in Germany. With all their patriotic talk and their charges against subversive activities, they have represented the most dangerous subversive threat to American ideals and government. We've got to awaken the American people to this danger, and I believe that our public hearings will accomplish that."

"I've heard enough from Dean," I advised Ervin, "to be satisfied that we should recommend final action on immunity for him at tomorrow's committee meeting."

"You're perfectly right, Sam," Ervin said. "We'll put it on the agenda for tomorrow's meeting and I know we'll get the necessary two-thirds vote. "Senator Weicker is voting with us on this question. Dean's a mighty clever person. His talk with Lowell won him over completely."

The major item on the agenda for the committee's meeting on Tuesday morning, May 15, was my recommendation that Judge Sirica be asked to grant an order of immunity for Dean. The committee had voted favorably on a number of immunity requests I had made earlier. The most notable of these were for Hunt, Liddy and Magruder. On these prior occasions when I had requested an immunity vote for a witness, I had provided the committee with a summary of the evidence that could be expected from the witness in order to justify a grant of immunity. This time, under my agreement with Shaffer, I could not do this.

The tension in the room was noticeable as the pre-meeting chatter abruptly stopped when Ervin called for order. The senators and staff all knew that an important decision about John Dean was to be made which could rip apart the polite curtain of bipartisanship the committee had been displaying. Dean had already emerged in public reports as the most dangerous threat to the Nixon White House. Only later would we learn, through the White House tapes and transcripts, how much of Dean's accusations delivered to the prosecutors were known from the start by Nixon through briefings he received from Kleindienst and Petersen. It is not difficult to imagine the White House pressure on Baker and Gurney to work against Dean at the time of this committee meeting.

Ervin announced that I had met with Dean, but only under special conditions, which Ervin had approved, where I was the only one present on behalf of the committee. He then asked me to continue with the report. I explained why Dean had insisted on meeting with me alone and concluded by saying, "Although I cannot reveal Dean's facts to the committee at this time, I can report to you, as chief counsel, that Dean's evidence is vitally important to the committee's investigation, that we cannot obtain this information from any other source, and that it, therefore, meets the committee's standards for implementing its use immunity powers."

I held my breath. I knew I was presuming on the prerogatives and egos of most of the senators in the room. What I was doing was simply not done at the United States Senate. However, I had the chairman's authorization and support—and that was enough.

Senator Gurney's face was contorted with anger. "That's nothing but sheer nonsense!" he shouted. "Dean's just trying to use this committee to escape punishment for the crimes he's committed. I think it's an insult to this committee to be told that its members can't be trusted, and that it should grant a witness like Dean immunity without even knowing anything about his testimony. The minority certainly has a right to know the factual basis for such an immunity recommendation. I think it's outrageous and we should not succumb to this transparent effort to manipulate this committee."

"I thoroughly agree with Ed Gurney," Baker spoke out, casting a bitter glance in my direction. "From what I hear, Dean is the principal culprit in this Watergate affair. Our investigation should be directed towards building a case against him, rather than trying to shield him with immunity." Baker was seated to the left of Ervin at the end of Ervin's desk, close to the side wall of S-143. He rose as he spoke and braced himself against the wall. His voice had become loud and belligerent. "Let me tell you," he continued, "we'll rue this day if we grant Dean immunity. History will not treat kindly with us. This committee has already voted to subpoena Dean to testify. I want to press that decision and have Dean brought down here and asked a lot of questions. If he wants to, he can take the Fifth Amendment. Then we can decide on a question-by-question basis, whether to offer Dean immunity for a particular answer. Ed's absolutely right that this committee can't let itself buy a pig in a poke, and suffer, in addition, the indignity of letting a witness tell us he won't let us know what he's got because he doesn't trust us. Damn it, we're United States senators, and we shouldn't let a criminal suspect like Dean push us around!"

I had expected Gurney and Baker to put up a fight. But Baker's wild attack on Dean only served to support Dean's suspicions of Baker. However, I concurred that the law required that Dean first plead the Fifth Amendment to a line of questions before the committee could grant him immunity.

"I don't agree with you at all, Howard," Weicker challenged Baker. "I think that John Dean is a key witness who has a very valuable story to tell this committee and the public. I think Sam Dash is right in urging us to grant him immunity and I support him a hundred percent."

We now had one Republican vote. When Ervin spoke up, Talmadge, Inouye and Montoya would surely follow him, and we would have the needed two-thirds majority.

"I authorized Sam Dash to meet with John Dean," Ervin said, "because I believed that Dean could reasonably fear that his story would leak from this committee. I'm not saying that I agree with his accusations about any members of this committee, but frankly, we've never been able to hold a secret when it's generally known by the committee. I think Dean will be the most important witness this committee will be able to present to the public. I am convinced that he has testimony that will get to the very heart of the Watergate scandal and reveal how the cover-up was carried out by all the persons who were involved." Ervin paused. The room was completely silent. Ervin's face was lifted with his mouth open. He then dropped his gaze and said matter-of-factly, "I move that the staff be authorized to request a grant of immunity for John Dean under the provisions of the appropriate statute."

Senator Weicker seconded the motion. The vote was five to two in favor of Senator Ervin's motion. Senator Baker and Senator Gurney had voted against the motion.

I waited expectantly, and was not disappointed. "Mr. Chairman," Baker said in a soothing voice after the vote, "I don't think it's good for this committee at this early stage of its work to present a divided image to the public. Our work is going to be tough enough, without it looking like we are acting in a partisan manner. Therefore, in a spirit of harmony, I'd like to change my vote, and if Ed Gurney is willing to join me, your motion will have the unanimous support of the committee."

"I'll go along with Howard Baker," Gurney said, "but before I vote, I would also like to say I think we're making a mistake." The vote was taken again, and it was unanimous for approval.

The meeting was adjourned. Ervin and Baker went out into the hall of the Capitol to appear before the waiting crowd of reporters and cameramen. Ervin began to announce the committee's action when Baker interrupted him and took over the microphones. "The chairman and I want to announce that our committee has unanimously voted to grant John Dean use immunity," he said in an obvious effort to convey the appearance of harmony within the committee.

That evening I drove to Alexandria to meet with John Dean at his home. I found 100 Quay Street at the corner of a row of recently constructed expensive town houses. Though new, the town houses preserved the traditional colonial design of old Alexandria. The street ended at the waterfront, and Dean's house overlooked the Potomac. His view of the river, however, would soon be blotted out by a large condominium building, whose construction was announced on a billboard at the waterfront across from Dean's house. Perhaps more offensive to Dean than the blocking of his view was the name of the building that was to loom in front of his home and cast a shadow for a considerable part of each day. The sign on the billboard announced in fat black letters: TO BE CONSTRUCTED ON THIS SITE SOON—THE WATERGATE OF ALEXANDRIA.

I rang Dean's doorbell, and a beautiful blond young woman opened the door. She had been expecting me, and introduced herself as John Dean's wife, Maureen Dean. "Everybody calls me Mo," she said with a sweet smile. "John is out with Charlie Shaffer, and he just called and said they were on their way home. Can I get you something cold to drink?"

I followed Mo Dean into the kitchen of the richly furnished split-level home. She had the kind of beauty that makes most men self-conscious. But she offset this initial reaction by her simple, direct, and pleasantly innocent conversation. As I sipped the iced tea she gave me, she told me about the daily ordeal she experienced with newspaper reporters, who had staked out their house and frequently came to the door seeking interviews. She said she turned them all down, and frequently did not answer the doorbell. Ever since she had married John Dean, in October 1972, life had been hectic for them. She had once liked to go out, but now, she said, she stayed mostly in the house, to avoid being "gawked at."

"People are so mean," she complained. "Why, they have even written a story that John is going out with another woman. He was seen driving in our car with one of my girlfriends. She had visited us, and John was driving her home. They make a big story out of that!"

"I suppose the sign across the street doesn't help much," I said.

"Oh, that! It's terrible! We bought this house because of the view, and now that building is going to ruin it. And isn't it a scream, the name they want to give it? John is so upset. The neighbors around here are all fighting to keep the building from going up. It really violates the zoning restrictions."

I wondered how Mo Dean was coping with her crushing change in fortune. In the several months since their marriage she had seen her husband transformed from the prestigious, influential presidential counsel to the unemployed, frequently reviled informer and self con fessed participant in the most serious criminal and political scandal in the country's history. She showed no outward sign of concern or com- prehension of her husband's—and consequently, her own—desperate plight. Indeed, except for her annoyance over the press's intrusion into her private life, her attitude and behavior seemed to show that she chose to ignore the existence of the problem. Such a remarkable display of indifference, under the circumstances, reflected either insensitivity and shallowness or an extraordinary ability to submerge feelings of personal turmoil. I was unable to detect which was true in Mo Dean's case.

The front door opened, and Dean, Shaffer and McCandless entered. We gathered in the living room and sat down in sumptuous chairs and sofas. Mo brought iced tea for everybody. Dean was informally dressed in slacks and a sports shirt and appeared to be in excellent spirits. He excused himself, went down to his study and returned with a pile of notes and documents.

"I have gone through a lot of these papers I took from the White House," Dean said, "and I think I have been able to reconstruct the important meetings I had with the President." "There must have been many," I speculated.

"That's the interesting thing," Dean replied, "there weren't. A very important fact is that from the time I was appointed counsel to the President in 1971 until September 15, 1972, when the Watergate indict- ments came down, I never had a face-to-face business meeting with the President. September 15, 1972 was the first time, and I was flabbergasted when I was told the President wanted to see me in the Oval Office. That's the time Bob Haldeman was there and the President con- gratulated me on the good job I had done in containing the Watergate investigation so that the prosecution went no further than Liddy."

Dean then described in detail his meetings with the President during February, March and April, 1973. He claimed that his rash of Oval Office meetings during this period was a strategy of the President's to repair a flaw in the reason he gave for refusing to allow Dean to appear as a witness at the Gray confirmation hearings or before our committee.

Nixon had asserted executive privilege, and Dean said he had remarked to Ehrlichman at the time that the President could hardly make such a claim when he had met only once with him. It was shortly after this statement to Ehrlichman, Dean said, that the President began calling him to the Oval Office on a regular basis.

Although Dean had trouble remembering the exact dates of meetings, he vividly recalled the subject matters discussed. Meetings with the President were not events he was likely to forget. He explained that the Oval Office had a magic to it which put the visitor—even a presidential counsel—in a state of awe. "Perhaps this sounds like an apology for my willingness to go along with the cover-up," Dean said earnestly, "but you really have to experience the feeling of being with the President in the Oval Office to understand what I mean. It's a disease I came to call 'Ovalitis.' "

As I sat in Dean's living room listening to the story that would be his sworn testimony, the unimaginable became startlingly real to me. Dean's evidence could destroy President Nixon. He was a witness to the President's actual statements and conduct in the Oval Office which directly implicated the President in the crime of obstructing justice in the Watergate investigation.

Shaffer had been following Dean's recitation closely. When Dean had finished telling me about his meetings with Nixon, Shaffer held up his hand toward Dean to halt Dean's narration. "Now, you understand, Sam, that all this information Dean has just given you about his meetings with the President is covered by our understanding that he hasn't told you anything officially, and you can't use any of it if the President can assert a proper legal privilege against Dean's disclosing anything about these meetings." I acknowledged that Shaffer had correctly stated our agreement, and assured him that the voluminous notes I had been taking would not be put in any file in the Senate office building, but would be kept in a safe place in my home.

I had prepared a long list of questions, based on my review of the prior two meetings with Dean, that required Dean to go over, point by point, most of the facts he had given me. I used this procedure for the double purpose of challenging information that had appeared vague or inconsistent when I reread my notes, and of checking Dean's retelling of the facts for discrepancies with his earlier version. Once again, Dean met this challenge by providing a sharper focus on the information he had previously given me and by producing new factual information, often with supporting documents, as a result of recollection refreshed by my questions.

I found that cross-examination failed to throw Dean off guard, but instead, provided an opportunity for him to strengthen his testimony. From my courtroom experiences as a prosecutor and a defense lawyer, I knew this to be characteristic of a truthful witness. I became more convinced of Dean's credibility and, consequently, his extraordinary importance as a public witness before the committee.

By the end of this third meeting Dean had given me most of the facts relating to the Watergate matter that he could recall. I suggested that he begin to prepare a complete written statement for the committee. When he had finished his first draft, I wanted to read it and cross-examine him on it.

"When do you think Dean will go before the committee?" Shaffer asked.

"Not before the middle of June," I replied. "The Department of Justice will insist that we wait for the full thirty statutory notice days before he gets an immunity order. This should give Dean plenty of time to prepare his written statement."

"And Dean won't be forced to reveal his testimony to the committee until just before he appears in public session?"

"That's right. Senator Ervin has backed me all the way on this agreement. And the committee has supported him. Baker and Gurney yelled bloody murder at first, but they didn't have the votes. They finally went along with the committee, since they didn't want to show their partisan position publicly. I have arranged that Dean will appear in executive session before the committee just a day or two prior to his public testimony."

Shaffer smiled. "Sam, when we first met I wasn't sure we were going to be able to work this. But I have to say that you and Sam Ervin have really shown that you know how to play in this dirty ballgame and still come up clean."

Dean laughed. "He's not used to giving praise. He's really a bastard." Dean paused for a moment, then said, "It's going to be a long and lonely trip for me before your committee. But it's one I've got to make, if I'm ever going to regain any respect for myself and pay the American people back for the damage I helped cause the country."

I left 100 Quay Street in Alexandria exhausted but satisfied. It was three-fifteen in the morning and it had begun to rain. The sound of my windshield wipers provided a backdrop rhythm for the thoughts that crowded my mind as I contemplated the historic appearance of Dean in the Caucus Room.

Major obstacles still lay ahead in the effort to produce Dean as a public witness. One would come from an unlikely source—the new special prosecutor—and force me into a court battle for the public testimony of both Magruder and Dean. The other would cause me to break my promise to Dean that all of his testimony would remain concealed from the committee until one or two days prior to his first public appearance in the Caucus Room.

Yet, in the early morning hours of May 16, when I left John Dean's home in Alexandria, I could not anticipate these threats to Dean's testimony that would shortly confront me. I thought I could now safely turn to the more pressing and urgent task of preparing for the opening of the committee's public hearings the following morning. Of course I would have liked more time to prepare. I was still recruiting lawyers and investigators who would staff the task forces directed by each of my three assistant chief counsel. When the hearings started, there was still only a handful of lawyers and investigators on the staff. Although in a period of one and a half months we had interrogated numerous witnesses and had subpoenaed hundreds of records and documents, I still considered that our investigation had just begun.

The committee's rush toward public hearings seemed in marked contrast to the unhurried pace of the Watergate prosecution team at the federal courthouse. They had been fully staffed and had begun working on the investigation long before we did, and still they had not obtained new indictments. It was obvious that they would not be presenting their evidence publicly, at a trial, for at least another year. It was because of this delay in the criminal prosecutions that I knew we could not postpone our hearings. Senator Ervin was worried that the loss of confidence in government by the people had reached so critical a stage that a national calamity was imminent unless there was some highly visible and responsible action by a branch of government. At this time he believed that only a public airing of the facts of Watergate by our Senate committee could meet the need for responsible government action.

It was especially fitting, Ervin thought, for a Senate select committee to serve this function, since, by so acting, it would be implementing the Constitution's concepts of separation of powers and checks and balances. "Where there is wrongdoing in the executive branch, Sam," he told me, citing Supreme Court authority, "it is the constitutional duty of the Congress to inform the public and provide remedial legislation." He was also fond of quoting President Wilson's statement that in a situation of corruption in the executive branch, "the public-informing function of Congress is even more important than its legislative function."

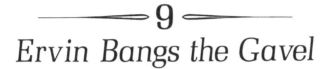

9

Ervin Bangs the Gavel

THE COMMITTEE HAD SCHEDULED FIVE DAYS OF HEARINGS FOR THE first two weeks—May 17, 18, 22, 23 and 25. Each of the witnesses scheduled to appear during these five days had been thoroughly interviewed in advance of his public testimony and notified or subpoenaed to appear on the day he was expected to be reached.

These were the foundation-laying witnesses. Robert Odle, former director of administration for the Committee to Re-Elect the President, and Bruce Kehrli, special assistant to the President, would explain the organization of CRP and the White House with the aid of giant charts my staff had prepared. Sergeant Paul Leeper and Officers John Barrett and Carol Shoffler would tell the story of the arrest of the burglars in the National Democratic Committee headquarters on the sixth floor of the Watergate Office Building on June 17, 1972. James McCord and Bernard Barker, two of the arrested burglars, and Alfred Baldwin, the lookout man, would each tell about his special role in the planning and carrying out of the two break-ins at the Watergate. McCord would also introduce the evidence showing that officials higher up than Liddy participated in Watergate and that a cover-up began immediately after he was arrested.

Ervin had arranged with the Senate Rules Committee for the committee to hold its public hearings in the historic Caucus Room, which had been the scene of the Teapot Dome scandal hearings, the Army-McCarthy hearings and the McClellan committee labor-racketeering hearings. Its chandeliered high ceilings, gracefully columned walls and dramatic mahogany backdrop for the long committee table provided a unique setting.

On Thursday morning, May 17, I was the first from the committee to enter the Caucus Room. It was ablaze with lights and alive with people, who already filled the spaces allocated for the press and the public.

Reporters walked back and forth between the long press tables set up in parallel lines the length of the room, dominating the large center space between the witness table, immediately in front of them, and the public section in the rear. At fixed positions along the wall and corner of the room opposite the entrance, TV cameramen adjusted their equipment for live, video tape and film coverage. Dozens of still photographers competed for choice positions in the space that formed a well between the witness table and the long baize-covered table soon to be occupied by the members of the committee and their counsel.

The sound, movement, equipment and lights all combined to create an electrifying atmosphere of anticipation, excitement and tension. My immediate reaction to this scene was a sense of awe mixed with a feeling of inadequacy. My discomfort arose in part from my apprehension that the committee's initial presentation would fall short of the high drama awaited by our vast audience, disappointing them and perhaps, even worse, losing their interest and attention. In part, also, the splendid Caucus Room setting and the actuality of exposure to a huge audience of observers and critics heightened my dissatisfaction with our state of preparation and readiness.

I walked over to where Sara was sitting in the front row of the public section. She rose and kissed me, saying, "Good luck, honey, and don't worry, you'll be terrific." Sara was beautiful—my greatest booster when I was hesitant or self-deprecating and my severest critic when I needed deflating.

I took my seat at the committee table in front of a pair of microphones and a nameplate. Soon the members of the committee and the minority counsel, Fred Thompson, entered the hearing room and took their seats. Staff assistants sat against the wall directly behind the committee table. A row of rectangular television lights that stretched above our heads and in front of us from wall to wall suddenly lit up.

The committee members were seated according to their political affiliation and seniority. To Ervin's left sat the Democratic majority: Senator Talmadge, senior Democrat after the chairman; then Senator

Inouye; and at the end, Senator Montoya. To Senator Ervin's right sat the Republican minority: Senator Baker, vice chairman and ranking minority member; Senator Gurney; and then Senator Weicker. I sat immediately to the left of Senator Ervin, and Fred Thompson sat immediately to the right of Senator Baker.

I had asked Rufus Edmisten, my deputy chief counsel, to sit behind me to transmit my directions to the staff as the need for facts, legal memos, documents or additional witnesses developed at the hearings. Rufus initially took this position. But he had arranged to have a swivel chair with wheels provided for him, and he would glide more often to a position between Ervin and Baker. As a result, his face appeared in practically every news photograph of the committee.

I learned later how Rufus' photographic exposure had been contrived. At the opening of the hearings Ervin insisted that the army of still photographers be stationed at either end of our long committee table and not in front of it, facing the witness. He wanted to protect the witnesses from being distracted or intimidated by the constant snapping of pictures directly in their faces. The photographers sought Rufus' intervention. He persuaded Ervin to permit the still photographers to occupy the exceptionally advantageous position in front of our table by assuring him they had promised not to take pictures once the witness was sworn and began to testify. This promise they frequently broke. But they faithfully kept their commitment to Rufus in return for the location he had won for them by including him in as many camera shots as possible. Rufus cooperated in this effort by maneuvering his rolling swivel chair.

It is customary at the opening of public congressional hearings for the chairman and committee members to read opening statements. I had prepared a statement for Ervin, which he modified to include some of his own personal thoughts. There was one passage I particularly liked but thought even Ervin might find too colorful. I had inserted it in the statement to permit Ervin to dramatize to the public the crucial difference between the Watergate burglary and ordinary burglaries aimed at property theft. It read:

> If the many allegations to this date are true, then the burglars who broke into the headquarters of the Democratic National Committee at the Watergate were, in effect, breaking into the home of every citizen of the United States. And if these allegations prove to be true, what they were

seeking to steal were not the jewels, money or other property of American citizens, but something more valuable—their most precious heritage: the right to vote in a free election.

Rufus told me this language was "corny" and he didn't think Ervin would want to use it. However, Ervin liked the passage, and when he came to it in reading his public statement at the outset of the hearings, his voice took on an accentuated tone of indignation. He continued solemnly to state the special mission of the committee:

> "The hearings which we initiate today are not designed to intensify or reiterate unfounded accusations or to poison further the political climate of our nation. On the contrary, it is my conviction, and that of the other committee members, that the accusations that have been leveled and the evidence of wrongdoing that have surfaced have cast a black cloud of distrust over our entire society. Our citizens do not know whom to believe, and many of them have concluded that all the processes of government may have become so compromised that honest governance has been rendered impossible. We believe that the health, if not the survival, of our social structure and of our form of government requires the most candid and public investigation of all the evidence and of all the accusations that have been leveled at any persons, at whatever level, who were engaged in the 1972 campaign. My colleagues on the committee and I are determined to uncover all the relevant facts surrounding these matters, and to spare no one, whatever his station in life may be, in our efforts to accomplish that goal. At the same time, I want to emphasize that the purpose of these hearings is not prosecutorial or judicial, but rather legislative and informative."

After Ervin presented his full statement, the other committee members gave their opening statements—beginning with Senator Baker and then, alternately, a Democrat and a Republican, according to seniority. For the most part, they spoke of the bipartisan nature of the investigation and its historic meaning. Senator Gurney, however, warned that although it was important for the committee to get at the truth, the committee must be aware of the impact its proceedings might have on the rest of the world, which faced many dangers, since the United States was in the same boat with the other countries of the world. "Thus," he emphasized, "the rocking of the boat by Watergate, its catastrophic effect upon the institution of the presidency, is indeed the object of serious concern of everyone at home and abroad."

As I heard Gurney make this statement I leaned over to Ervin and whispered, "Gurney doesn't want us to rock the boat." Ervin whispered back, "It appears to me that this is the time the occupants of the boat Gurney speaks about would benefit much more from the cleansing effect of being dumped into the water."

In a very brief statement Senator Weicker focused on a major theme of Ervin's statement, and expressed it in a way that foreshadowed Weicker's repeated display of almost youthful fervor for moral government. Weicker looked directly at the audience in the Caucus Room when he spoke:

> "The gut question for the committee and country alike is and was how much truth do we want? A few men gambled that Americans wanted the quiet of efficiency rather than the turbulence of truth. And they were stopped a yard short of the goal by another few, who believed in America as advertised. So the story to come has its significance not in the acts of men breaking, entering and bugging the Watergate, but of the acts of men who almost—who almost stole America."

As the lackluster witnesses of the first day of hearings gave their detailed testimony, the news reporters grew restless. They were impatient for the appearance of a headline name like Dean or Colson or Mitchell. Therefore, when they learned that James McCord was featured the second day, they complained of boredom. Mary McGrory of the Washington *Star* commented to me wryly, "Everything McCord has to say has already leaked to the press. Is tomorrow going to be a retread of McCord's old testimony?" I smiled at Mary and said, "Why don't you wait and see?"

I had a surprise for the press. McCord's testimony the next day would be treated by the press as the first "bombshell" of our hearings. McCord told me about his new evidence only three days before his appearance as a public witness. He had concealed it from me and the grand jury at his prior interrogations. In the meticulous procedure he had employed earlier, McCord submitted this information to me in a carefully prepared memorandum.

His statement revealed for the first time the story of how McCord had been promised executive clemency by a White House agent if he kept his silence during the first Watergate trial and afterwards. It was a complicated narrative involving a number of meetings McCord had with Jack Caulfield at a prearranged location on the George Washington Memorial Parkway where Caulfield communicated the offer of executive clemency, claiming it came "from the very highest levels of the White House." At the time, Caulfield was a Treasury official, but previously he had worked in the White House as an investigator, frequently for John Dean.

McCord stated he had been directed to the initial meeting with Caulfield in a series of telephone messages he received at a booth on Maryland Route 355 near the Blue Fountain Inn and close to his home. The caller had first telephoned McCord at home and told him to go to the booth. McCord did not recognize the voice on the telephone in any of the calls and could not identify the voice even at the time he testified before the committee. He said he spurned the offer of executive clemency, even though Jack Caulfield, who had been a friend of his, made an implied threat as to the consequences McCord might face from the "administration" if he did not go along with the "game plan."

At the public hearing on May 18 I asked McCord why he had not told any investigating body about these events before. He replied simply that they involved a good friend, Jack Caulfield, and that they might involve the President of the United States. For these reasons, he said, he wanted to be very sure of his facts and had waited until he could accurately reconstruct them in his prepared statement for the committee.

When McCord testified that he could not identify the voice of the person who talked to him on the telephone, Terry Lenzner, who was sitting behind me while I was questioning McCord, whispered, "We know whose voice it was!" I was surprised, because the identification of an anonymous voice is usually an impossible task. If we really did know who called McCord, then we would have fitted another link in the chain of conspirators responsible for Watergate. At the lunch break I asked Terry to join me in my office.

"How the hell were you able to find out who called McCord?" I asked Terry. "We just learned about that incident only three days ago."

"I had been following a different line of inquiry based on what Kalmbach told us in his interviews," Terry replied. "You remember, Kalmbach told us that he used a former New York policeman, Tony Ulasewicz, to make the cash hush payments to the Watergate defendants. We've just interviewed Ulasewicz. In addition to confirming Kalmbach's story, Ulasewicz independently told us Caulfield asked him to call McCord and give him the message about executive clemency and arrange for the meetings with Caulfield on the George Washington Memorial Parkway."

"Then," I said, "after we put on Caulfield to hear his side of the story, we've got to put on Ulasewicz to reveal publicly the owner of the mysterious voice."

"Shit, Sam, that's going to blow Ulasewicz as a witness!"

"What do you mean?" I asked.

"Tony's call to McCord is only a tiny part of his testimony. He's a fascinating witness. Actually, he's funny as hell, although he doesn't mean to be. After receiving thousands of dollars in hundred-dollar bills from Kalmbach, Tony's the one who contacted Mrs. Hunt to find out the names and amounts of the payoffs. He didn't use his real name, but called himself Mr. Rivers. He then made deliveries of the cash by means of 'drops' all over the Washington area."

Terry was clearly upset at the prospect of calling Ulasewicz at this time. "You know, once we have to give the fact sheet on Ulasewicz to the senators, they're not going to be satisfied to question him only about his call to McCord. They'll go all over the fucking map about his working with Kalmbach and his deliveries of the hush money before we've laid a foundation for that part of the narrative. It will screw up your whole strategy of giving the public the facts in some coherent order."

"Don't we have the same problem with Caulfield?" I asked. "Your reports of interviews with Caulfield indicate that he was involved in a lot of the dirty tricks and political espionage."

"That's right," Terry replied. "If the committee gets into those matters, then they're going to ruin the dirty tricks phase of our public hearings, which you've assigned to me."

"There is only one way to handle this," I said. "I'll talk to Ervin and alert him to these dangers. I'll ask him to urge the senators to hold their questions about deliveries of hush money and dirty tricks until the appropriate time when these witnesses will be recalled."

"Do you think that has the slightest chance in hell of working?" Terry exclaimed. "With the television cameras on them and a guy like Tony Ulasewicz as a witness, those senators will go crazy with these facts. It would make a sensational show for them and give them a hell of a lot of publicity."

"I think if Ervin is strong enough, we can carry it off," I said with more assurance in my voice than I actually felt. As Terry, disgruntled, was leaving my office, I asked, "Was there any significance in Ulasewicz using the name Rivers?" "Oh yes." Terry smiled faintly. "Tony says that he was going to be a runner making the cash deliveries, and rivers run."

Caulfield was not due to appear before the committee until Tuesday, May 22. I met with Ervin the day before and told him of our need to call Caulfield and Ulasewicz to expand on McCord's testimony concerning the offer of executive clemency made to him. But I emphasized how imperative it was, for the preservation of coherent public testimony, to limit Caulfield's and Ulasewicz's testimony at this time just to that subject. I asked Ervin to request the committee members to cooperate with this strategy of our presentation of evidence.

Ervin agreed to call a meeting and told me that he thought he could persuade the members of the committee to go along. "However," he said, with a twinkle in his eyes, "you know that you can't really tell a senator what to do, and I suppose I can't guarantee that one or two of them might not go running off at the mouth."

The meeting the next morning in Ervin's office took only fifteen minutes. I briefly explained the problem. Ervin reinforced my statement by urging each of the members of the committee to discipline himself by postponing his questions on hush money payments and dirty tricks until a later time in our hearings.

"I'm willing to go along with that, Mr. Chairman," Weicker said. "Only I want to be sure that Tony Ulasewicz and Jack Caulfield are going to be recalled. I have a lot of questions to ask Caulfield, particularly, that deal with the dirty tricks area."

I had worried most about Weicker's being willing to restrict questioning. He had asked Terry to brief him on the dirty tricks evidence Caulfield and Ulasewicz could give, and Terry believed Weicker was preparing to open up the whole dirty tricks area. I quickly assured him that Ulasewicz and Caulfield would be recalled and that there would be ample opportunity to question them about other matters. The meeting ended with the committee agreeing to follow what Senator Inouye jokingly called "Dash's game plan."

When Caulfield testified and was followed by Ulasewicz, Terry hovered behind me impatiently sweating out what he firmly expected would occur—a total destruction of our hearing strategy. But the committee stuck firmly to their agreement and exhibited a self-discipline that is exceptionally rare in congressional hearings dealing with volatile facts. The control displayed by the committee was especially remarkable with regard to Ulasewicz. He proved to be such an entertaining witness, evoking frequent bursts of laughter in the Caucus Room, that it was obvious the committee members were sorely tempted to hold him as a witness and explore all the information Ulasewicz was capable of giving the committee. However, the committee restrained itself, and let Ulasewicz go after he had testified about the telephone calls he made to McCord.

I turned around and winked at Terry. Terry grudgingly responded, with a note of humor in his voice, "So the bastards have a sense of honor, after all."

McCord's dramatic testimony and Caulfield's confirmation that he had made the clemency offer to McCord, on John Dean's instructions, suddenly shifted the focus of our committee's public hearings. Now presidential involvement in Watergate could be inferred from the testimony before the committee. Only the President of the United States had the power to grant executive clemency. Caulfield acknowledged this and testified that Dean had told him that the offer had come from the highest levels in the White House. He said he understood this to mean that the offer of clemency had at least been transmitted to Dean by Ehrlichman.

The press noted the full implications of this testimony, and for the first time there was serious speculation by reporters, editors and columnists about a Richard Nixon Watergate connection. This threat to Nixon led Senator Gurney to try to scuttle my witness schedule. He urged the committee to call immediately the major witnesses, such as Mitchell, Colson, Haldeman and Ehrlichman, who he claimed could answer the question of whether the President was involved in Watergate. Gurney received some Democratic support from Senator Talmadge, who appeared to be motivated by a fear that lengthy hearings would be harmful to his reelection campaign. But Talmadge withdrew his objection to continuing with my witness list when I assured him we would reach Magruder, Dean and the other principal witnesses by the middle of June.

Baker agreed with Gurney's complaint that the committee was wasting time on minor witnesses. However, he elected not to make a fight of it when Ervin strongly opposed Gurney's move and was backed by Talmadge, Inouye, Montoya and Weicker. To Baker's dismay and, at times, open resentment, Weicker now was voting regularly with the Democratic majority.

The early feuding between Weicker and me had ended, and I had good reason to count on his support. About the third week in May, Weicker had called me to his office to tell me that he would turn over to me all information or evidence he received. He said he could not trust Fred Thompson because he believed Fred leaked information to the White House. Weicker also asked me to tell Senator Ervin that he would have his vote on most matters, since his views coincided with Ervin's on the course and scope of the investigation.

The sudden shift in the importance of the Watergate break-in and cover-up phase of our public hearings, with the attendant wide newspaper and TV coverage, also had a sharp impact on my top staff. After Ulasewicz's testimony, Dave Dorsen and Terry Lenzner asked to meet with me privately. They were obviously disturbed, and Dave looked embarrassed. "What Terry and I have to say," Dave began, "fully recognizes that when we began working together we all agreed to chop up the investigation in three distinct areas, and that each of the assistant chief counsel would help you in a particular area. I was happy to direct the investigation on campaign financing and Terry took on the dirty tricks phase. That left the Watergate break-in and cover-up to Jim Hamilton." Dave spoke haltingly, emphasizing particular points with hand gestures. "That all seemed fair at the beginning," Dave continued. "But now Watergate has become the most exciting phase of the committee's work and undoubtedly will receive the lion's share, if not the only share, of live TV coverage. That will give Jim Hamilton the limelight and leave Terry and me little or no opportunity for public exposure."

"So what do you suggest?" I asked, sensing the answer to my question.

Terry, who had been sitting with a scowl on his face as Dave spoke, replied, "Dave and I think we should change the whole deal. We have more trial experience and public reputation than Hamilton. We want to be able to share in the questioning of the Watergate witnesses." They debated in this vein for a while, but all I could promise them was that I would present the problem to Jim and recommend a solution.

Jim immediately approved the idea of giving Terry and Dave opportunities to question Watergate witnesses. In fact, he indicated to me that he had been expecting such a proposition. He was well aware of the expanding importance of the Watergate investigation that had been made his responsibility. I was impressed with Jim's sense of fairness, and I told him that he made my job a whole lot easier.

However, Jim was worried, too. "Now, look, Sam, I don't mind moving over and letting Dave and Terry share Watergate witnesses with me. But when the Watergate hearings are over, and we move into the dirty tricks hearings and the campaign financing hearings, I want Terry and Dave to agree to let me question some of the witnesses in those hearings." Terry and Dave were delighted that the issue had been settled so easily, and they readily agreed that Jim should share in their areas of the investigation.

10

White House Memos and Computer Print-Outs

THE COMMITTEE HAD ACCESS TO AN EXTRAORDINARY SOURCE OF documentary evidence. This was the National Archives collection of CRP files containing thousands of memos and records. CRP administrator Robert Odle had, in fact, been instrumental in providing this storehouse of evidentiary material.

On November 6, 1972, the day before the presidential election, Odle included the following in a memorandum he issued to all staff members of CRP:

> We are very anxious to preserve *all* committee papers, records, documents, etc., so that some day they will be included in the records of the President's library. As previously mentioned in a memorandum to the division directors from Mr. MacGregor, all files should be considered committee property and preserved here.
>
> Beginning Wednesday morning, Martha Duncan will distribute to all offices uniform packing cases for the files and also printed labels. After you have packaged all your files please call Martha and they will be picked up.
>
> Please do not take any files or papers with you—some day the committee's records at the Nixon library will be an invaluable aid to researchers in examining the 1972 campaign.

How true Odle's prediction was to be! The packed records of CRP were then collected and shipped to the National Archives. Perhaps it was because of the innocence of those packing the records that no one screened them first to remove any that might prove embarrassing, damaging or incriminating. If it was not innocence, then surely it was arrogance; for included in these boxes at the National Archives were not only the records of the daily activities of CRP but thousands of memoranda written by top White House officials, such as Haldeman, Buchanan and Malek. They were there because Jeb Magruder, as deputy director of CRP, was on the distribution list of all the political White House memos—even the "confidential" and "eyes only" memos that had nothing to do with him.

The Nixon White House probably put down on paper more of its ideas and activities, lawful and unlawful, than any other administration in the country's history. Magruder once told me that the huge flow of paper work in the White House was the result of Haldeman's many years in the advertising and public relations business, a business dominated by memos. A number of the "eyes only" memoranda dealt with contemplated unlawful or improper activity, sponsored by White House leadership, and occasionally contained the caution, "It would be very embarrassing to the administration if this program became publicly known."

When we first learned that CRP's records had been sent to the National Archives, we did not anticipate that they would contain significant evidentiary material for our investigation. We assumed they had been screened and cleansed of any sensitive items. Yet, following my practice that became a policy for the staff—to not overlook any possible source of evidence—young college and high school students, who were working as research staff assistants, were sent over to the National Archives building to sample the files, which were contained in approximately 1,100 cartons, occupying 1,500 cubic feet of space. I received Ervin's approval to subpoena the general counsel to GSA, the agency officially responsible for the National Archives, to produce these CRP records. The subpoena was complied with through a procedure which permitted my staff research assistants to comb through the boxes and identify documents that appeared to be relevant to our committee's investigation. The staff of the National Archives made photocopies of these identified records and gave them to our research assistants. A duplicate copy of every document we received was also provided to counsel for CRP.

It was when the research assistants came back to the committee offices with the first collection of memos that we knew we had uncovered a gold mine. During the total period of our investigation five separate teams of researchers went to the Archives to review the CRP records. Over 32,000 pages of documents were photocopied by the Archives staff and brought back to the committee.

My daughter, Judi, a senior at Brown University, was a member of the first team of researchers who discovered the treasure of memoranda in the CRP records at the Archives. They had expected the assignment to prove boring, but the discovery of the confidential memos transformed their work into an exciting detective adventure. Judi was working that summer for the Senate Separation of Powers Subcommittee. She was assigned, along with a number of other staff members of the Separation of Powers Subcommittee, to assist the staff of the Senate Watergate committee; this was made possible by a provision in the resolution of our committee authorizing the borrowing of staff assistance from other congressional committees. When Judi returned to Brown in the fall of 1973, my younger daughter, Rachel, who had just graduated from high school, joined the Separation of Powers staff for a brief period. Rachel became a member of a subsequent team of researchers to go through the boxes at the Archives, and experienced the excitement of finding her sister's I.D. marker in some of the boxes Judi had gone through months before.

By the opening of the second week of our public hearings I was ready to make use of our computerized records system. This was the first time a computer had been used in a congressional investigation. Our investigation entailed the questioning of hundreds of witnesses and the compiling of many thousands of documents. In addition, we would be conducting lengthy private and public hearings, which would provide thousands of pages of testimony. Also, we had collected the enormous record of information that existed prior to the creation of the committee, which included the full transcript of the first Watergate trial, voluminous depositions in the civil litigation, and the thousands of news clippings covering events since the time of the break-in on June 17, 1972, which the staff at the Library of Congress was providing us on a continuing basis.

I had become convinced it was a near-impossible task to manually locate quickly needed facts in this enormous storehouse of information that would ultimately fill over a hundred full-size filing cabinets. It was no wonder that when the Library of Congress staff came to my office to offer their assistance in setting up a computer system I immediately accepted. Bob McNamara, my research assistant at the Law Center, joined the committee staff to add his computer technology experience to that of the Library of Congress staff.

Quickly, McNamara recruited a team of law students, who were trained by Library of Congress staff to abstract committee records for storage on computer tape for the Bibliographic System (BIBSYS) we had chosen. McNamara augmented our automated records system by adding a microfilm component. Every document abstracted on the computer was also photographed on microfilm and given an index number which permitted it to be speedily located by the use of a microfilm viewer. The viewer was equipped to print out a copy of the document as needed by the staff. This permitted us to protect the original subpoenaed document in the secure file section of the auditorium.

Throughout the months of April and May, day and night, our committee records were stored on the computer with elaborate security precautions being taken at the same time. By the middle of May McNamara provided me with samples of the types of print-out reports that we could expect to receive from the computer. I was amazed. One report reduced thousands of pages of evidence from various sources relating to a specific individual to a thin set of print-out sheets supplying, in chronological order, abstracts of everything we had in our files relating to that individual. Each abstract identified its original source and page number, enabling me to go back to the file to read the full account if I needed to. But, with the computer print-out I could see at a glance everything we had collected about what the witness himself had said, what had been written about the witness and what other witnesses had said about the witness.

Another print-out report offered me an even thinner set of print-outs providing me with a more selective retrieval of information we had about the witness in connection with a particular subject matter. Still another print-out report correlated statements made by a number of selected witnesses concerning a specific event.

McNamara pointed out that other selective print-outs and cross correlations could be made according to names, dates, places and subject matter. "For example," he explained, "suppose you have a known event, a meeting, or something like that, and you want to recall all the persons who participated and what they said or did. If there is no file on that particular event, which is likely, since most of our files are organized according to names of witnesses and their testimony, rather than subject matter, you would be lost if you tried to get this information by going to the files." However, with the computer, he said, the problem was simple. He could request the computer to print out everything we had collected about the event. "In almost an instant," McNamara concluded, "you can have in your hand a digest of everything that our investigation has revealed about the subject of your inquiry. And I mean *everything,* since the computer won't overlook any data."

"What about discrepancies in testimony?" I asked. "It's a long and laborious task to examine the testimony of a number of different witnesses to identify where they disagree on specific facts."

"That's easy," McNamara said with enthusiasm. "Just ask the computer to correlate the specific subject matter of the testimony you're interested in with the names of the witnesses you want to compare, and instantly the computer will give you a print-out which will tell you at a glance what each of the witnesses has testified about the particular matter. Again it will give a source reference and page numbers if you want to explore the abstracted testimony more thoroughly."

"Another beautiful thing about this program," Bob added, "is that it will practically write your final report for you. The computer can analyze our entire data chronologically, topically, or according to the activities of individuals, as you may desire. The material will have already been abstracted and will save you the time of boiling down many thousands of pages of evidence. In addition, it will permit you to speedily analyze the huge amount of information our committee will have collected and to make all kinds of comparisons of different versions of the facts, so that the report can be written in an objective and balanced form."

As it later turned out, the special prosecutor adopted our computer program for his investigation shortly after he was appointed, and his staff was trained in its use by our staff. Moreover, the House Judiciary Committee, which months later conducted the impeachment inquiry against Richard Nixon, received from us a duplicate copy of our computer tape, and was able to use our computer program in making the factual presentation to the House Judiciary Committee members and in formulating the articles of impeachment against the President.

One of the last assignments given the computer program provided a kind of poetic justice and clearly a touch of irony. When Haldeman, Ehrlichman and some of the other Watergate defendants were facing trial brought by the special prosecutor, they complained that the prosecutor's computer program placed them at a disadvantage. Turning to our committee, they requested access to our computerized data system, offering to pay necessary costs to the Library of Congress. The committee unanimously approved my recommendation that this request be granted. Thus these former witnesses before the committee whom we had questioned with the aid of the computer now used our computer program in their turn in the preparation of their defense.

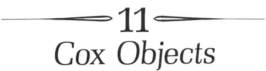

11

Cox Objects

AS I PREPARED TO PRODUCE MAGRUDER AND DEAN AS PUBLIC WITnesses the committee was unexpectedly confronted with a serious threat to the continuation of its hearings. It came from an unlikely source— the newly appointed special prosecutor, Archibald Cox.

Following Kleindienst's resignation as Attorney General and Nixon's appointment of Elliot Richardson to replace Kleindienst, the Senate Judiciary Committee was urged by the public, the press and a number of its own members to make it a condition of Richardson's confirmation as Attorney General that he be willing to appoint a special prosecutor to take over the criminal investigation and prosecution of Watergate. Our Senate committee could expose the facts and recommend legislative reforms, but it had no power to prosecute criminal charges against Watergate offenders. Richardson agreed to appoint a special prosecutor. After unsuccessfully offering the post to a number of qualified men, he finally appointed and won the acceptance of Professor Archibald Cox, of Harvard Law School, who had formerly been Solicitor General of the United States.

The choice appeared to be an excellent one. Cox was undoubtedly a scholar, a brilliant appellate advocate and a man of great integrity. I was personally pleased by Cox's appointment. He had been my labor law professor at Harvard Law School, and we had continued to have infrequent contacts over the years at professional meetings or during my visits to the law school.

Cox was confirmed by the Senate on May 23 and immediately arrived in Washington to set up his office. To help him get started he appointed a colleague of his at Harvard Law School, Professor James Vorenberg. Once again I experienced the uncanny shift in relationships that seemed to punctuate my activities as chief counsel. I had met Vorenberg seven years before during his earlier sojourn in Washington as director of President Johnson's National Crime Commission. Later Vorenberg and I had frequent contacts as he directed a criminal justice research center at Harvard Law School similar to the research institute I had been directing at Georgetown University Law Center—both funded by the Ford Foundation.

As soon as I learned that Cox was in Washington, I called to welcome him and to offer my help. Cox was pleased that I had called and told me he wanted to meet with me as soon as possible to discuss some important relationships between the Senate committee and the special prosecutor's office. We agreed to meet the next day, May 30, at his office.

I experienced a strong pang of nostalgia as I walked down the hallway of the Justice Department I had frequently used over twenty years before when I served as a trial lawyer in the Appellate Section of the Criminal Division. Cox and Vorenberg were waiting for me, and greeted me warmly in their temporary quarters. Packing cases on the floor and disarrayed tables and chairs gave evidence of the recent occupation of the offices.

Cox was a very tall, slim man, with a crew cut. His pale blue eyes gazed frankly under prominent eyebrows, and apparently by sheer habit, he often grimaced as he spoke. Vorenberg was also tall—about my height. His dark hair and bushy eyebrows accentuated a pensive, almost sad expression on his long, narrow face.

Cox had the habit of speaking slowly, often in drawn-out sentences, in a high-pitched voice that sometimes cracked. After a few preliminary inquiries about the committee's general plans, he asked me if we intended to put on Magruder and Dean. When I said yes and that we would welcome his help in expediting their immunity procedures, he replied, "That's just my problem. Not only am I unwilling to expedite your production of Magruder and Dean as public witnesses, I don't want you to put them on at all."

"What do you mean?" I became suddenly aware of a tension in the room. Vorenberg's face was expressionless, although he was watching me steadily.

"Well, it should be clear to you that many things have changed now," Cox replied slowly, almost haltingly. "No one doubts the responsibility your committee had to fully investigate and expose the facts at a time when the Department of Justice could not be trusted to do that job. But now, as a result of the urging of the Senate itself, an independent special prosecutor has been appointed—me—with a broad mandate to investigate all the Watergate charges, and even more, to prosecute those who are indicted by the grand jury. It doesn't seem to make any sense that there should be two investigations, does it?"

I still had not realized the full implications of Cox's statement, because it was completely unexpected and unthinkable. Vorenberg saw that I was perplexed. "Let me put it this way, Sam," Vorenberg said, "You've had an important job to do, and you've done it very well so far. Now Archie has been brought to Washington as an independent special prosecutor, probably with more power, and certainly with more resources than your committee has. He has the terribly difficult and complex job of conducting a criminal investigation limited by all the procedural requirements that you yourself know so much about. I'm sure you don't question his integrity, ability, or courage. You know that he's going to do as thorough a job as can be done. The question, therefore, is—if the job *is* going to be thoroughly done, why is it necessary for your committee to do it also? The question is not only one of duplication, but of the dangers that can be caused by the publicity of your hearings to the complicated and sensitive criminal prosecutions Archie now will be engaged in."

"Are you saying," I asked, trying to control my anger, "that we should close down our Watergate public hearings?"

"That is exactly what I am saying," Cox replied, his face contorted in a reflex grimace that was maddening under the circumstances.

"But that's absolutely ridiculous!" I half shouted. "Our tasks are entirely separate and distinct. You were appointed to conduct a criminal investigation, which will end up in decisions that certain persons are guilty of criminal offenses and might have to go to jail. We have a broader responsibility. Under our mandate and constitutional duty, our Senate committee must find and publicly expose the facts involving corruption and abuse of power in the executive branch. We also must recommend remedial legislation, but we can't do that without producing the facts that support such legislation. The committee can't abdicate these responsibilities now. I can tell you quite definitely that Senator Ervin and the other members of the committee would be absolutely opposed to shutting down our public hearings."

Cox's eyes looked coldly at me. "Are you and the committee willing, for the sake of publicity, to prejudice the outcome of this crucially important criminal investigation and prosecution that has now been placed in my hands?"

"I think you're making an assumption that is unreal," I replied. "How soon do you expect to have your grand jury return indictments in the Watergate case?"

Cox looked at Vorenberg, and Vorenberg replied that it would be at least ninety days. I then pointed out that they probably wouldn't be able to go to trial for nine months to a year after the indictments were returned. "The lights in the Caucus Room will be darkened for a year or more before you open up your trial. No court in the country would uphold a claim of prejudicial pretrial publicity under these circumstances."

Cox posed some further objections about the committee's publicity and ended up by saying, "What you're really saying to me, Sam, is that I should go back to Harvard."

"And what you are really saying, Archie," I replied flatly, "is that I should go back to Georgetown."

As I was about to leave, I thought of another, particularly powerful argument in favor of our hearings. "You have ignored the question of presidential involvement," I said. "If we don't hold hearings that will reveal the facts concerning whether the President was or was not involved in Watergate, and you can't indict the President, then possibly the most important Watergate information needed by the people in the country today—on whether the President of the United States was involved in these crimes—will never be officially disclosed to the public."

Cox looked uncomfortable. "Well, we can always include what information we uncover about presidential involvement in our report to the Congress. I'm required to file a final report to the Congress."

"A written report to Congress," I replied, "is clearly no substitute for public hearings or a public trial of the facts. But that's another matter you can take up with Senator Ervin." I agreed to set up a meeting with Senator Ervin as quickly as possible. Cox and I both pledged that we would say nothing to the press about our discussion, and if asked, would only acknowledge that we had met.

I left the Justice Department building feeling I had just witnessed an unparalleled display of arrogance. In effect, Cox had told me that now that he, "Mr. Clean," had come to Washington, everybody else had to stop what he was doing and get out of Cox's way to let him attack the Watergate dirt all by himself. His attitude also expressed his indifference to the doctrine of separation of powers and to the constitutional responsibilities of Congress. I still believed, however, that Cox was the right choice for special prosecutor to carry on—independent of the Department of Justice—criminal investigations and prosecutions relating to Watergate.

The battle came quickly, to the great delight of the White House. Cox was proving to be an unexpected ally of Nixon and his threatened colleagues by seeking to shut off our hearings. Already my secret meetings with Dean had been leaked to the press, and the published juicy tidbits of Dean's revelations to me about his Oval Office meetings suggested how dangerous he could be to the President. The leaks had to come from someone close to Dean. Why the leaks were made always puzzled me—unless Dean was behind them to build up pressure on the prosecutors in his bid for complete immunity.

A few days after my meeting with Cox, as soon as the senators returned from the Memorial Day recess, Cox moved to try to persuade the committee to overrule me. The speed of his action may have been prompted by a news leak of the substance of our meeting. Cox first met with Ervin and me alone in an effort to persuade Ervin to put off the Watergate phase of the public hearings for at least ninety days. Ervin flatly rejected the request. "Professor Cox, I greatly respect you," Ervin said firmly, "but the executive branch has had almost a year to prosecute these cases and have done nothing but convict some underlings. If we wait ninety days until you get indictments, then you'll want us to postpone again until after the trials—and the appeals." Ervin paused and allowed a smile to light up his face. His eyes twinkled as he added, "You know, that could be until the last ringing echo of Gabriel's horn trembles off into silence." It was a favorite quip of Ervin's and I was to hear it repeated frequently in the future. But Cox saw no humor in the situation. "The prior delay is not my fault, Senator. Surely you don't want to prejudice this vital criminal investigation now entrusted to me." But Ervin wouldn't be budged from his position.

"We won't prejudice your investigation," Ervin said, assuming a serious expression again. "You won't be trying your cases for a long,

long time. But I'm frank to say that with the state of crisis in the country today due to the public's loss of confidence in its government —I believe it is more vital that the public be informed of the facts right now than that some people go to jail."

The next day, a Sunday, Cox sent a long letter to the full committee restating his opposition to public, televised Watergate hearings. He also released it to the news media at a press conference. In his letter Cox warned that continued public hearings at this time would seriously jeopardize his criminal investigation and might well lead to all those guilty of Watergate offenses going free.

The Nixon White House, eager to keep John Dean's testimony from the public, rushed to Cox's aid. White House loyalists Bill Safire and Joe Alsop immediately produced columns criticizing the committee and urging that the courts and the special prosecutor be allowed to pursue their responsibilities to achieve justice without interference from meddlesome senators and their staff.

Alsop took on the dirty job of smearing John Dean. Calling Dean a "bottom-dwelling slug," Alsop proceeded to link the fate of Nixon and the American dollar to the "lies" of the former counsel to the President. However, Alsop's facts were so inaccurate that it seemed to me that he had merely reproduced copy given to him by White House aides. At the same time, other columnists as well as editors rejected Cox's position and supported Ervin's stand for the need for immediate public revelation of the Watergate facts.

On Monday, June 5, the committee met and unanimously voted to refuse Cox's request for a postponement of public hearings until he obtained indictments. Cox went to court. Pending at that time before Judge Sirica were the committee's applications for orders granting immunity to Magruder and Dean. Cox petitioned Sirica either to deny these applications or to impose conditions on the immunity orders requiring private hearings for Magruder and Dean, or if the court allowed public hearings, to require that they be held without television or radio coverage.

The law was overwhelmingly against Cox, and he knew it. He was either bluffing, or as Vorenberg later claimed, he was making a record to preclude any defendant from having a basis to contend that the special prosecutor had allowed pretrial publicity to prejudice the criminal prosecution.

I looked forward to arguing the case against my former professor. However, I and the crowded courtroom of lawyers, reporters and spectators were disappointed when Cox did not show up but sent an assistant to argue the case for him. Judge Sirica was visably displeased that Cox himself did not see fit to come before him and argue the important question.

Under the circumstances, Sirica was even more appreciative of the irony of my strongly relying on a position Archibald Cox had once taken as Solicitor General in the Supreme Court, in *Hutchinson* v. *United States.* He had claimed then, as we claimed now, that the pendency of criminal prosecutions could not justify judicial interference with congressional public hearings under the doctrine of separation of powers. The Supreme Court's ruling in the Hutchinson case upheld Solicitor General Cox's argument and served, therefore, as a uniquely binding precedent supporting the committee's position before Judge Sirica.

Four days after the argument, on June 12, Sirica handed down an opinion, rejecting Cox's requests for limitations on the committee hearings, and signed the orders granting Magruder and Dean immunity. Cox announced that he would not appeal Sirica's ruling. The way was now clear for us to call Magruder and Dean as public witnesses.

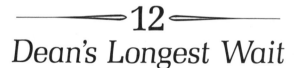

12

Dean's Longest Wait

I HAD ONLY A DAY TO PREPARE FOR MAGRUDER'S PUBLIC TESTImony. James Bierbower, Magruder's lawyer, had refused to produce his client for private questioning until the immunity order had been signed by Judge Sirica. That made June 13 the earliest date I could schedule an executive session hearing to get Magruder's story under oath—and we would reach him on the witness list for his public testimony the following day, June 14.

Although we had called it close, the time was sufficient. Maurice Stans was testifying publicly before the committee on June 13, and I had assigned Rufus Edmisten to question him. That left me free to question Magruder in executive session, and Senator Ervin temporarily excused himself from the public hearings to administer the oath to Magruder and to preside for a brief period at the private hearing. Magruder's testimony was precise and detailed about his role in the Liddy bugging plans and the burglary of the DNC headquarters at the Watergate. He was not in doubt anymore about Mitchell's final approval of the plan in Key Biscayne, Florida. He said that Mitchell definitely "signed off" on it.

He went further to testify that Mitchell actually received the fruits of the bugging operation and that Mitchell was displeased with the "junk" that Liddy was producing. This testimony corroborated information Dean had given me. Dean told me that Liddy had complained to him on June 19, 1972, that the reason he got his burglary team to make the fateful second break-in at the Watergate on June 17 was that Magruder was pushing him to get better information because of Mitchell's displeasure over the malfunctioning of the wiretap on Lawrence O'Brien's telephone.

Magruder never directly implicated Haldeman. However, he testified that he had kept Gordon Strachan, Haldeman's assistant and liaison to CRP, fully informed of the progress of the Liddy bugging plan. He said he provided Strachan with copies of Liddy's Gemstone planning memoranda and showed Strachan the Gemstone wiretap logs and the photographs that had been taken from the files in the DNC headquarters.

I wondered, as I listened to Magruder, how this handsome, young executive could so coolly describe the outrageous crimes—conspiracy, burglary, wiretapping, perjury and obstruction of justice—he had committed. He appeared totally insensitive to the nature of these offenses and to their impact on the country. The following day at the public hearing I watched the hypocrisy of Magruder's instant conversion as he earnestly expressed contrition and regret for his crimes to the senators and the TV audience.

In any event, Magruder was now a cooperative witness. His public testimony before our committee presented to the American people the first eyewitness account of the Gemstone political intelligence and bugging operation—from its planning stage to the cover-up of the Watergate break-in. In a remarkable way, Magruder's testimony both supplemented and set the stage for the explosive testimony of John Dean, who would follow him as a witness before the committee.

With Magruder safely locked in, I turned my attention to Dean and the preparation of his statement and testimony. Once again I made my trips to Charlie Shaffer's office in Rockville, Maryland, and to Dean's home in Alexandria, Virginia. Only, this time I did not have to go alone. As Dean's public appearance before our committee was rapidly approaching, I wanted the assistance of Jim Hamilton in assessing Dean's statement and in preparing for Dean's interrogation. By this time, during the final stage of preparation, Shaffer and Dean were readily agreeable to Hamilton's joining me in our secret meetings.

Instead of driving in the same car to these meetings, Jim followed behind in his own car. Sara thought this would be safer in case something happened to one of us. If nothing else, it certainly heightened my sense of adventure.

Our first meeting was in Shaffer's office, where his secretaries had just completed typing the first portion of Dean's statement. Jim and I were each handed a copy, and after reading for a while I broke the silence by saying, "This won't do—you put your finger on everybody but yourself. John, when you told me the story before, it was very clear to me that you were as much a part of this cover-up as the others. In fact, you were directing a large part of it under instructions from Haldeman and Ehrlichman. Now, unless you admit that under oath, you're just not going to be a credible witness."

"What have you got to say about that, John?" Shaffer sharply asked Dean.

Dean looked startled by my criticism. "I think my involvement is all there implicitly. I couldn't be making these statements if I didn't know what was going on."

"But that's just it," I said. "You were in it all, up to your neck, and you can't imply it—you've got to spell it out. Otherwise, your testimony won't be worth a damn."

"I still don't understand what you want from me." Dean's voice was hesitant.

"Well, let me show you," I replied. "You state here that Ehrlichman and Haldeman wanted you to see that Magruder got through the grand jury all right. And then you state that Magruder gave a perjured story to the grand jury concerning why he paid Liddy so much cash. Now, since you were supposed to get Magruder through the grand jury, did you know, in advance, that Magruder was going to lie to the grand jury?"

"Sure," Dean said. He then admitted to having coached Magruder before he went to the grand jury.

"Now, that's what I want you to put in the statement!" I declared.

"The moment you hedge, you open the way for all kinds of doubts and attacks which then put the rest of your statements in question."

Dean was clearly unhappy. "I don't want to hide my role, Sam. That's why I want to come forward and tell everything I know publicly. I still think that anybody who hears my statement will have no doubts as to my involvement. But you're suggesting I specifically blacken myself, and I wonder if that will hurt my credibility more. What are people going to think about me if I spell out the fact that I coached Magruder to lie?"

"That you're telling the truth, because that's quite an admission." I suggested to Shaffer that we talk to each other alone for a moment. We went into the hallway outside his office. "Charlie, I'm dead serious about this. His statement is lousy. Unless John tells it all, it won't do."

"Now, don't get excited," Shaffer replied. "You'll get what you want. It's just hard for a guy like Dean to spell out all the dirt about himself when he's finally confronted with it."

"Well, you've got to tell him that he must do it all the way through the statement or I simply will recommend to the committee that they not offer him immunity, even though we have an order from Sirica giving us power to do so."

"Let's go back and talk to John," Shaffer said.

We returned to the office. Shaffer gave Dean a hard look. "You've got to make a decision, John," Shaffer said sharply. "Either you're going to tell everything, or you're not going to tell anything at all. Now, perhaps, as your lawyer, I should not say this to you in front of Sam Dash, but damn it, if you've got something to hide or you want to hold things back, I suggest you cut out this fucking business of looking like you want to cooperate with everybody and let them indict you and you'll plead not guilty and we'll fight like hell to keep them from trying you or convicting you. Believe me, there are a lot of things going for you." Shaffer's voice had the ring of an advocate.

"On the other hand," he said, "if you want to do just what you told Sam Dash you want to do, that is, fully cooperate with the Senate committee, then you've got to tell every last fucking thing you did, no matter how bad or lousy it sounds or how distasteful it is to you to admit it. You can't have it two ways."

Dean looked stunned at his lawyer's outburst. But he quickly replied, "I haven't changed my mind in the slightest way about fully cooperating with the Senate committee. What I've written so far is just a draft. I'm not trying to excuse myself of anything. I know how wrong my actions were. I just want an opportunity to right things as best I can by publicly telling the full story. I don't have any hesitancy in painting myself black if that is necessary. However, I want what I did to be seen in the context of the whole picture—in proportion to what others did. Because although I was all over the place, I was basically a messenger boy carrying out the instructions of Haldeman and Ehrlichman."

"Okay, okay," Shaffer interrupted Dean. "Then we're going the cooperation route. So let's keep in mind it's got to be the whole story." Shaffer said Dean would go over the draft and would rewrite it and spell out exactly what his role had been, and that I would have an opportunity to review it again.

The tension that had built up in the room relaxed, and we spent the rest of the meeting until 3 A.M. going over the draft line by line, cross-examining Dean repeatedly about his basis for making particular statements and what evidence he had to support them. Dean made frequent notes to remind him to locate a particular document or memorandum and to consult his notes further to amplify a response he had given. I repeatedly made it clear to Dean that I was not suggesting any answers to him in my effort to obtain the complete and accurate statement. My questions were meant to probe his recollection and his ability to support his accusations. I did not want Dean to get the idea that I wanted to influence his testimony in any way.

Shaffer saw my predicament and sought to clarify the relationship. "We all recognize what your role is. John knows that you're not suggesting that he testify in any particular way, except to give you the true story as he knows it. And your questions are aimed at helping him do that."

I was grateful to Shaffer for providing this clarification. A meeting of this kind with a principal witness could be later misunderstood. Even Dean might misunderstand my purpose and attempt to shape his answers in a way he might think would please me. It was just as important for me to learn from Dean that certain accusations were unfounded as it was to obtain facts supporting culpability.

Most of the following meetings were held at Dean's home, which was much more pleasant. We were periodically interrupted by Mo Dean serving iced tea and club sandwiches. Dean was more relaxed at home and found it easier to provide the supporting information I constantly required of him, since he kept the documents he needed in his den. Dean's public testimony was scheduled for Tuesday, June 19, and by

Friday, June 15, the statement was completed in a form that satisfied me as to its fullness and credibility.

As we reached the eve of Dean's public appearance, I began to worry that the secrecy we had been able to maintain might now begin to work against us. Dean's testimony could be marred if Senator Baker and Fred Thompson publicly declared that Dean had been sprung on them as a witness for the first time in public session, and that they had not been given an opportunity to prepare for his interrogation.

I mentioned this concern to Shaffer and suggested that the only solution was to have Dean appear in executive session, the next day, on Saturday, June 16, and give an overview of his testimony in the presence of Fred Thompson and subject himself to questioning by Thompson. Shaffer did not object to this procedure. "Well, Sam, it will just be a couple of days before John gives his public testimony. They won't be able to exploit what they learn in that short period of time."

I faced another sticky problem. Dean's evidence exposed the private meeting Senator Baker had had with the President shortly after the committee was created. Dean also had information about the undercover White House contacts one of Baker's assistants had been making. These revelations would be harmful to Senator Baker, and Baker knew that I had been secretly meeting with Dean and getting his story. As vice chairman of our committee, he could reasonably expect, as a matter of courtesy, that I would advise him of this potentially volatile information that was going to be made public.

This question became even more disturbing to me after a call from Bob Woodward of the Washington *Post.* There had obviously been a leak to Woodward from a knowledgeable source, since he asked me to verify for him whether Baker had privately met with President Nixon, at Baker's request, soon after his appointment as vice chairman of our Senate committee. I told Woodward that I could not make any comment on his question.

"Well, I know Baker did have the meeting," Woodward said, "because I have one very reliable source on it. And that bastard Baker specifically denied he had the meeting when I recently asked him about it. Okay, Sam, I'll just have to wait until Dean testifies, and if Dean gives evidence of Baker's meeting with Nixon, I'm going to roast Baker."

I decided I had to alert Fred Thompson about the information I had received. On Friday, June 15, I walked into Fred's office and told him what Dean would say about Senator Baker. Fred looked astonished. "Shit, Sam," he exclaimed, "that's bad news. I'm sure Senator Baker will appreciate this advance notice and has a positive explanation for the meeting if it took place."

I also told Fred that I wanted him to have an opportunity to prepare for Dean's interrogation, and was setting up an executive session the following day to permit him and Baker to question Dean. On Monday, June 18, Dean would appear in executive session before the full committee, and he would begin his public testimony on Tuesday, June 19. Fred's face broke into a broad smile. "You're finally going to take the wraps off your mummy, huh? That's great, I've been itching to hear what he's got to say."

Prior to Dean's appearance before our committee, Earl Silbert, now working for Special Prosecutor Cox, made a frantic effort to persuade Dean to plead guilty to one count of obstructing justice. Dean told me that he was unhappy with the treatment he was receiving from Silbert and the newly appointed special prosecutor. They did not appear to take him too seriously and the special prosecutor had not even shown an interest in talking to him or Shaffer.

I had called Cox to tell him that Dean would be his most vital witness and that he should personally arrange to interview Dean on an informal basis. Cox reacted to my suggestion by indicating that he had serious questions about Dean's credibility and motivation.

Although Magruder readily accepted Silbert's deal of pleading guilty to one count of obstructing justice, Dean refused this same offer, claiming that the testimony he had to offer merited a grant of immunity from the prosecutor. Silbert immediately took Dean before the grand jury, hoping to preempt our committee and force Dean to tell his story under oath. But Dean pleaded his Fifth Amendment privilege. For the moment, Dean had slipped out of the prosecutor's hands and was cooperating completely with our committee. He believed our public hearings gave him the best forum to get his story out—and consequently to win him public support to use as leverage for a better deal with the prosecutor.

On Saturday morning, June 16, Dean appeared in my office for his executive session. Senator Baker presided and administered the oath to Dean. No other senator was there. Dean would appear before the full committee in private session two days later. This session was primarily for Thompson's preparation.

Solely to create a record that would protect Dean's legal interests,

Shaffer made a preliminary motion to Baker that Dean be excused from testifying before the committee and that if the committee would not totally excuse him, Dean's testimony should be taken only in executive session. Shaffer explained that Dean had been informed by the prosecutor's office that he was a target for prosecution and that his public testimony before television cameras could prejudice his right to a fair trial. He therefore wanted to be able to raise this claim of prejudice should Dean be indicted and brought to trial, and he did not want Dean to be waiving his right to make this claim by voluntarily agreeing to give public testimony and thereby contribute to the prejudice created.

Baker denied Shaffer's motion for the purpose of this executive session, but indicated that he would have an opportunity again to make this motion when the full committee met in executive session on Monday, June 18, to hear Shaffer's other motions on attorney-client privilege, executive privilege and national security.

To protect himself Dean still had to withhold his testimony. Although Judge Sirica had signed an immunity order for Dean's testimony, the law provided that immunity could not be granted to Dean unless he first refused to give testimony on the ground of his Fifth Amendment privilege, and then was compelled to do so by the committee on the basis of Judge Sirica's immunity order.

Therefore we had to engage in a little charade. I put several incriminating questions to Dean, and he refused to answer, asserting the Fifth Amendment. I then turned to Baker and asked him to order Dean to testify under the grant of immunity signed by Sirica. Baker read the immunity order to Dean and gave a copy of it to Shaffer. He then directed Dean to answer my questions under the grant of immunity. The legal groundwork had now been laid so that Dean could give his testimony protected by an immunity grant that would prevent the special prosecutor from using his testimony against him in a criminal proceeding.

Baker announced that he had to leave to attend to other duties but that he could return should he be needed to rule on any other matter. I assumed Baker wished to avoid a confrontation with Dean and was relying on Thompson to discover the worst that Dean might say. But Dean did not want to speak about Baker in his absence. "Senator, I have one point," Dean said. "In my informal discussions with Mr. Dash, I raised the matter that your name does come up in my testimony, and I didn't want you to be caught off guard when that occurred."

Baker resumed his seat. Dean then briefly gave his account of White

House efforts to contact Baker to influence his conduct on the committee; Baker's request for a secret, off-the-record meeting with President Nixon, shortly after he was appointed to the Senate Select Committee; and the meeting Baker did in fact have with Nixon. Dean also testified that Baker's staff had sought to establish a White House relationship and had indicated that Baker was looking for guidance from the White House. If Baker was disturbed, he did not show it. His face was impassive.

"Mr. Dean," Baker interrupted, "could I ask you whether you knew that the question of whether the President should assert executive privilege before our committee virtually occupied all of the conversation that I had with the President? Was there any feedback to you what my advice was in that respect?"

"Yes there was," Dean replied. "You told the President you thought he ought to waive executive privilege and send the White House staff up to the committee as quickly as he could get them up there."

"Was there any feedback on the President's reaction?" Baker asked.

"He said he was going to hold the line on written interrogatories," Dean replied, but added, "After your meeting with the President, I had a discussion with Mr. Haldeman, and subsequently with the President about the meeting. The White House must have perceived the meeting differently than you. They felt there was going to be cooperation and possible assistance from you as a result of your seeking the meeting and that the discussion included suggestions from the President to you on how you could help him with the committee." Dean explained that some of these suggestions were included among the items on an agenda he had prepared for the President in advance of the Baker meeting.

Baker glanced at me and pursed his lips. He was obviously disturbed by Dean's last statement and the fact that it would be part of Dean's public testimony; there was the suggestion of worry in the frown that appeared on his face. He rose and made a statement for the stenographic record to the effect that the only conversation he had with the President dealt with his recommendation that the President "send the White House staff to the committee, beating on the doors for the opportunity to testify, instead of evoking the executive privilege."

In regard to his staff's efforts to establish White House contacts, Baker simply said that Jim Jordan had called down to the White House for the purpose of getting organizational charts and that his administrative assistant, Mr. Branson, had had further discussion with someone, perhaps William Timmons, the White House liaison to the Congress, about questions of executive privilege. Dean, however, had stated that Baker's staff had contacted the White House after Baker's meeting with the President to make it clear that Baker was seeking guidance from the White House. And, according to Dean's testimony, when Timmons reported to President Nixon about the concerns expressed by Baker's staff over unsatisfactory White House contacts, the President called Attorney General Kleindienst and said, "Why in the world are you not meeting more frequently with Senator Baker?"

As Senator Baker left my office, Dean and Shaffer assured him that Dean's testimony would not reveal any improprieties on his part. Baker expressed his satisfaction that Dean's testimony accurately reflected his relationship with the White House. Although Dean had earlier revealed to me a more dubious relationship between Baker and his staff and the White House, he was now before our committee and at its mercy. He told me that he did not want to get Baker angry and was willing to soften his testimony with regard to Baker so that he could fully present the rest of his story before the committee. Dean's strategy worked. Because of his innocuous treatment of the Baker-Nixon meeting in his public testimony, Baker went out of his way to handle Dean with kid gloves, and did not cross-examine him or challenge his credibility at the public hearing when the world watched on television.

Although I was troubled about my own responsibilities concerning Dean's testimony regarding Baker, I reasoned that any efforts on my part to attempt to refresh Dean's recollection by referring to his earlier statements would be hazardous, especially if Dean contradicted me. It would appear I was going out of my way to injure the vice chairman of our committee and therefore would be publicly demonstrating a partisan attitude. Also, I wanted to maintain the public's confidence in our committee. Discrediting the vice chairman of the committee at this time would defeat that purpose.

Just one additional private committee meeting had to be held before John Dean would begin presenting his public testimony. It was the scheduled executive session meeting of the committee on Monday, June 18, when Shaffer could argue a number of preliminary legal objections for the record to put Dean in a position where his testimony would be compelled, rather than volunteered. I expected the meeting to be brief and perfunctory.

As I walked to S-143 of the Capitol I was deeply disturbed by information given to me by a reporter in the hall. Senator Mike Mansfield, the majority leader, and Senator Hugh Scott, the minority leader, were requesting that the committee postpone its hearing that week during the meetings between Brezhnev and Nixon. I couldn't believe it! This seemed like a plot. I had succeeded in getting Dean to the brink of giving his public testimony without his story getting out, until he talked to Fred Thompson and Senator Baker at Saturday's executive session. Now, suddenly, Dean was to be stranded and exposed for a full week.

The meeting opened with Shaffer making his for-the-record requests. Then Dean and his lawyers left the room and the committee voted to deny the requests.

While Dean and his lawyers were still out of the room, Ervin brought up the subject of postponing the hearings during the time Brezhnev was meeting with President Nixon. He said Mansfield and Scott were sending the committee a letter requesting the postponement. The letter arrived as Ervin was referring to it. Baker immediately moved that the public hearings be postponed until Monday, June 25. He also moved that in the interim the chief counsel and the minority counsel should continue to question John Dean in executive session and that members of the committee could, as usual, attend such executive hearings.

Senator Weicker opposed the postponement, asserting that it would be good for Brezhnev to personally witness how strong America was to be able to have such hearings. However, Senator Baker's motion for postponement was approved by a vote of six to one.

Mansfield and Scott had known about the Brezhnev visit for several weeks. Why had they waited until the very day before Dean's testimony to try to postpone the hearings? Two weeks before the Mansfield-Scott letter, Baker had alerted the committee to the problem. But at that time the Committee, with Baker concurring, decided not to call off the hearings during the Brezhnev visit. This action lulled me into ignoring Brezhnev's meeting with Nixon.

Obviously, if I had had advance notice of the week's delay, I would have put off Dean's executive session with Thompson and Baker until a day or two before we were ready to resume public hearings. My heightened suspicions led me now to speculate whether the administration was behind this last-minute "big gun" effort to stay John Dean's testimony for a week, after he had revealed a substantial part of his story to the minority, to buy time to publicly discredit Dean and his story. Although the matter was out of my control, I couldn't help feeling that somehow I had personally betrayed Dean.

Senator Talmadge inquired whether the committee should still resolve any questions connected with John Dean's testimony which involved attorney-client privilege, executive privilege and national security. I reported that Leonard Garment, counsel to the President, had informed me that the President would not interpose any attorney-client privilege or executive privilege objections to John Dean's testimony. Garment also said it was the President's view that the committee should handle national security questions in accordance with its own discretion. There remained no further legal impediments to Dean's being able to testify.

Dean, Shaffer and McCandless were asked to come back into the meeting room. They were told of the decision to postpone Dean's public appearance for one week. Dean's mouth dropped open. It was as though he had been punched in the stomach. He knew he had dangerously exposed himself, and now was in the position of hanging from a cliff, open to the all-out attacks from his enemies in the White House. I looked helplessly at him, angry at myself for not having been able to prevent this dangerous situation. Baker informed Shaffer that he expected Dean to continue to appear in executive session before Fred Thompson and me to provide the staff with the remainder of his testimony that had not been revealed to Thompson at the executive session hearing on Saturday, June 16.

The morning after our June 18 committee meeting a Seymour Hersh story in *The New York Times* revealed that Dean had used approximately $4,000 from cash funds belonging to CRP in order to pay for his honeymoon expenses. Dean himself had disclosed this information during Saturday's executive session hearing with Thompson. He also explained he had recently reiumbursed the fund through a special escrow account arranged by his attorney. Hersh's story included other parts of Dean's testimony, citing Senate sources. In a number of news stories announcing the postponement of the committee's hearings because of the Brezhnev visit, Baker was quoted as stating that the postponement should not be interpreted as meaning that the committee believed that Dean was an important witness or had significant testimony to give to the committee. I thought this was an attempt by Baker to downgrade Dean and to diminish his credibility.

Shaffer came to my office with *The New York Times* in his hand. He pointed to the Dean honeymoon story and exploded: "I can't allow Dean to give any more testimony before Fred Thompson or Senator Baker until his public appearance! There has been a deliberate leak to the newspapers on his Saturday session, and I don't have any doubt where it came from."

"Why don't you simply take that position before the committee, Charlie," I suggested. Shaffer was worried whether this would upset Senator Ervin. I said the best way to find out was to ask him.

When he outlined his problem to Senator Ervin, Shaffer said he was fearful that the leaks would provide Dean's White House enemies with an opportunity to develop counterattacks in the press which would unfairly jeopardize the credibility of Dean's testimony. "Frankly, Senator," Shaffer concluded, "With all due respect to you, and I deeply respect you, I'm not going to allow my client to give any more testimony before your committee until his public appearance, even if he's held in contempt or I'm held in contempt."

Ervin smiled broadly. "I wouldn't worry about any contempt proceedings, Mr. Shaffer. If you think it's against the best interest of your client to give further private testimony to the committee, then you take whatever action you feel you have to to protect your client. I always respect a lawyer who fights hard for his client."

"You're very generous and understanding, Senator," Shaffer said with a tenderness that I had never noticed in his voice.

"No, Mr. Shaffer," Ervin replied. "I just respect the able performance of a good lawyer."

When we left Ervin's office Shaffer told me he thought he should talk to Fred Thompson, as a matter of courtesy, and explain his reasons for not producing Dean for any further executive session hearings. Thompson became angry at Shaffer's position, and when he found that I was supporting Shaffer he complained to Baker. Baker met a solid wall of resistance from Ervin—and further executive sessions to hear John Dean, prior to his public testimony, were called off.

During the week-long postponement of Dean's public testimony, the newspapers daily reported speculations on and leaks of Dean's testimony. The staff summary on Dean's testimony that I finally had to distribute to each of the senators just prior to Dean's expected appearance on June 19 was released in its entirety by some committee source.

Every day the leading newspapers carried a major story on Dean, most of them depicting him in an unfavorable light and many of them bearing the unmistakable stamp of a White House release. Pro-Nixon columnists spewed out their venom, describing Dean as a latter-day Judas. Even anti-Nixon columnists characterized him with a critical pen in a clumsy effort to appear objective. Dean's worst fears of premature exposure appeared to be coming true during this Brezhnev-week postponement.

One day, during that week of suspense, Fred Thompson walked into my office and gave me a typed copy of what he called Fred Buzhardt's reconstruction of Dean's meetings with President Nixon. Buzhardt was special Watergate counsel to the President and the reconstruction was obviously prepared in anticipation of Dean's testimony. Indeed, about the same time Thompson gave this to me it was leaked to the press in an attempt to jump the gun on Dean.

Anonymous White House sources claimed that this "authentic" version of the meetings would hang Dean because it demonstrated that Dean never warned the President of his culpability but, on the contrary, had misled the President. From my knowledge of Dean's testimony, I knew Dean could contradict this charge. But I was intrigued at how close the Buzhardt reconstruction tracked what Dean would say. Of course, it omitted major areas of presidential culpability, but on the other hand, it admitted some significant knowledge on the President's part by attributing statements to the President relating to the payment of blackmail money to Hunt. "My God!" I said to some of my staff, "Look at what they are admitting. They must believe Dean can prove this." We would learn later, from the White House tapes, that Nixon and Haldeman believed Dean had his own tape of his meetings with Nixon. The Buzhardt reconstruction was prepared to provide a version close to what Nixon believed Dean's tape would reveal, but it was edited to protect Nixon and harm Dean.

The following week, during the questioning of Dean, I referred to the document as "Buzhardt's reconstruction of the Dean-Nixon meetings." As soon as I returned to my office from that particular session, my secretary told me that Garment had been repeatedly trying to reach me from the White House. I called Garment and found him in a state of agitation. "Who told you that Fred Buzhardt or anybody in the White House submitted a document reconstructing the conversations between the President and John Dean?"

When I replied that Fred Thompson had, Garment claimed that Buzhardt had given a version of the conversations to Thompson in a telephone call and Thompson must have prepared the typed document I was using at the hearing. He asked me to publicly correct the erroneous reference to a Buzhardt reconstruction. Thompson verified Garment's account, but insisted he had given me an accurate restatement of what Buzhardt had told him on the telephone.

I called Garment back and said I was satisfied it was still a Buzhardt reconstruction given to Thompson. But to ensure we were not misquoting Buzhardt, I asked Garment if he and Buzhardt could come to my office immediately to examine Thompson's typed recollection of the telephone call.

They arrived a half-hour later. Buzhardt carefully studied Fred's version of their telephone conversation, and said, "Well, it seems to be all there. I may have provided a little more information about some of the meetings and said it slightly differently than Fred Thompson has here, but all in all, it's basically accurate."

"Good," I said. "I want to make sure we're not misquoting you when we refer to your reconstruction of these meetings and put it in evidence as an exhibit. By the way, how did you go about reconstructing the meetings? Didn't this require your talking with the President?"

Buzhardt, who had a bespectacled, pinched face and spoke in a raspy voice, replied, "I just asked around the right places. And you know damn well I'm not going to tell you about any discussions I might or might not have had with the President."

Garment remained uneasy that we were introducing as an exhibit a document that we were labeling a White House "reconstruction" of the President's meetings with Dean. "I don't see why you have to use that," he said. "It's not really evidence and Fred Buzhardt merely provided this information to Thompson to assist him in the questioning of Dean."

"I disagree with you, Len," I said. "It constitutes a representation by the special Watergate counsel to the President regarding very relevant meetings between Dean and the President."

Garment shrugged his shoulders and he and Buzhardt left my office.

In addition to the "Buzhardt reconstruction," Fred Thompson also received from Buzhardt two documents that were being submitted by the White House to the committee with a request that the committee use them in cross-examining Dean. One of the documents contained a long list of questions the White House wanted Dean to answer. They were leading questions, obviously biased and poorly phrased. When I showed them to Jim Hamilton, I commented that I thought there was something self-destructive about the White House crowd. It was surprising that the President's men wanted to be identified with these kinds of questions.

But the most astounding document was the White House theory of the Watergate break-in and cover-up. While it viciously attacked John Mitchell and John Dean, it was excessively protective and defensive of the President, Haldeman and Ehrlichman. It was an unsophisticated and superficial piece of hatchet work, written in the shrill tones of adolescent name-calling. Again, I expressed my amazement to Hamilton that the President's assistants had been willing to expose their hatred or desperation so transparently.

A copy of this document went straight off from me to William Huntley, Mitchell's lawyer. But I had miscalculated and given Mitchell a weapon against the President rather than a reason for cooperating with us. When we released the document the following week during the questioning of John Dean, President Nixon issued a statement that it did not have his approval and was not an authorized position of the White House. Obviously, Mitchell had gotten a message to the President that unless this hysterical attack on him was retracted, he would be forced to retaliate in his testimony before the committee.

During the week of our committee's recess that had been called because of the Brezhnev visit, Dean told me how unhappy he was with his image that was emerging before the public as a result of newspaper stories. "I think I've been badly hurt," he told me despondently. "This is exactly what I feared would happen if my testimony leaked out prior to my giving public testimony. They pulled a fast one on us, that's for sure."

"Who do you think 'they' are?" I asked.

"The White House, Baker and Scott. Mansfield probably never knew the score. They must have made him feel that it was some kind of national emergency."

My staff was worried too. Some were sure that the whole thing was a White House plot. One investigator said he had heard from a reporter with good sources in the White House that we had been set up. I mentioned these glum views to Ervin, but he discounted them, saying that the delay would only make Dean's appearance seem more dramatic.

I trusted Ervin's judgment, and his optimistic assessment was comforting. But I was suddenly faced with a more serious problem. Sometime in the middle of the week of June 18 my secretary rushed a letter to my desk. It was a death threat against John Dean. The anonymous note was brief and printed in large block letters. It said: "JOHN DEAN WILL NEVER BE A WITNESS. HE WILL BE DEAD." The committee had received other hate notes or threats, mostly incomprehensible mutterings representative of the "kooky" mail known to all government agencies. This note was different. It was simple, direct and seemed serious.

When I showed the letter to Ervin, he, too, feared that it was a real threat. He said that the Capitol police could protect Dean in the Caucus Room, but that was about all. The Senate had no way to provide Dean with security outside any of the buildings of Congress. I suggested that Dean needed the protection of U.S. marshals in his home and on his way to the public hearings, and while he was sitting in the Caucus Room. The special prosecutor was the only one who had the authority to assign marshals to Watergate-related tasks, and we turned to him for help.

Cox, at first, was dubious. The problem involved a congressional committee hearing, not a prosecution under his control. Besides, he wasn't sure he should take such unusual action as providing security for a Senate witness on the basis of a single threat, which might be a hoax.

I thought Cox's judgment was being muddied by his own distrust of Dean. Fortunately, Cox called back in an hour to tell me that he had ordered full security measures to be taken to protect Dean's life.

A marshal would be placed in Dean's home. A detail of marshals would keep Dean's house under surveillance. He would be delivered each morning and taken home each day by marshals during his public testimony before the committee. During his testimony two marshals would sit behind him and Capitol police guards would be at the entrance of the Caucus Room and throughout the room.

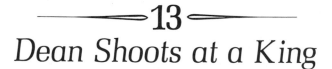

13
Dean Shoots at a King

ON THE MORNING OF JUNE 25, 1973, I ENTERED THE ALREADY crowded Caucus Room to take my seat at the committee table. The press tables were filled to capacity, and not only was every seat in the public spectators' section taken but a large standing crowd lined the walls in the rear of the Caucus Room. An augmented contingency of Capitol police guarded the entrance doors, and inside the Caucus Room uniformed and non-uniformed Capitol police were at their stations, intently watching every inch of the crowded room. John Dean had already entered the old Senate office building and had been escorted to a waiting room near the Caucus Room.

I informed one of my aides to notify the marshals to bring Dean in When he entered, flanked by U.S. marshals and Capitol police guards, and accompanied by his lawyers and his wife, a stir of excitement rippled through the room. Senator Ervin banged the hearing to order with his large gavel with the Indian-beaded handle. "The committee will come to order." Ervin's deep voice resounded through the room as he spoke into the microphones. "Counsel will call the first witness."

"Mr. John W. Dean, the third," I said, in as solemn a tone of voice as I could muster.

After Dean was sworn in, Ervin made a statement for the record that Dean appeared before the committee under subpoena and not as a volunteer, and that he was compelled to answer questions because he had been granted immunity. Baker added for the record that the committee had been informed by the President's counsel that the President waived any claim of executive privilege or attorney-client privilege with regard to Dean's testimony. Also noted were Shaffer's prior record objections to Dean's appearance at televised public hearings which might prejudice him in future criminal proceedings and the committee's ruling against these objections. Finally Ervin announced that the committee would make rulings on any national security objection with regard to Dean's testimony or documentary evidence when the question arose during the hearing. When all of the record statements were made, which placed John Dean in the official position of appearing involuntarily before the committee and testifying under compulsion by a grant of immunity, Dean was ready to read his statement to the world. Beginning at 10:30 in the morning, he read his lengthy statement throughout the entire day, completing it at 6:00 P.M. in the evening. The committee then adjourned at 6:05 P.M. until the following morning, when the questioning of Dean would begin.

Dean's daylong statement stunned the press and the country. It presented a devastating mosaic of intrigue, illegality and abuse of power participated in by the highest officials in government, including the President of the United States. The worst fears of most Americans, which had been building by speculation, were now realized. Their

President, Richard Nixon, had been involved in crimes more serious than the Watergate burglary. He had authorized illegal police-state methods and had abused the power of executive law enforcement agencies to crush dissent and to destroy his enemies. And he had participated in the greatest obstruction of justice and cover-up in the history of the country to conceal his involvement and the involvement of his subordinates in illegal activities. The preciseness of Dean's statement and the frequent documentary exhibits he used to support his allegations made it all clear and credible.

Ervin had been right. Dean's story had not been diluted by the week's delay and the efforts made to discredit him. Indeed, those efforts appeared puny in the face of the powerful and persuasive force of Dean's mountain of facts. During the next four days Dean elaborated on his statement and provided additional fresh facts and documentary evidence in response to questioning from me, Fred Thompson and members of the committee.

I limited my questioning of Dean to pinpointing the highlights of his testimony. A number of viewers, most of them lawyers, wrote to me complaining that I had not subjected Dean to rigorous cross-examination at the hearing.

Of course, these people did not realize I had interrogated Dean for a month before his public testimony. It was now up to the rest of the committee and the press to tear him apart if they could. But they could not. Baker, wary of Dean, and fearing to provoke damaging revelations about himself, approached Dean with broad general questions. His most famous question, one that projected Baker to his TV audience as a seeker of truth, was, "What did the President know and when did he know it?" The answer I thought Baker wanted from Dean—but could not get—was that the President knew little, and what little he knew he knew late in the game.

The strongest cross-examination Dean received was from Senator Gurney. Except for an irrelevant mix-up on Dean's part between the Mayflower coffee shop in the Statler Hilton Hotel and the Mayflower Hotel, Dean not only withstood Gurney's cross-examination and held fast to his previous statements, but added new material and new insights prompted by Gurney's probing. The only point Gurney scored was in getting Dean to accept Gurney's rephrasing of his answer that he left the September 15 meeting with the President only with *the impression* that the President knew of the cover-up.

However, when I questioned Dean again, I took him through every item of his testimony concerning the September 15 meeting, and then asked him, "Now, after all those events, after the President having told you how Bob Haldeman had kept him posted on your handling of the Watergate case; and that he appreciated how difficult a job that was; and your statement to the President that you had only contained it, and that someday it might unravel; and your own statement to the President that in a civil case, an ex parte relationship had been established to influence the judge; and then the discussion on the Patman hearings— frankly, and honestly, Mr. Dean, when you left the President on September 15, did you just have an impression as to his knowledge of the cover-up, or did you have a conviction concerning that?"

Dean quietly replied, "Mr. Dash, there was no doubt in my mind that the President was aware of it and I would have to, to use your language, say I had a conviction, or I was convinced."

I turned to look at Senator Baker and caught him frowning at me.

After Dean completed his public testimony on June 29, the committee adjourned its hearings until Tuesday, July 10, because of the July 4 recess of the Congress. Dean's testimony capped the accusatory phase of the committee's Watergate presentation. We were now ready to call the principal witnesses who were implicated by that presentation. They were mainly Mitchell, Ehrlichman and Haldeman. We had little more than ten days to complete our investigation of these major witnesses. Dean and Magruder had already provided us with a strong basis for confronting them. But judging from my private interrogations of them, they were going to try their best, in Ehrlichman's language, to "stonewall" us.

Terry, Dave and I had confronted this kind of problem before when we were prosecuting organized and white-collar criminals—I as district attorney of Philadelphia, and Terry and Dave as assistant U.S. attorneys in the Southern District of New York. To organize an effective investigative strategy, I assigned each of my three assistant chief counsel to supervise the investigation of a particular major witness who had been accused by prior testimony. Under each of these top aides I assigned a task force of committee lawyers and investigators.

The strategy assumed that the target witnesses spoke, acted or collaborated in the presence of subordinate people during the time they were engaged in conspiratorial activities, and that they were confident or arrogant enough to believe they were impervious to future investigation, so that they would have left numerous tracks behind them.

The subordinates who would be aware of these tracks would be aides, secretaries and associates, who might have kept records or remembered. We termed these identified subordinates "satellites" of the targeted witness and plotted them on a satellite chart of each witness. The plan called for each of the satellites to be brought in for questioning by task force members and to produce whatever written records he or she might have kept. It was a plodding, tedious method of investigation— a far cry from the more glamorous but purely fictional Perry Mason approach.

When John Dean told me he suspected that President Nixon had recorded the April 15, 1973, meeting between himself and Dean, each of the task forces was directed to ask White House satellites whether they had any reason to know or believe that the President recorded telephone or room conversations. I had no idea what spectacular and determinative information would ultimately be produced.

My primary goal was to provide corroboration for John Dean's testimony. Credible as he was—polls showed 70 percent of the public believed him—he still stood alone as the only accuser of President Nixon and as the witness providing most of the incriminating evidence against Ehrlichman and Haldeman. I doubted whether John Dean's solitary testimony, as powerful and unshaken as it had been before our committee, would be sufficient without independent corroboration to persuade the majority of our committee members to make a hard finding against Ehrlichman and Haldeman or any finding at all against the President. Ervin, however, spoke frequently about the inference of culpability the law of evidence allowed him to make against the President when the President failed to produce documents or testimony to refute the strong and specific charges Dean had made against him. Ervin made a distinction between a criminal prosecution and a congressional hearing. He recognized that the right of a criminal defendant to remain silent permitted a jury to draw no adverse inference against him, but the President was not a criminal defendant and our committee hearings were not a criminal trial.

"One doesn't have to be a lawyer to understand what I'm talking about," Ervin said, when asked by a reporter to explain what he meant by an inference of culpability. "It's simply part of human experience. Any darn fool would suppose that the President must have something to hide if he's unwilling to produce relevant papers or to respond to questions and direct accusations that have been made against him."

I had not realized the full extent of the challenge to Richard Nixon's presidency caused by John Dean's public accusation until the fourth of July 1973. I was working in my office when I received a call from Jerome Zeiffert, general counsel of the Judiciary Committee of the House of Representatives. "Would you have time to meet with me and the minority counsel of our committee?" Zeiffert asked.

"Of course," I replied. "When would you like to meet?"

"Now," Zeiffert said. "We can come to your office."

I was surprised at the urgency in his voice and told him that I would be pleased to see him right away. In less than half an hour, Zeiffert, accompanied by a young man, entered my office. Zeiffert, a short, round-shouldered man, appeared to be in his late fifties. Wearing steel-rimmed glasses, his soft round face seemed frozen in a perpetual smile.

"Do you mind?" Zeiffert asked in an intense voice as he shut and locked my door from the inside. Although I wondered at Zeiffert's action, I simply shrugged my shoulders. Then Zeiffert and his colleague moved two of the chairs in my office close to my desk and sat down. "I want to impress upon you, Mr. Dash," Zeiffert almost whispered, "that this meeting has to be kept very, very confidential. It is only exploratory, but it could be very explosive for our committee and yours if what I'm going to talk to you about becomes generally known."

I promised Zeiffert that I would keep our discussion in strictest confidence.

"What I'm about to say to you must be considered as a hypothetical matter," Zeiffert said. "Our committee has taken no action whatsoever, not even a suggestion of an action. Only Chairman Rodino has talked to me. He wanted me to raise with you—hypothetically, mind you— the question of what help your committee can give our committee in an impeachment inquiry against the President of the United States." Zeiffert paused and stared steadily at me to let his words sink in.

Needless to say, the subject matter we were discussing had the greatest implications for the country. I chose my words carefully. "I'm sure that Senator Ervin would want our committee to give the House Judiciary Committee the fullest cooperation possible. We, of course, have a substantial investigative start on any inquiry your committee might wish to make, and I would recommend to Senator Ervin that we share our investigative data with you."

"If we go ahead, we may not have time to make a complete investigation," Zeiffert said. "Therefore, we would be dependent, to a large extent, on the evidence you could supply us and on any other evidence we could obtain from other committees or the special prosecutor."

"The special prosecutor would be in a difficult position to assist you," I cautioned. "He is burdened by the secrecy rule governing the grand jury. However, I'm sure he will help you as much as he can." I then assured Zeiffert that I would put my staff completely at his disposal to assist him in preparing for the inquiry.

"That would be excellent," Zieffert said. We then discussed the next step that should be taken to establish an official relationship between our two committees. He agreed that Chairman Rodino should write to Senator Ervin as chairman of our committee and formally request assistance of our committee in an impeachment inquiry to be undertaken by the House Judiciary Committee. I made this suggestion because the White House and some people in the Congress had already accused our committee of trying to get the President. It was important that our committee not be in a position of a volunteer to assist the House Judiciary Committee. It should act only on invitation by Rodino's committee.

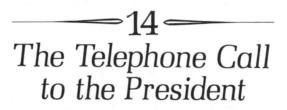

14

The Telephone Call to the President

THE MORNING OF JULY 12 WAS THE FIRST TIME SINCE THE RECESS that the committee could get together. As usual, I arrived first at Senator Ervin's office and took a seat close to the desk. It was a large comfortable room. The massive, ornately carved desk and high-back judge's swivel chair sat in front of a window alcove opposite the entrance to the office. About five feet in front of the desk was an overstuffed leather sofa. Two matching leather chairs were on each side of the desk. The length of one wall, facing the entrance door, was lined with bookshelves, crammed with books. The opposite wall exhibited plaques, framed citations, a number of Indian tokens and other memorabilia, some of which rested on the mantel of a white marble fireplace. The walls of the alcove behind the desk were covered with framed original cartoons that had featured Ervin on the editorial pages of newspapers throughout the country from his early days in the Senate to the Watergate committee period.

Shortly after nine the senators began to arrive, one at a time, each accompanied by a member of his own staff. They took the same seats they had used since the very first meeting of the committee. Inouye came in, winked at me good-naturedly, and took his seat in front of the bookshelves. Montoya entered right behind Inouye and sat beside him, to his left. Weicker strode in, towering over everybody else in the room and sat in a chair next to the sofa on the far side of the room from the entrance. "Jesus," he said, "the hall is littered with the press and cameras—it was damned difficult to get in the door." Weicker's office was just across the hall from Ervin's.

Talmadge appeared and sat on the side of the sofa closest to the entrance. As usual, he said nothing, crossed his legs, took a long cigar from his jacket, lit it and began to puff quietly. Gurney came shortly afterwards, limping and in pain from the wounds he had suffered in World War II. He carried a flat, hard cushion with him and took a seat on the other side of the sofa, placing the cushion behind him. Baker then sauntered in, greeting everybody gaily, and moved his chair close to Ervin's at the far side of Ervin's desk.

Although Ervin had no difficulty working late each day, 9 A.M. meetings were not easy for him to make. He entered at nine-twenty, and as he sat his heavy frame in his chair behind the desk he cheerfully said, "I apologize to you all for being late, although I set the meeting time, but as you know—" and with a chuckle, he left the rest unsaid.

With a nod from Senator Ervin, I began my presentation to the committee. It was very brief. I reported that Nixon had sent Ervin a letter on July 6 in which he refused our request for White House documents relevant to our investigation, claiming executive privilege and separation of powers. There could be only one response from the committee. The documents we had requested from the President were relevant to the mandate of the resolution that had created the committee and were absolutely essential for a complete investigation. There was no valid basis for a claim of executive privilege. I requested that the committee authorize a subpoena directed at the President for the documents.

Senator Ervin picked up my request. "The way I see it," he said, "the President can't use executive privilege to deny us these papers. They deal with political matters or criminal activities in the Watergate affair. Executive privilege is supposed to protect as confidential only those conversations between the President and his aides which assist the President in carrying out his statutory or constitutional duties. None of the papers we want has anything to do with the President's lawful duties."

"Has the Congress ever subpoenaed papers from the President before?" Senator Talmadge asked me in his matter-of-fact, dry tone of voice.

"No," I replied. "This would be the very first time in the history of the country."

"But that don't make a difference," Ervin added, his voice rising in volume. "The President isn't above the law, and if he has evidence relevant to a lawful investigation, he is subject to subpoena like any other citizen. Chief Justice Marshall held that in the Aaron Burr case."

Gurney, who had appeared to be drowsing, looked up. Biting his words between clenched teeth, he said to Ervin, "But surely, Sam, we should be able to achieve what we want without subpoenaing the President of the United States. The committee will only be blasted by the public, and rightly so, for seeking some cheap publicity. I think we should put our case to the President again, and more persuasively. I haven't read all the cases, but I'm not sure we have a right to those papers."

Weicker, sitting next to Gurney, said, "Ed, I don't agree with you. The only language the President will understand is a subpoena from this committee. I think we should go ahead with it."

"So do I," chimed in Senator Montoya.

Talmadge took a puff on his cigar and said slowly, drawing each word out, "Sam, if as chairman of this committee you think the committee should issue a subpoena on the President, I will go along with you."

Baker stood up from his chair. I had expected it to come, and I was not disappointed. Soothingly he said, "Now, Sam, I am one hundred percent behind you, as I have always been, in insisting that this committee get all the information it has a right to." Baker sounded as if he meant it. "But I am concerned with the image of this committee. We have a good image and we have done some very good things, but I agree with Ed Gurney that we are going to look lousy if we shoot from the hip with a subpoena, without first trying to negotiate this thing out with the President. I'm basically an optimist, and I think the President is going to give us the papers we want to see. I think we should write to him again, and better still, you should try to arrange a meeting with the President to talk it out with him."

"Yeah," added Gurney, "that would be much better than a subpoena, and makes more sense to me."

"But, Howard"—Ervin addressed himself to Baker, his eyebrows wiggling rapidly—"I don't see how that's going to do us any good. He turned us down. He probably won't even agree to meet with me, and I can't see where a meeting is going to change anything anyway. Although I'm not proud, and if I thought it would work, I wouldn't mind asking kindly. But I don't like the idea of begging the President for something we have a right to have, knowing that he's going to turn me down."

"I disagree with you, Sam," Baker replied. "I think if you explain the committee's need of these papers to the President, personally, he's going to give them to us. I'll go down the line with you for a subpoena if that fails, but I hate to think we didn't try everything we could to work out something with the President before getting into a very ugly confrontation, which isn't going to make us look any better than the President. I just got a feeling in my bones that this will work, although I may be eating my words later if it doesn't. But then, there's always time to serve a subpoena on the President."

"Well, I don't mind meeting with the President, even though I doubt it will do any good." Ervin always sought to avoid the appearance of being unreasonable. "But I don't think I should see him alone. I think you should go with me, Howard, as vice chairman, and our chief counsel and minority counsel should be there, too."

Baker, perhaps still smarting under Dean's revelations that Baker had had private contacts with the President when the committee was first created, said that he thought the chairman should go alone to meet with the President, but that he would be willing to accompany him. Weicker added that he didn't mind efforts to arrive at a reasonable accommodation with the President, if that was possible, but he urged that this action be taken immediately, and if unsuccessful, that a subpoena be issued. A consensus in the committee was quickly forming. Baker had accomplished it. The confrontation would be avoided for the time being and, instead, an effort would be made to set up a meeting with the President to negotiate the committee's request for the White House documents.

Baker quickly dictated aloud to my secretary a letter to the President for Ervin's signature:

"Dear Mr. President:

I acknowledge receipt of your letter of July 6, addressed to me with a copy to Senator Baker. The Committee feels that your position as stated in the letter measured against the Committee's responsibility to ascertain the facts related to the matters set out in Senate Resolution 60, present the grave possibility of a fundamental Constitutional confrontation between the Congress and the Presidency. We wish to avoid that, if possible. Consequently, we request an opportunity for representatives of this Committee and its staff to meet with you and your staff to try to find ways to avoid such a confrontation.

"We stand ready to discuss the matter with you at your convenience. We would point out that the hearings are ongoing and that time is of the essence. We trust that this may be done very promptly.

Very truly yours,

Sam J. Ervin, Jr., Chairman"

When he completed dictating the letter, Baker said, "You know, Sam, I think in addition to the letter, you should telephone the President, refer to the letter, and personally push the idea of a meeting."

Ervin resisted the idea of a telephone call, saying that he thought the letter was enough. But other members of the committee supported Baker's telephone call suggestion, and Ervin agreed. However, it was now about ten minutes after ten. We all knew that the Caucus Room was crowded, the press was waiting, and former Attorney General John Mitchell was ready to resume his testimony. "We won't be able to make the telephone call now," Ervin said, "but we can get the letter delivered to the President this morning, and let's reconvene in executive session here at one P.M. after the morning hearing. We will make the telephone call then."

The meeting broke up with this resolution of the question, and I instructed my secretary to have the letter to the President typed as quickly as possible and sent to the Caucus Room for Senator Ervin's signature. It would then be delivered to the President during the morning session of our hearings.

Although I believed that Gurney's and Baker's strategy of a meeting with the President preceded by a telephone call from Ervin was a delaying action, I was not disturbed by the outcome of the meeting. We certainly would present a public appearance of reasonableness by this approach, and I knew if it failed, the committee's vote for a subpoena to the President would then probably be unanimous.

As I walked down the third-floor hall of the old Senate office building from Senator Ervin's office to the Caucus Room I was surrounded by news reporters clamoring to find out what we had done. I suppose I repeated a dozen times, "I cannot comment on anything that occurred in an executive session meeting of the committee." When I entered the Caucus Room, it was crowded with visitors, many standing against the back walls. The press were at their tables, the overhead TV lights were blazing, the cameras were ready and Mitchell was at his place ready to testify. I took my seat next to Senator Ervin at the table. That morning I would begin my cross-examination of Mitchell.

Senator Ervin adjourned the hearing early, at eleven-thirty, so that we could eat lunch and reassemble in his office at 1 P.M. for the telephone call to the President. The White House had been informed of our one o'clock meeting by Rufus Edmisten, and we had learned that the President would place a call to Senator Ervin during the meeting.

At one o'clock all the committee members were back in Senator Ervin's office. No one wanted to be late. The atmosphere in the room was one of excitement and tension. Something different was going to happen—different not only from what the committee had done before, but from what any committee had ever done in the history of Congress. We all felt that we were attending a historic meeting and we appreciated the privilege of being present.

This unique feeling was especially noteworthy with regard to the senators. United States senators are a rare and powerful elite, who have reached the top of the political ladder. One would not think that they would be particularly impressed by a telephone call from any political leader—even the President. Yet the seven senators of the Watergate committee behaved like nervous teenagers as they awaited the President's call. I realized the power of the presidency more clearly then than at any other time. It was not that Richard Nixon would be calling that electrified Ervin's office; it was that *the President* would be calling.

During the brief period of waiting, the senators entertained themselves with jokes and storytelling. Ervin matched some North Carolina tales with Baker's lawyer stories from Tennessee. Even Talmadge broke out of character, and smilingly asked, "Should we all stand when the telephone rings?" Baker surprised everyone by replying with a giggle, "I suppose we should, and then all sing 'Bail to the Chief.'" That convulsed everyone in the room with laughter and Inouye shook his finger at Baker in mock disapproval. Baker blushed deep red.

Then the telephone rang—it seemed unusually loud. Instinctively everyone leaned forward, and there was a sudden hush. My deputy, Rufus Edmisten, picked up the telephone and announced in as solemn a voice as he could manage, "Senate Watergate committee!" After a pause, he looked confused, composed himself, and said, "Oh, yes, oh yes, we understand, I will report that to Senator Ervin." Rufus turned to the inquiring faces in the room and said, "That was just Timmons, the White House liaison guy. He says the President thinks it is more appropriate for Senator Ervin to call him, and has given me this number to call."

"Well, if the President is too proud to call me, I'm not too proud to call him," Ervin said with a sweet smile. "Dial the number, Rufus."

Rufus dialed the number Timmons had given him and said inadvertently to the White House secretary who answered, "Ma'am, Senator Ervin wants to get the President." He handed the telephone to Ervin. Ervin hunched forward over the telephone, waited for the President to come on the line, and when he did we all heard Senator Ervin's side of the conversation with the President:

"Mr. President, this is Senator Ervin. Our committee had a meeting this morning and we sent you a little note. I suppose you got it . . . I don't know how it got in the paper . . . We just don't agree with your interpretation with respect to presidential papers . . . The committee is hoping that they can work out some arrangement that some members of the committee staff and some members of the White House staff . . . Maybe Senator Baker and I can come down and talk to you about this . . . I was at home when your letter was written and I didn't get back until Tuesday. There was a death in my family and I had to stay there . . . But Mr. President . . . But Mr. President . . . We can't give you a detailed request for papers when we don't have access and can't describe them. We want any papers that are relevant to any matters that the committee is authorized to investigate . . . Mr. President . . . But

Mr. President . . . Mr. President, if nobody can go through them and if we can't see the papers, we can't identify them . . . All except those that are of a purely confidential nature . . . Anything that reflects any wrongdoing on the part of any of the White House aides . . . Not on the part of the President . . . But Mr. President . . . But . . . But Mr. President . . . But we are not out to get anything, Mr. President, except the truth . . . We are not out to get anybody . . . Well, Mr. President . . . Frankly I don't believe there is much hope for us working out anything . . . I'll have to report to the committee that you are willing to see me sometime next week if it is convenient and sort of defer to the wishes of the committee . . . But Mr. President . . . But . . . But . . . But . . . Well, as far as I am concerned and as far as the committee is concerned, we are not out to get anyone. There is nothing that would give me greater delight than to be able to say that there is nothing in the world to connect you with the Watergate in any way and I would be happy if the committee could reach that conclusion, Mr. President. Goodbye."

Ervin looked up from the telephone, his face flushed, his eyes deeply disturbed. "You know," he said to us, who had listened unbelievingly to his utterances on the telephone, "the President was shouting at me on the other side of that telephone that all we wanted to do is to get him. He kept repeating it, and I could hardly talk to him. But he did agree to a meeting next week."

I was asked to keep in touch with White House counsel and report back to the committee the date for the meeting. The telephone call had so shaken the senators that none of them appeared to want to say anything, and the meeting broke up, each of us going out quietly.

Later that afternoon, the President entered the hospital. His doctors said it was pneumonia.

15

The White House Tapes

THE DAY AFTER NIXON WENT TO THE HOSPITAL OUR SATELLITE chart system for spotting and questioning witnesses paid off in a truly spectacular way. For the superstitious, the day had portents of trouble for someone—it was Friday the thirteenth of July.

Alexander Butterfield arrived at G-334, our interrogation room, for routine questioning. There was no special significance to his appearance. Although at that time Butterfield was head of the Federal Aviation Administration, we were interested in him because he had once sat at a desk outside the Oval Office as a top aide to Haldeman. Indeed, so routine was Butterfield's appearance that neither I nor any of my assistant chief counsel thought it necessary to be present during his interrogation. Instead, Butterfield met with majority staff members Gene Boyce and Scott Armstrong and deputy minority counsel, Don Sanders.

I spent the day in the Caucus Room, where members of the committee were questioning Richard Moore, a White House counsel. Moore, a shrewd, public relations adviser in the White House, was one of the witnesses the White House had specifically requested me to call after John Dean's testimony. Leonard Garment, who had made the request, claimed it would be only fair, since Moore had been present on many of the occasions about which Dean testified.

Terry Lenzner had grilled Moore the day before and had challenged the credibility of his prepared pat testimony by a withering cross-examination during which Moore had stammered and fumbled, unable to recall events contemporaneous with, and collateral to, the events about which he had testified. All day Friday, Fred Thompson and Senators Baker and Gurney sought to rehabilitate Moore, while Ervin, Talmadge, Inouye, Montoya and Weicker extracted responses which revealed Moore's role as a White House apologist and genteel hatchet man against John Dean.

Often referred to as "the fox" by his colleagues at the White House, Moore managed to appear befuddled during the questioning and won the sympathy of many watchers of the hearing. Lenzner's tough cross-examination was especially resented. Ervin was nettled when he read newspaper complaints that the committee had mistreated an elderly, white-haired witness. "Elderly, my foot!" the seventy-seven-year old Senator exploded. "That fella Moore is a young man of fifty-eight."

When Ervin adjourned the hearing at five-thirty, I gathered my files and took the long basement corridor walk between the old and new Senate office buildings to my office. Usually, after each hearing day, I would spend a couple of hours with my senior staff aides reviewing the proceedings that day and discussing plans for the next witnesses or actually interviewing witnesses.

However, I had promised Sara that I would not come home late on this particular Friday evening. She had planned a special Sabbath meal and the Edmistens and the Millers had been invited to dinner. The pace of the investigation had been so hectic that there had been little time for us to relax together. Sara and I both wanted this Friday evening to be different, especially since the following day was our wedding anniversary.

As I started to leave the office my phone rang. It was Scott Armstrong. "Sam, can Gene Boyce and I come up to see you right away?" Scott's voice seemed breathless. "It's important," he urged. It occurred to me that Scott always thought everything was important. "Can't it wait until tomorrow, Scott?" I asked. "Sara made some special plans for dinner tonight and I promised her I wouldn't come home too late."

Scott was persistent. "I can't talk to you about this on the telephone. But it will only take us a couple of minutes to get over to your office. And when you hear what we have to say, I think you'll agree that it's important enough for you to know about it now."

I sat down at my desk and waited. In a short while Scott and Gene came into my office. They both looked wild-eyed. Scott was sweating and in a state of great excitement. As soon as he had closed the door the words tumbled out of his mouth as he told me about Butterfield's astounding revelation of the White House taping system, which had recorded every conversation Richard Nixon had in certain key rooms in the White House, the Executive Office Building and at Camp David —twenty-four hours a day—since the spring of 1971. Scott, Gene and I became overwhelmed with the explosive meaning of the existence of such tapes. We now knew there had been a secret, irrefutable "witness" in the Oval Office each time Dean met with Nixon, and if we could get the tapes we could now do what we had thought would be impossible —establish the truth or falsity of Dean's accusations against the President.

Since I wanted more information from Scott about Butterfield's statement, I called Sara and told her I was going to be delayed. She sounded upset but said she understood.

When I asked Scott why Butterfield had given us this remarkable evidence, he explained that he had put Butterfield through three hours of detailed questioning of his duties and had carefully led up to asking him to examine Buzhardt's reconstruction of Dean's conversations with Nixon. Butterfield remarked that the details in Buzhardt's statement had to be based on more than memory. Scott said Butterfield was asked (but did not say by whom) whether Dean was correct in suspecting that the President had recorded one of his conversations. At this question, Scott continued, Butterfield reexamined the Buzhardt reconstruction and replied that Dean didn't know about any recordings. He then told them in a tone of resignation that they did not have to look for *one* recorded conversation. He revealed that the President recorded *all* room or telephone conversations he had in the Oval Office, the President's Executive Office Building office and the Cabinet Room, as well as conversations on the telephone in the Lincoln Sitting Room of the White House and the telephone at the President's desk in the Aspen cabin at Camp David.

Butterfield himself had supervised the installation of the microphones and the recording equipment in the spring of 1971. The system was a voice-activated one, which meant that the microphones would spring on as soon as a tracer light, to which they were connected, would indicate that the President had entered the room. The recording equipment itself would begin to operate only when persons began to speak.

Scott added that Butterfield had stated he didn't think he was telling the committee anything it hadn't already discovered. He knew we had questioned Haldeman and Higby and believed they had probably told us about the tapes. No one else could have told us, Butterfield had reasoned, since he knew we had not questioned the only other persons who knew about the White House taping system: the President, Haig, Stephen Bull (who took his job), a few Secret Service men who maintained the system, and his own secretary. Butterfield found himself in a "squeeze play"—not knowing what Haldeman or Higby had told the committee and not wanting to be caught making a false statement, he decided to tell the truth about the taping system when confronted with a direct question.

What Scott Armstrong and Gene Boyce did not tell me during the excitement of that Friday afternoon was that neither of them had asked the crucial direct question that had prompted Butterfield's historic response. It had been the minority staff member present, Don Sanders, who had asked it. It would be ironic if the question had been put not for the purpose of producing the facts revealed but to alert Butterfield to the direction of Scott's questions and to give Butterfield an opportunity to crush Dean's suspicion of an Oval Office recording. For it had the opposite impact on Butterfield, who, believing the committee knew more than it did, decided to tell all.

"Who else knows about this now?" I asked Scott.

"Those attending the session with Butterfield were myself, Gene, Don Sanders, and also Marianne Brazer, who took notes," Scott replied. "When Butterfield left, Don said he would just tell Fred Thompson and we said we would only tell you. That's it."

I started to think out loud. "We've got to present this information publicly through sworn testimony," I said.

"Then you're going to have to move fast," Scott said. "Butterfield told us he was leaving for Russia this coming Tuesday to negotiate some treaty. He made it clear that he does not want to be a public witness on the White House taping system."

"Well, he has no choice," I snapped. "He installed the damn system and knows all about it. We'll have to put him on Monday, before he gets out of the country, and before Nixon thinks about using executive privilege." I told Scott and Gene that I would make this recommendation to Senator Ervin, and if he approved I would call Scott later and tell him to inform Butterfield to be prepared to testify on Monday. We would issue a subpoena to compel his testimony rather than request him to be a voluntary witness, to make it easier for him to explain his appearance before the committee to his superiors at the White House. We would also issue subpoenas for Haig, Bull, Higby and Haldeman, who would follow Butterfield as witnesses, to corroborate the existence of the taping system and its current operation by Nixon.

A soon as Scott and Gene left, I called Senator Ervin at his Washington apartment, across from the Supreme Court. When Ervin heard my news, he replied in an awe-stricken voice, "That is the most remarkable discovery of evidence that I have learned about in my entire experience in the practice of law, as a judge on the bench and as a United States senator." He paused and stuttered, as if searching for words. Then he continued excitedly, "Why, Sam, this is nothing less than providential. Now there is uncontrovertible evidence to determine whether John Dean's testimony can be corroborated. The President should have read the warning in the King James version of the Bible: 'There is nothing covered, that shall not be revealed; neither hid, that shall not be known.' " Ervin authorized my preparation of a subpoena for Butterfield's public testimony on Monday.

I arrived home about nine o'clock, and although our guests had arrived and Sara announced that the dinner was overdone, I added to her consternation by grabbing Rufus and whisking him off to my den. Since he was my deputy chief counsel, he should know of our discovery. After pledging Rufus to secrecy, we emerged to finish an evening that was full of tension. It was only later that night that I could tell Sara what was happening. She realized at once how busy I would have to be that weekend and said quietly, "Honey, why don't we postpone celebrating our wedding anniversary until later." I had been about to make the same suggestion and was feeling like a heel. It was not easy for Sara to put her own emotional life on the shelf. But I was grateful that she helped share the burden of seemingly endless hours of work and stress.

On Sunday I called Scott and told him to notify Butterfield that he would be a witness on Monday. Scott called back a little later to tell me that Butterfield was unhappy and extremely reluctant to be a witness. He could not understand why we were unwilling to call some of the other persons who had knowledge of the taping system. After receiving Scott's call, Butterfield got in touch with Fred Thompson and Senator Baker, and met with Baker at Baker's home on Sunday to seek Baker's help to prevent his having to testify before the committee. Thompson had earlier, on Friday evening, tipped off Buzhardt about Butterfield's revelation. Baker advised Butterfield to tell someone at the White House that he had informed the Senate committee about the taping system.

Butterfield called Len Garment on Sunday and told him what he had told our committee. This was the first time Garment heard about the White House taping system. The President was still in the hospital and the news of Butterfield's revelation must have taken the senior White House staff by surprise; no plan of defense had been developed when subpoenas signed by Ervin were sent to the White House for Haig, Higby, Bull and Butterfield's former secretary.

On Monday morning Jim Hamilton, who had made some of the original contacts with Butterfield for his appearance at the informal staff interrogation session, volunteered to serve the subpoena on Butterfield.

Later, I was called away from the committee table in the Caucus Room, where the committee was winding up its interrogation of Richard Moore, by an urgent phone call from Jim Hamilton. His voice was troubled as he explained that he had located Butterfield and had served the subpoena on him, but Butterfield had told him he was not going to honor it and refused to be a witness. I told Hamilton to stay on the line until I could inform Ervin of this problem and that I would come right back to him.

When I whispered to Ervin about Butterfield's attitude, he thought for a minute and then said, "Tell Jim to tell Butterfield that if he does not appear in compliance with that subpoena, I will send the sergeant-at-arms out after him to arrest him." I looked at Ervin, and he wasn't smiling. Hamilton was then told to call in Butterfield's reply immediately.

About ten minutes later Hamilton informed me that Butterfield had agreed to come to Room G-334 at the lunch recess to meet with Senator Ervin, Senator Baker, Fred Thompson and me to discuss the need for his testimony. Ervin decided to adjourn the morning session of the hearing early to allow for the meeting with Butterfield.

Ervin, Baker, Thompson and I went to G-334, where Butterfield was waiting for us. He was visibly agitated as he immediately launched into a plea to be relieved of having to testify in open session. He emphasized that the exposure he would get with such testimony would compromise him as a representative for the United States in the treaty negotiations he was to carry on in Russia. "You don't need me as a witness on this subject," Butterfield pleaded. "You can call Haig, Higby, or Stephen Bull just as well."

Senator Baker cleared his throat. "You know, Sam, I think Alex is right. Why don't we just excuse him and let him go to Russia to serve his country in the treaty. I think it would be a shame if we did anything to embarrass the government's position with the Soviet Union in this matter just to put Alex on as a witness when, as he says, there are substitute witnesses that can replace him."

Ervin was standing and his face had taken on a stubborn expression. "Howard, I think it's more important that the people of this country hear about the White House taping system from the man who super-

vised the installation of that system than that he go to Russia to participate in some treaty negotiations. I think it's absolutely essential that
Mr. Butterfield take the stand this afternoon and tell everything he
knows to the American people about the recording system by which the
President recorded all his conversations in the White House."

"But what about my job at the Federal Aviation Agency?" Butterfield asked plaintively. "You're asking me to stick my neck out and it's
bound to get chopped right off."

"The best way for you to keep that job as administrator for the
Federal Aviation Agency is to testify this afternoon to what you know
about the taping system," Ervin said with a smile on his face. "After
you appear on public television as a witness to the truth, I guarantee
that nobody in the White House will dare lift a finger to touch you."
Baker agreed with Ervin that Butterfield was not jeopardizing his position by testifying before the committee. When he saw that Ervin was
adamant in his position about Butterfield's testimony, Baker joined in
advising Butterfield to comply with the subpoena. "It will be your best
job insurance," Baker told Butterfield.*

I had a clinching bit of information which made it difficult for
Butterfield to squirm out of testifying at this point. Fred Buzhardt
had called and told me that if Butterfield took the stand and testified to the existence of the taping system, the President had agreed
that Buzhardt should send a letter for the President to the committee conceding the truth of Mr. Butterfield's testimony, making any
other subpoenas unnecessary. Buzhardt said a White House messenger would appear with the letter the moment Butterfield completed
his testimony. On hearing this, Butterfield agreed to testify at two
o'clock that afternoon.

Then a strange thing happened. Baker took me aside as we were
leaving G-334 and said, "Since it was a minority staff member, Don
Sanders, who asked the question which produced Butterfield's revelation of the taping system, I would appreciate it very much, Sam, if you
would let Fred Thompson open up the questioning of Butterfield. This
is going to be quite a blow to the administration, and I don't want the
minority on the committee to look like it got caught with its pants
down, when in fact it played a key role in discovering the tapes."

I was taken aback. Baker's information about Sanders' question to
Butterfield was news to me. I told Baker that I would check with Scott

*Butterfield survived until Richard Nixon resigned. He was fired by President Ford.

Armstrong and Gene Boyce, and that if they confirmed Sanders' version of what happened I would be pleased to let Fred Thompson open up the questioning of Butterfield.

After making a hurried search in staff headquarters, I finally located Scott in the Senate cafeteria. He was sitting at a table with Marc Lackritz, whose curly Harpo Marx hair style could not be missed. Marc was one of the most brilliant young lawyer-investigators on my staff, but you couldn't tell it by looking at him. He dressed and looked like one of the dead end kids of the movies. However, with a mind like a calculator for detail, he was a relentless prober. Scott, a shorter, squatter counterpart, with unruly Afro-style hair, long sideburns and ruffled appearance, looked like anything but a Senate committee investigator. Yet no one on the staff was more courageous, honest or persistent.

I joined them. Immediately I told Scott about Baker's claim that it was Don Sanders who had elicited Butterfield's statement about the White House tapes. Scott fidgeted with his fork. He looked troubled about my statement. "Well, I suppose it is literally true that Sanders put the specific question to Butterfield about tape recordings," he said, "but it's a gross exaggeration that he developed the Butterfield testimony. As I told you, I had been gradually probing Butterfield about the likely sources for Buzhardt's reconstruction of Dean's conversations with Nixon."

Scott insisted that Butterfield revealed the taping system because he believed the committee staff already knew about it and their questions about the Buzhardt reconstruction and Dean's suspicions of a tape recording in the Oval Office were a ploy.

"Nevertheless," I said, "Baker is in fact accurate that Sanders first questioned Butterfield about Dean's belief that one of his meetings with Nixon in the Oval Office was taped."

"Yes," Scott replied, "but that is a hell of a note!"

I got up from the table and told my staff members that I had no choice but to let Fred Thompson develop the Butterfield material. I personally resented it and felt cheated. This had indeed been the greatest find of our committee investigation. It was unlikely that we would be able to top it. Amazingly, there appeared to have been no leaks of our discovery of the White House taping system,* and our public

---

*I am puzzled by Bob Woodward and Carl Bernstein's claims in *All the President's Men* that they had a leak that weekend from a senior committee staff official and the hearings at two o'clock that afternoon would reveal to the world for the first time this most extraordinary information about Richard Nixon's White House.

It was approaching two o'clock and the senators and staff members were reassembling. When Fred Thompson walked into the Caucus Room, I told him I was pleased to concur with Senator Baker's suggestion that he open up the questioning of Butterfield. Fred's big, friendly face broke into a smile. "That's right generous of you, Sam," he said. "Well," I said quietly, "it's only fair."

We took our seats and Senator Ervin banged the table with his gavel. The next witness was expected to be Herbert Kalmbach. A murmur of surprise was heard in the room when I called out the name Alexander Butterfield. Butterfield was led into the Caucus Room by committee staff members and took his seat at the witness table. After a brief explanation from me, Fred Thompson began the unfolding of Butterfield's testimony. It drew gasps of shocked surprise at the press tables and struck the worldwide television audience like a bombshell.

As soon as Butterfield had completed his testimony a Capitol policeman brought an envelope to me, telling me it had been handed to him for delivery to me by a White House messenger. I handed the envelope to Senator Ervin, and he announced, after reading the letter enclosed: "The chair has received a letter from J. Fred Buzhardt, counsel for the President, dated July 16, 1973, reading as follows:

> 'Dear Mr. Chairman: This letter is to confirm the facts stated to your Committee today by Mr. Alexander Butterfield that the President's meetings and conversations in the White House had been recorded since the spring of 1971. I am advised that this system, which is still in use, is similar to that employed by the last administration* which was discontinued from 1969 until the spring of 1971. A more detailed statement concerning these procedures will be furnished to the Committee shortly.' "

This letter from Buzhardt was to be the last concession our committee was to receive from the White House. Indeed, we had moved none

---

Washington *Post* did not publish it because they could not confirm it. The story was too hot and they would have called me, even though they knew they would get a "No comment" from me. That never stopped them from calling me before on important stories, and neither of them called me that weekend.

*Buzhardt's claim that President Johnson had a similar taping system was mistaken.

too quickly in rushing Butterfield before the committee. Our next effort was to subpoena a small band of White House Secret Service men under the direction of Al Wong, who maintained the taping system and who stored the reels of recorded tapes. When our subpoenas were served at the White House, Buzhardt called and told me that the Secret Service men would be under instructions not to answer any questions.

When the Secret Service men appeared at a special executive session of the committee, they were accompanied by counsel for the White House and counsel for the Secretary of the Treasury.

After Wong refused to answer my opening questions, counsel for the Treasury submitted to Ervin a letter from Secretary of the Treasury George P. Shultz which referred to President Nixon's letter to him directing that "no officer or agent of the Secret Service shall give testimony to congressional committees concerning matters observed or learned while performing protective functions for the President or in their duties at the White House." Nixon's letter said that it specifically applied to the "Senate Select Committee which is investigating matters relating to the Watergate break-in and the current efforts which I am informed are being made to subpoena present or former members of the White House detail of the Secret Service."

Ervin excused Wong and counsel for the Treasury so that we could consider the question of the President's letter in executive session of the committee. At the meeting he pointed out that the committee was empowered to recommend contempt proceedings against Wong and the other Secret Service men who had been subpoenaed. But he expressed the view that this would not be fair to these minor public officials who were caught in the middle between an order from the President of the United States and a subpoena from a Senate committee.

He said the committee's dispute was with the President and not with these Secret Service men. He recommended that the Secret Service men be excused from testifying because of the President's letter and that the committee send a letter directly to the President requesting access to the White House tapes and renewing the request for the White House papers which had been made in June. The committee unanimously approved Ervin's recommendation and adjourned to the Caucus Room, where Ervin publicly announced that he was putting into the record the letter he had sent to the President pursuant to the meeting the committee had held that day. The letter was as follows:

The President
White House
Washington, D.C.

Dear Mr. President:

Today the Select Committee on Presidential Campaign Activities met and unanimously voted that I request that you provide the Committee with all relevant documents and tapes under control of the White House that relate to the matters the Select Committee is authorized to investigate under S. Res. 60. I refer to the documents mentioned in my letter to Mr. Leonard Garment of June 21, 1973, and the relevant portions of the tapes alluded to by Mr. Alexander Butterfield before the Committee on July 16, 1973. If your illness prevents our meeting to discuss these issues in the next day or two, I should like to suggest that you designate members of your staff to meet with members of the Select Committee staff to make arrangements for our access to White House documents and tapes pertinent to the Committee's investigation. I should like respectfully to relate that the Committee's investigation is ongoing and that access to relevant documents should not be delayed if the Committee is to perform its mission. May we hear from you at your earliest convenience? The Committee deeply regrets your illness and hopes for you a speedy recovery.

Sincerely,

Sam J. Ervin, Jr., Chairman.

The President's response came six days later. Practically on his return to the White House from the hospital, Nixon wrote Ervin a letter rejecting the committee's request for access to the White House tapes. He asserted the doctrine of executive privilege, and made the strange comment that the "tapes would not finally settle the central issues before your Committee." He claimed that he had personally listened to a number of them and that they were entirely consistent with what he knew to be the truth and what he had stated to be the truth. But he added, "However, as in any verbatim recording of informal conversations, they contain comments that persons with different perspectives and motivations would inevitably interpret in different ways."

The committee reviewed the President's letter at a meeting on July 23, 1973, and voted unanimously to issue a subpoena against the President for specific tapes relating to conversations between Dean and Nixon which took place in the Oval Office. When the committee reconvened in the Caucus Room in the afternoon session of Monday, July

23, Ervin publicly read into the record the President's letter to the committee.

Ervin announced that the committee had unanimously voted to authorize and direct the chairman to issue two subpoenas, one requiring the President to produce the tapes which would be described in the subpoena, and the other requiring the President to make available to the committee the presidential papers that would be described in the subpoena. Ervin added with a toss of his head, "This is a rather remarkable letter about the tapes. If you'll notice, the President says he had heard the tapes of some of them, and they sustain his position. But he says he's not going to let anybody else hear them for fear they might draw a different conclusion." The Caucus Room broke out into loud laughter.

Speaking in a more serious tone, Ervin entered into a discussion of executive privilege and separation of powers and concluded by saying, "I am certain that the doctrine of separation of powers does not impose on any President either the duty or the power to undertake to separate a congressional committee from access to the truth concerning alleged criminal activities.

"I was in hopes that the President would accede to the request of this Committee for these tapes and papers. I love my country. I venerate the office of the President, and I have the best wishes for the success of the present incumbent of that office, because he is the only President this country has at this time.

"A President not only has Constitutional powers which require him to see to it or to take care that the laws be faithfully executed, and I think it's his duty under those circumstances to produce information which would either tend to prove or disprove that criminal activities have occurred. But beyond that, the President of the United States by reason of the fact that he holds the highest office in the gift of the American people, owes an obligation to furnish a high standard of moral leadership to this nation, and his Constitutional duties, in my opinion, and undoubtedly his duty of affording moral leadership to the country places upon him some obligation under these circumstances.

". . . I deeply regret that this situation has arisen, because I think that the Watergate tragedy is the greatest tragedy this country has ever suffered. I used to think that the Civil War was our country's greatest tragedy, but I do remember that there were some redeeming features in the Civil War in that there was some spirit of sacrifice and heroism displayed on both sides. I see no redeeming features in Watergate."

The issue had been joined. That afternoon my staff drafted two subpoenas: one for certain specific tapes relating to conversations John Dean had testified had occurred in the Oval Office, and the other for a number of White House papers. Rufus Edmisten, incapable of passing up so historic a walk-on role, urged me to let him serve the subpoenas. I approved his taking on this mission—the first time a congressional committee had ever served a subpoena on the President of the United States. That same afternoon, by coincidence, Special Prosecutor Archibald Cox issued his own subpoena to the President on behalf of the grand jury, demanding the surrender of a number of White House tapes and other documents based on the investigation of our committee.

The committee and the special prosecutor's office knew they had taken an extraordinary step in subpoenaing the President for the tapes. But much more occurred that late Monday afternoon, July 23, 1973, than the service of two sets of subpoenas at the White House. History must record that this was the beginning of the end of Richard Nixon's presidency.

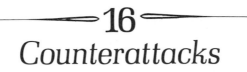

16
Counterattacks

NIXON PROMPTLY REFUSED TO HONOR THE SUBPOENA FOR THE TAPES, claiming executive privilege. The committee was now confronted with the problem of how to enforce its subpoena. It could, of course, call on the Senate to exercise its own enforcement power through a contempt proceeding initiated by the sergeant-at-arms of the Senate arresting the President and bringing him to the bar of the Senate. But the prospect of arresting the President for contempt was repellent and the committee rejected this procedure out of hand. Besides, as one member gibed, the sergeant-at-arms wouldn't be permitted to enter the White House and might be shot if he tried to force his way in.

The committee considered it equally unseemly to resort to the federal statutory offense of contempt of Congress which would require a grand jury indictment against the President obtained by the special prosecutor. Our subpoena was the first of its kind in history and the criminal process was a clumsy instrument to test this virgin exercise of congressional power. Also there was considerable disagreement on the question of whether a President could be indicted.

Under the circumstances, the committee decided that its best course of action was to sue the President in the federal district court. Cox had gone to court earlier to enforce his subpoena and we were now trailing his case.

Both lawsuits were heard by Judge Sirica. Cox's was based on Sirica's order on the President to show cause why he was not complying with a grand jury subpoena. Sirica ruled against Nixon in the Cox suit, holding that the President could not assert executive privilege with regard to taped conversations involving criminal activities or providing evidence of crime being investigated by the grand jury.

However, Sirica ruled against the Senate committee in its suit on the ground that it lacked jurisdiction to bring the suit. With certain exceptions, in federal actions a plaintiff must allege and prove to establish jurisdiction that the "amount in controversy" in the action is over $10,000. According to Sirica, we had failed to meet this requirement, despite our argument that the tapes were worth much more than $10,-000 to Nixon and would save our committee considerably more than that amount by shortening our investigation if we had access to them.

In October 1973 the committee appealed Sirica's adverse ruling to the United States Court of Appeals for the District of Columbia. As a safety measure Ervin introduced a bill in the Senate specifically giving our committee jurisdiction to sue the President for the tapes without regard to any "amount in controversy." The bill sailed through both houses of Congress in a few days without any opposition. Nixon could have vetoed the bill, but he was in an obvious conflict of interest. He let it become law without his signature.

The Court of Appeals remanded the case to Sirica to reconsider it in light of the new statute giving the committee jurisdiction to sue. Sirica, claiming he was overburdened with Watergate cases, transferred the committee's case to Judge Gerhard Gesell, one of the ablest judges on the court. Gesell elicited the views of the special prosecutor and Nixon. The special prosecutor took a neutral position. Nixon, however, suddenly claimed a sensitivity for the fairness of criminal trials. He also protested any violation of his confidential communications, despite the fact that he now was publicly referring to them and had allowed Haldeman to testify about Oval Office conversations with Dean.

Judge Gesell surprised us by ruling against the committee after finding in the committee's favor on every legal point. He simply exercised judicial discretion (which we claimed he did not have) in preferring criminal prosecutions in the courts over the Congress's legislative and investigative functions. He worried that giving us the tapes might prejudice the criminal trials, even though the Supreme Court had held that Congress as a separate, coordinate branch of government could not be subordinated to the criminal process in the courts. On February 20, 1974, we appealed again to the Court of Appeals. That court showed little interest in expediting its decision, although our committee's time was fast running out.

In July 1973, when we were beginning our suit against Nixon, the committee was in a state of exhaustion from the many long days of public hearings since May 17. Senator Ervin and his colleagues on the committee looked forward eagerly to August 3, when Congress would begin its long recess, which would not end until after Labor Day. However, I knew it would not be possible to close the hearings by the August 3 recess because there were too many witnesses remaining to be called in the Watergate break-in and cover-up phase of our investigation. Ehrlichman and Haldeman were next in line. They were the principal defenders for the White House and had clearly been assigned the task of destroying John Dean's testimony. Each of them could well take a week before the committee.

There were also a dozen other witnesses. Even more had been on the list, but we had gone through a tight pruning process, and what remained were the witnesses I believed were essential to provide a complete and balanced factual presentation to the public. Talmadge urged that the committee sit through the summer and complete its hearings, even though it meant working during the August recess. At committee meetings he repeatedly expressed the worry that the public was growing tired of Watergate and that if the committee dragged the hearings on too long, there would be a political backlash on the committee.

The committee's mail—which had been steadily increasing to about nine thousand letters a day, running 90 percent in support of the committee's work—did not reflect Talmadge's position that the public wanted the committee to terminate its investigation and hearings. It seemed more likely that Talmadge was getting local advice from his campaign advisers in Georgia, who were probably more worried about the time the committee work took away from the senator's ability to deal with the problems of his constituents. There was no doubt, however, that Talmadge was getting the message from home that his people thought that prolonging the hearings could be dangerous to him.

A problematic witness was Charles Colson. He had been eager to appear, and Fred Thompson was urging that I call him. However, Colson's testimony would probably take three days to a week and it would be necessary to follow him up with a number of rebuttal witnesses. I would be playing directly into the hands of the White House if I closed the first phase of the hearings with Colson alone and did not call other witnesses that could rebut or explain his testimony.

When the committee met to discuss the witness list, Gurney, Baker and Fred Thompson were insistent that the committee not adjourn without calling Colson. I said that I was willing to call Colson if the committee was willing to sit through their August recess to hear the other witnesses who had to be called in conjunction with Colson. Senator Ervin agreed that Colson could not be permitted to testify without calling the other witnesses and stated that he did not want to give up the recess.

After a vote was taken, it was decided that we would not call Colson until the recess ended. As it turned out, this would be too late to obtain Colson as a witness.

When I next contacted Colson's attorney to question Colson in preparation for his appearance before the committee after Labor Day, I was informed that Colson would now have to assert his constitutional privilege under the Fifth Amendment. The special prosecutor had already notified Colson that he had become a target for the grand jury investigation. The White House had looked forward to having Colson do battle for Richard Nixon and attack John Dean, but Colson, the head hunter, became the hunted, and he was removed from the list.

By excusing Colson we were implementing a policy Ervin and I had succeeded in getting the committee to adopt: no witness asserting his Fifth Amendment privilege would be forced to appear publicly before television cameras to repeat his refusal to answer questions on constitutional grounds. Other committees had engaged in the practice of exhibiting "Fifth Amendment" witnesses—some notoriously. But we concluded that public display of such witnesses could serve only an improper purpose of showmanship and did not perform any legislative or public-informing function.

In the midst of the pressure to complete a shortened witness list by the beginning of August, a nasty incident occurred that was clearly meant to sidetrack the committee and destroy or immobilize one of my most valuable staff assistants—Carmine Bellino, my chief investigator. On July 24, 1973, the day after the committee subpoena for the White House tapes was served on the President, the Republican national chairman, George Bush, called a press conference and released three affidavits, which he said revealed that Bellino had engaged in espionage and electronic surveillance activities against Republican party and campaign officials during the 1960 presidential campaign. Three days later, as if carefully orchestrated, twenty-two Republican senators signed a letter to Senator Ervin, urging the Senate Watergate committee to investigate Bush's charges and calling for Bellino's suspension pending the outcome of the investigation. Ervin was forced into a corner, and on August 3 he appointed a subcommittee consisting of Senators Talmadge, Inouye and Gurney to investigate the charges.

The White House knew that Carmine Bellino, a wizard at reconstructing the receipts and expenditures of funds despite laundering techniques and the destruction of records, was hot on the trail of Herbert Kalmbach and Bebe Rebozo. Bellino's diligent, meticulous work would ultimately disclose Kalmbach's funding scheme for the White House's dirty tricks campaign and unravel a substantial segment of Rebozo's secret cash transactions on behalf of Nixon.

I assigned Dave Dorsen to make a thorough investigation for the subcommittee and to make whatever additional inquiries he believed were necessary. Bellino, from the start, vehemently denied Bush's charges and provided the committee with an affidavit stating under oath that he had never engaged in any kind of electronic surveillance. Dave and his staff, particularly Barry Schochet, a young staff attorney, quickly went to work. Even though Ervin had not removed him from the investigation, Bellino had been rendered emotionally unable to work effectively because of the charges.

Dave Dorsen quickly learned that there was no credible evidence against Bellino. The principal accuser had died before Bush had made his public attack on Bellino. The other so-called witnesses, who had signed affidavits implicating Bellino in electronic surveillance, admitted when questioned that they had no personal knowledge about the subject but were only relating what some third or fourth person had told them. When the individuals they referred to were questioned, they denied ever making any such statements about Bellino. The charges became even murkier when our staff discovered that the person who had put them together was a man named Jack Buckley. In their dirty tricks investigation of the 1972 presidential campaign, Terry Lenzner and his staff had identified Buckley as the Republican spy, known as Fat Jack, who had intercepted and photographed Muskie's mail between his campaign and Senate offices as part of Ruby 1 (a project code named in Liddy's Gemstone political espionage plan).

When I received this report from Dave and Terry, I could not help exclaiming incredulously, "The dirty tricks didn't end with the election —they're still pulling them on us now!" Ervin had the same reaction when he learned the story and asked Senator Talmadge to bring the investigation to a close with a report clearing Bellino. However, we had not counted on the fact that the strategy to knock out Bellino included the help of Senator Gurney, with the support of Senator Baker, Fred Thompson and Thompson's deputy Don Sanders, whom Thompson had assigned to work with the subcommittee for the minority.

When Talmadge pushed for an early resolution of the investigation, Gurney stalled, claiming that Sanders had not completed his part of the investigation. The unsubstantial nature of the evidence had to be obvious to Sanders, yet he dillydallied, stating that there were a number of additional witnesses he still wanted to question. I told Fred Thompson that we had learned of "Fat Jack" Buckley's role and that we were considering making Buckley testify. Thompson warned that Buckley might be willing to make additional charges against Bellino, and that that would make it impossible for Gurney and Baker to join in any effort of the committee to provide a unanimous vote of confidence for Bellino.

It was clear to me that Fred was uncomfortable in giving me this message. I did not believe he was playing an active role in this dirty business; I thought that as minority counsel, he had no choice but to represent the partisan position of his bosses. Yet I smelled the ugly odor of blackmail on the part of somebody and I did not like it. I called a meeting of my top assistants—Dave, Terry, Jim and Rufus—to arrive at a strategy to recommend to Ervin. The staff consensus was that it was more important to get Bellino cleared as quickly as possible than to expose Buckley's role in the plot. Therefore we decided to wait out the subcommittee's report, which Dave said would ultimately be favorable to Bellino, according to assurances he had received from Don Sanders.

The matter dragged on through the fall while I repeatedly requested at committee meetings that the committee make a public statement clearing Bellino of the charges. It was not until November 13, 1973, that

Ervin finally forced the matter to a vote. By then hundreds of hours had been spent by Dave and his staff on these charges with the result that the committee's primary investigation was short-changed. Senator Talmadge and Senator Inouye filed a report completely clearing Bellino of the charges. Gurney filed a minority report which conceded that there was no direct evidence against Bellino, but that there was some conflicting testimony that had to be noted. The minority report was primarily based on the affidavit of the witness who had died before the public charges had been made. Ervin ordered that the committee's position clearing Bellino of the charges against him be printed in the Congressional Record, since the original charges had appeared there through the publication of the July 27 letter signed by the twenty-two Republican senators. Thus the matter ended with little fanfare and almost no newspaper comment. The reputation of a public official with many years' service as a dedicated and incorruptible investigator had been deeply wounded and tarnished, and Bellino would retire from federal service believing—rightly—that he had not been given the fullest opportunity he deserved to clear his good name.

John Wilson, the aged, white-haired veteran of many years of courtroom sparring, brought his Tweedledum and Tweedledee witnesses—John Ehrlichman and Bob Haldeman—to the Caucus Room for a decided change of pace of the committee's public hearings. Until Ehrlichman gave his testimony, most of the witnesses who had participated in the Watergate break-in or cover-up activities presented confessionals in repentant tones. They were the men in gray flannel suits who had been caught, said they were sorry, blamed too much power or too much money, and urged the committee to recommend broad reforms in the American political electoral system.

One major exception had been John Mitchell, who never brought himself to admit any wrongdoing, despite his admission of cover-up activities. Throughout his long testimony before the committee he sat placidly smoking his pipe, finding it difficult to recall the details of practically any given event, and claiming lack of knowledge of most relevant facts. Just as the White House tapes would later reveal what Nixon expected his loyal servant to do, Mitchell simply sat there in front of us and "put on his long face and stonewalled it."

But even Mitchell on occasion fell into the refrain heard frequently by the committee: "In hindsight I would have . . ." Not so Ehrlichman. He came on gnashing his teeth, fighting and slugging. His task was to take on the committee: the strategy involved his launching an offensive against the committee in an attempt to reverse the trend of the committee hearings—to break the momentum the committee had been steadily building since the first witness was called on May 17. I was fully prepared on the facts for handling Ehrlichman, but my real problem with Ehrlichman was his unwillingness to be questioned. Ehrlichman insisted on making speeches instead of answering questions. He used the witness chair as a platform to challenge the committee and to justify his conduct and that of Richard Nixon and Bob Haldeman. A frequent tactic employed by Ehrlichman was to try to anticipate many of my questions, and then interrupt me and object to what he complained were hidden assumptions or premises in a question.

Wilson, Ehrlichman's lawyer, also made numerous objections and statements of law. He even engaged in a memorable debate with Ervin on national security powers of the President. The committee gave the lawyers for other witnesses equal latitude. This was unusual, since in most congressional hearings lawyers for witnesses are only permitted to whisper legal advice to their clients on their legal rights concerning the answering of questions and are not permitted to make arguments to the committee.

Like Dean, Ehrlichman took a full week for his public testimony before the committee. He was defiant to the end, and turning his face to the television cameras, he made a closing speech to the television audience about the contributions of the Nixon administration. After his testimony one news reporter came up to me and said provokingly, "That guy was tough as nails—you couldn't break him down."

"Well, what do you think after hearing him?" I asked the reporter. "Was he involved in the cover-up?"

"Oh! Up to here!" the reporter exclaimed, placing his hand on the top of his forehead. I shrugged my shoulders and said, "Then what more do you want the committee to show?"

John Wilson switched horses with Haldeman. He presented Haldeman as a responsive, cooperative witness. There was none of the Ehrlichman wrangling and scrapping in Haldeman's testimony. Haldeman sought to maintain a pleasant smile on his face and to appear as a respectful witness as he responded to the committee's questions. But he also appeared as an absent-minded witness who could not recall any details of practically anything that had happened during the relevant periods about which he was questioned. The Haldeman testimony was very much like a replay of Mitchell's testimony, but without the pipe.

There were brief periods where the fire of hatred showed in Haldeman's eyes when he was pushed in a corner and confronted with damaging memoranda he had prepared or on which he had written brutal comments—it was as though his thin veneer of pleasantness had been pricked by a knife point. However, he would quickly recover his calm, and generally maintained a public relations attitude toward the committee until the end of his testimony.

Haldeman also carried out a special mission for Richard Nixon when he appeared before the committee. He provided the first "ear witness" account of a White House tape-recorded conversation between John Dean and the President. Haldeman explained that at the President's request he had listened to certain tapes of conversations in the Oval Office, including the one that took place on March 21, 1973. He said that when Dean had testified before the committee he had mistaken the date of that conversation and had placed it earlier, on March 13.

Haldeman told Senator Ervin that he had been present at only the latter part of the March 21 meeting and had been instructed by President Nixon not to reveal, on the ground of executive privilege, any parts of conversations to which he himself had not been a party. Ervin rejected the executive privilege claim made by Haldeman and Wilson and directed Haldeman to reveal the entire conversation between Dean and the President on the March 21 tape. What followed made it clear that Wilson, Haldeman and presumably the White House had engaged in a ploy to permit Haldeman to present his version of the March 21 meeting under circumstances where the White House could still pretend to be invoking the doctrine of executive privilege against disclosure of the tapes. Haldeman immediately reached into his file and picked out a sheet of paper he claimed contained a typed summary of the taped Dean-Nixon conversation in the Oval Office on March 21, 1973, and read it to the committee in compliance with Ervin's directions.

Haldeman's purpose in revealing this version of the President's conversation with Dean became obvious. Dean had told the committee that the President had asked him how much it would cost to meet Hunt's blackmail demands and he had said it might cost as much as a million dollars. Dean said the President had remarked that it would not be difficult to raise the money. Haldeman testified that the tape of the March 21 conversation revealed that the President told Dean he could raise the money but "it would be wrong." Senator Baker had Haldeman repeat this for the record, stressing that according to what Haldeman heard on the tape, the President made it clear that he thought it would be wrong to pay Hunt blackmail money.

Ironically, these replies by Haldeman to Baker's questions later formed the basis of a perjury count against Haldeman by the Watergate grand jury. When the actual recording of the conversations was finally released to the grand jury, it revealed that Haldeman had testified falsely before the committee. No doubt, at the time of Haldeman's testimony before the committee, both he and Richard Nixon believed that this tape would never be heard by unfriendly ears.

Indeed, in the summer of 1973, Nixon believed that simply by asserting that the tapes were in his custody and control he made it impossible for anybody to obtain access to them without his consent. He felt free to launch a counteroffensive to demolish John Dean's charges and to claim that the tapes exculpated him because only he possessed the clinching evidence. Nixon was not concerned that the special prosecutor or the Senate committee had subpoenaed the tapes and had gone to court to enforce the subpoenas. For, as he would have his lawyers argue in court, he, as President, had absolute, unreviewable power, and was not subject to the process of any court, except a court of impeachment (which he ignored because he felt that Congress didn't have the guts).

One question is asked everywhere, by everyone—university presidents and cab drivers—Why didn't he destroy the tapes? If he had, Nixon would have served out his full term as President; John Dean's word alone could not have unseated a President—or even convicted the top Watergate conspirators. Why didn't he? Simply because in his arrogant perception of his powers, Nixon believed that no one could ever force him to release the tapes.

Part Two

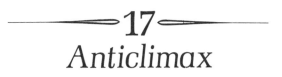

17
Anticlimax

WHEN THE SENATE WATERGATE COMMITTEE RECONVENED AFTER the long August recess, the members displayed little of the vim and vigor that had got them through the extraordinary pace and high drama of the committee's public hearings during the spring and summer. They had had a good vacation and looked rested. But they had also had the occasion to pause a while with their advisers and constituents to look back at what they had done during the past few months. For most of them it had been both an exhilarating and unsettling experience.

Through their hearings and subpoenas, they had thrust themselves directly into the Oval Office and had come close to destroying the presidency of Richard Nixon. They were like mountain climbers who had successfully scaled two-thirds of a treacherous, lofty mountain, and now looked down from their dizzy perch in wonderment that they had come so far—and in fear that if they climbed further toward the peak they might slip to their doom.

Most of the senators spoke from the viewpoint of the politician and referred to the ever-impatient public, who most of them claimed had grown tired of our public hearings and wanted an end to Watergate. The committee's heavy mail still negated this assessment of public opinion, but the senators, four of whom were coming closer to their reelection bids, preferred to rely on their "back home" advisers. Talmadge reminded the committee that Congress would go on recess again on October 15 and urged that date as a cutoff date for all further public hearings of the committee. He reminded the committee that the Senate resolution called for a final report by February 28, 1974, and that his suggestion would give the committee four good months to prepare and review a report for submission to Congress.

I was disappointed when Ervin appeared amenable to this suggestion and agreed with Talmadge that he wanted to have the committee complete its work strictly within the time limit allowed by the resolution. The Watergate break-in and cover-up was only one part of the committee's mandate, I argued. Perhaps more important for the political reform of the electoral process and the education of the American people, I insisted, was the committee's responsibility to investigate unethical and illegal political espionage and campaign financing during the presidential campaign of 1972. I also reminded the committee that we had begun a lawsuit to enforce the committee's subpoena against the President for the White House tapes. Looking directly at Ervin, I declared that our report would be incomplete and vulnerable to criticism if we did not have access to the White House tapes.

Talmadge took the cigar out of his mouth and asked me, "Well, then, how much time do you require to put on the rest of your witnesses?"

"We will at least have to go into November," I said. To do justice to the two remaining phases of the investigation, I didn't believe we could complete public hearings in November or even December. In fact, I thought we would still be hearing witnesses in January. But I decided to let the committee confront the reality of the situation when it arose. Once we were in the midst of taking testimony, I did not expect the committee to shut off the hearings. After all, I reasoned, despite Ervin's and Talmadge's desire to get out of the Watergate limelight, they were men of integrity, and would not lend themselves to anything that would even appear to be a cover-up of relevant evidence.

The senators were not the only ones who were worried about our next set of public hearings. By September 1973 Terry Lenzner had failed to develop a successful investigation which would produce an exciting set of public hearings comparable to the Watergate hearings. And his phase of the investigation—political espionage, which we were now calling campaign practices—was next on the agenda for public hearings. This had not been Terry's fault. Throughout most of the Watergate hearings, Terry and his staff had helped me investigate and prepare for the questioning of the major witnesses; these hearings had absorbed the resources of the committee's entire staff.

Although Terry and his staff had done some preliminary investigative work in the political espionage area during the spring and summer, most of it was done after the August 7 recess. And at the end of this exhaustive field investigation, Terry had come up with a story on Donald Segretti's dirty tricks operation that was only slightly more detailed than the one already revealed in the newspapers about a year earlier.

Terry's staff was still unable to break the "canuck letter" dirty trick mystery which had such a devastating effect on Senator Muskie's presidential campaign. But their investigation did provide information on the identities and activities of a couple of additional CRP infiltrators into the primary campaigns of Democratic candidates, and they collected a large assortment of exhibits and samples of fraudulent literature used in the Republican dirty tricks program. These, however, were not dramatic breakthroughs. Indeed, so dissatisfied was Terry with his investigation that he became impatient with me when, in talking to either the committee or the press, I emphasized the importance of the public hearings on campaign practices. He complained that my statements would lead everybody to expect exciting hearings and they would be disappointed with what he would actually be able to produce.

There was one promising subject in his investigation. In August, while following a lead in Las Vegas based on Magruder's claim that Mitchell had instructed Liddy to break into the safe of Hank Greenspun, the publisher of the Las Vegas *Sun,* Terry found dramatic evidence. He learned that Howard Hughes had made a secret political contribution of $100,000 to Nixon through Nixon's close friend, Bebe Rebozo.*

According to the division of responsibility among my assistant chief counsel, this subject fell within Dave Dorsen's jurisdiction, since it related to campaign contributions. However, Dorsen had more than he could handle—the campaign financing area had developed into a vast investigative field. Indeed, it initially included Robert Vesco's activities and the highly publicized ITT political contribution. Dave quickly realized that these two areas alone could occupy all of his time, and we both agreed to recommend to the committee that since they were major targets of investigation by the U. S. attorney's office in New York (Vesco) and by the special prosecutor (ITT), we would not include them in our investigation. This still left Dave and his staff the task of investigating political contributions by corporations, unions, trade as-

---

*Actually, Jack Anderson had published this story in his column in 1971, but it appeared to receive little notice except at the White House. Also, Hughes' former major-domo, Robert Maheu, in a suit against Hughes for libel, revealed this Hughes-Rebozo transaction in a deposition in the spring of 1973. And Washington *Post* reporter John Hanrahan wrote about it in a story on September 25, 1973.

sociations and special interest groups. Dave's concern with his projected hearings related not to the scope of the material he could produce —he knew he would have too much—but to the possibility that it would be boring and appear to be not significantly different from what had been political practice, on the part of both Democrats and Republicans, in every presidential campaign over the years.

Perhaps the most dramatic part of Dave's investigation related to the substantial political contributions of the milk producers to persuade Nixon to overrule the decision of the Secretary of Agriculture and raise the price of milk in 1972. Dave was particularly worried about this investigation. The more he probed, the more he learned of major contributions made by the same dairy people to United States senators. Dave suspected that the campaign financing investigation would be a thorny one for the committee members to confront, and he wondered whether it would ever reach the stage of public hearings.

The worst fears of most of the senators that the campaign practices hearings might injure the committee's image appeared to them to be realized when I called Pat Buchanan as a witness. This was not true of Ervin. He strongly supported my bringing Buchanan before the committee. My plan in leading off with Buchanan was to offer an explanation of what led the Nixon team to engage in political espionage and dirty tricks in 1971 and part of 1972 when Nixon had become a "shoo-in" after the convention and won reelection by an overwhelming vote. That this was one of the most frequently requested explanations in all parts of the country indicated that many people had forgotten that in 1971 and early 1972 Richard Nixon was by no means certain of reelection. Indeed, the polls showed him trailing behind Senator Ed Muskie of Maine. For the Nixon team a victory for Muskie would have been not just a transition from a Republican to a Democratic administration but the virtual destruction of the United States. The architect of this point of view in the White House was Patrick Buchanan.

Over a period of years he had written more than a hundred memoranda, many of them to Nixon, setting forth in the rhetoric of what he called "hard ball politics" his fears and hatreds of the liberal establishment and his philosophy of the literal application of the spoils system. According to Buchanan, the winner should take everything provided by tax dollars, and the losers—Nixon's enemies—be denied any benefit of federal funds.

In the 1972 campaign Buchanan plotted to destroy Muskie by using "any stick available." In one of his memoranda he said, "We ought to go down to the kennels and turn all the dogs loose on Ecology Ed. The President is the only one who should stand clear, while everybody else gets chewed up. The rest of us are expendable commodities; but if the President goes, we all go, and maybe the country with us."

After recommending strategies for destroying Muskie, he wrote a memorandum in which he said, "What we need now is the decision on whom we want to run against. We believe that McGovern is our candidate for dozens of reasons. He could be painted as a left-wing radical candidate, the Goldwater of the Democratic party; and at this point in time we would inundate him." On April 27, 1972, Buchanan sent Mitchell and Haldeman a memorandum gloating over the fact that Muskie had withdrawn, giving McGovern a good chance at the nomination. He said, "With the great success of McGovern and subsequent pull-out of Muskie, the chances of a McGovern nomination are eminently improved. Thus, we must do as little as possible, at this time, to impede McGovern's rise." He closed the memorandum with this warning: "The temptations will be high in many quarters to go after McGovern, but word ought to go out to lay off with few exceptions. We have plenty of time to attach labels later, and the same labels which will defeat McGovern for the presidency are the same labels which will prevent him from getting the nomination. Let's not do Hubert's work for him." Buchanan, in his memoranda, also recommended covert operations, the use of political pranksters and the exploitation of racial and ethnic groups.

My purpose in calling Buchanan was not to establish that he had participated in any wrongdoing. Rather, it was to identify the draftsman of the blueprint that the Nixon storm troops sought to follow. Subsequent witnesses would tell how they carried some of these ideas to an extreme—even by committing illegal acts.

Buchanan probably decided that Ehrlichman had been successful as a witness by being aggressive and attacking the committee, because he adopted the same tactic. He started out accusing the committee of leaking unfavorable statements about him to the press. I went on record as joining him in deploring any leaks by our committee concerning his proposed testimony or reflecting on his character. Senator Baker surprised me by coming to my defense and strongly supporting me on this issue.

I took Buchanan over a series of his memoranda for the purpose of publicly revealing his philosophy of "hard ball" politics and the political spoils system, as well as his strategy of manipulating Democratic primaries. While reviewing his memoranda, I was constantly challenged by Buchanan as to what was wrong with this or what was wrong with that. And I found myself constantly replying that I was not suggesting anything was wrong, but was merely making a record of what was done, so that the committee could ultimately pass upon the propriety of such practices, even if they had been condoned in the past or used by both Democrats and Republicans.

However, Buchanan, with his sharp tongue and articulate sense of humor, repeatedly appealed to his many friends at the press tables to whom he had leaked many a story. Each time the press responded with laughter the senators at the table fidgeted uneasily and nervously. Indeed, when the committee's turn came to question Buchanan, most of the questions were aimed at showing that the Buchanan memos were nothing more than a recitation of old-fashioned politics. Ervin, however, sharply challenged Buchanan's claim that the spoils system allowed the winning administration to spend the taxpayers' money primarily on its friends.

Buchanan was finally excused as a witness, with the senators feeling that he had devastated the committee and that they had been made to look like fools. The press treated Buchanan as the best defender of the Nixon White House that had appeared before the committee, and I was depicted as having been destroyed by Buchanan's withering replies to my questions.

It did not appear that any of the reporters or columnists had read Buchanan's memos or understood Buchanan's role as a witness. They had become so accustomed to assuming that each witness called before the committee was there to be accused of wrongdoing that they were oblivious to the possibility that a witness might be called simply to establish a set of objective facts to lay a foundation for the calling of other witnesses.

Terry Lenzner, already insecure over the lack of strength of his campaign practices hearings, left the hearing room distraught. He, too, believed that Buchanan had seriously damaged the committee. It was to no avail that I explained to Terry that the committee and the press had misunderstood Buchanan's role as a witness. He replied, "That may be, but Buchanan got away with establishing his own role."

It was not until a couple of months later during a lull in the committee's work that news reporters began to look at the Buchanan memos. They became shocked at the brutal and savage blueprint that Buchanan had laid out for the White House. Some of them came to see me and asked why I had not briefed them on the significance of these memoranda prior to calling Buchanan. I became angry and replied that I did not see it as my duty to take them by the hand before I called each witness and explain what I planned to show through the witness. I expected them to be competent enough to sit in the Caucus Room, listen to the testimony, review the exhibits and understand what was going on in their presence.

The networks ended live television coverage of our hearings after Donald Segretti's appearance before the committee on October 3, 1973. They had concluded that the public would be bored with witnesses testifying about campaign practices and illegal campaign contributions. During parts of Segretti's testimony Dan Schorr of CBS acted out for me an exaggerated yawn in pantomime. During a recess of the testimony I kidded Schorr about not being able to stay awake. "Sam," Schorr replied, "your stuff is so dull and old-hat that you're losing your audience. What you put on this summer was sensational, and you should have left it at that—but you've got to be politically naïve to think that the stuff you're now dealing with is worth the bother."

I was stung by his accusation of political naïveté. Several news reporters had used the same charge against me in their stories, referring to certain anonymous Senate committee sources who were supposed to be furious with me for what they thought was the committee's humiliating encounter with Buchanan. "The trouble with you, Dan, and some of the other so-called sophisticated Washington press corps," I said, "is that you think you know all there is to know about political foul play, that you cannot recognize a new and more dangerous form even when it's right under your nose. And so you don't write about it or expose it on television. You fellows have become the great censors of what the public will know and will not know. If it tickles your fancy, or is sufficiently sexy or controversial, you'll let the public in on it. However, if it 'bores' you, you shut the public out. This is what you call the great free press. I disagree with you that the public is not interested in how their political campaigns are run. I think you underestimate the intelligence of your viewers."

Schorr shrugged his shoulders and said, "Well, it's not my decision —we'll go dark after today and stay that way until you bring in somebody like Rebozo or Connally."

"See what I mean?" I chided Dan, and walked back to the table.

The committee's disenchantment with the future subject matter of the public hearings so seriously threatened the continuation of the hearings that I asked Terry to suppress his passion for secrecy in the interest of salvaging the investigation. Although far from complete, Terry's investigation into the secret gift of $100,000 from Howard Hughes to Richard Nixon and a series of additional Hughes relationships with Richard Nixon through Nixon's brother, F. Donald Nixon, held the promise of important new revelations and understandings about the Watergate affair.

Terry went all out and offered the material to the committee as a new explanation for the break-in and wiretapping of the offices of the Democratic National Committee headquarters in the Watergate. Most knowledgeable people had found it difficult to understand why the Liddy operation had taken place, since it could never have offered the promise of much significant political information. Terry explained to the newly aroused senators that it wasn't political strategy that the burglars and wiretappers were expected to secure—it was information that might embarrass Nixon.

He revealed the close relationships between Robert Maheu, who had been fired by Howard Hughes as Hughes' top executive officer, Las Vegas publisher Hank Greenspun and Democratic National Chairman Larry O'Brien. O'Brien had been a highly paid consultant to the Hughes empire. He had been brought in by Maheu and suffered Maheu's fate when Maheu was dismissed by Hughes. This occurred at the time when Hughes mysteriously disappeared from Las Vegas and Hank Greenspun was boasting that he had the largest collection of personal memos written by Howard Hughes outside of Hughes' own secret files.

Into the pot Terry threw tidbits of evidence his staff had been collecting concerning questionable dealings Donald Nixon had been having with a Hughes official; a mysterious trip Donald Nixon and the Hughes official made to Central America; the mission Kalmbach received from Ehrlichman to find out from Hank Greenspun what he had in his safe; and Mitchell's instructions to Liddy to break into Hank Greenspun's safe which led to plans made by Hunt and Liddy to carry out this burglary in cooperation with the security officer of the Hughes Tool Company. Terry believed that all these facts provided Richard Nixon and his collaborators with a better reason to want to tap the Watergate headquarters telephone of Larry O'Brien, who was in regular communication with Maheu, than simply to pick up political intelligence. However, he acknowledged that it was all speculation at the moment.

Ervin, who had been kept advised of these investigative developments, nevertheless showed his excitement at hearing various threads of the investigation pulled together. "It looks like we might be able to put on hearings concerning the Hughes matters as important and as exciting to the public as our hearings this summer." Inouye, Montoya and Weicker also commented favorably on Terry's report and urged that his investigation be pursued to the exclusion even of other matters on the committee's agenda. Talmadge, Baker, Gurney and Thompson, however, wanted more specific facts before any committee decisions were made.

When Special Prosecutor Cox won his lawsuit to enforce the grand jury's subpoena against the President for certain White House tapes, Nixon faced a dilemma. Even though Nixon believed he had absolute, unreviewable power to withhold the tapes (he told Sirica the President was as absolute a monarch as Louis XIV had been—but only for four years at a time), he realized that short of delivering the tapes, he had to come up with some compromise plan to make his avoidance of the order of the Court of Appeals palatable for public consumption.

The scheme Nixon and his advisers devised was a variation of the old shell game. Cox was told that he would get a typed summary of the tapes which would be verified by Senator John E. Stennis, a much respected elder of the Senate, who had just recovered from a street robber's bullet wound. When this plan was revealed to Cox by Attorney General Elliot Richardson, Cox made it clear that he could not fulfill his responsibilities as special prosecutor to the grand jury and in later criminal prosecutions by limiting himself to secondhand evidence which would not be admissible in court. This unfolding crisis during the week of October 15 was a tightly held secret between Nixon and his top aides and Cox and his senior assistants.

On Friday, October 19, I received a call from a reporter which struck me as amusing. "We've been hearing a rumor that the President will be meeting with Ervin and Baker this afternoon on the tapes question. Any truth to that?" I laughed and told the reporter that he could completely disregard the rumor, since Ervin was in Louisiana and Baker was in Chicago; in any event, if there was any meeting planned I would certainly know about it and be present. I thought at the time this was a wild rumor that a prankster had floated to make an otherwise dull Friday more interesting.

Later that afternoon the Washington *Post* called me and asked why Ervin and Baker had spent part of the afternoon with President Nixon in the Oval Office. When I replied that I didn't believe they had, I was told that there was no question that they had been with the President that afternoon, and the reporter wondered why I wouldn't know about it. All I could reply was I wondered the same thing.

When I tried to reach Ervin and could not locate him, I called Baker's office. "Sam," Baker said exuberantly, "we just made a breakthrough!" He then went on to explain about the Stennis plan which he said the President had offered Ervin and him as a compromise for the tapes. Baker's version was that we would receive a third-party summary of the tapes prepared by the White House which Stennis would authenticate. When I asked if we would have to give up our lawsuit, he said no, but didn't see any reason for us to pursue the tapes. He was enthusiastic over the Stennis plan compromise and said Ervin was also.

"But why weren't Fred and I given a chance to be there?" I asked. Baker explained that it all had been done in such a hurry.

When I hung up, I exploded. " 'Hurry'— Nonsense! There is always time for a phone call. What are they trying to pull?" Shortly afterwards the phone began to ring with reporters' calls. The White House was releasing the tapes compromise agreement with the chairman and vice chairman of the Senate Watergate committee. I told the first callers that I couldn't comment, since I hadn't been there. Then I left my office and drove home determined not to answer any further newspaper calls until I had a chance to speak to Ervin, who had returned to Morganton.

At nine that evening I got in touch with Mrs. Ervin and told her it was very urgent that Ervin call me as soon as he arrived home, no matter what hour of the night that might be. She promised to give Senator Ervin the message. I waited up all night to receive Ervin's call, but it didn't come. I was disappointed. Could it be that he did not want to speak to me? I was becoming angry and beginning to feel that I might have no alternative but to resign.

Early Saturday morning Ervin called and apologized for not telephoning me the evening before. When he finally arrived in Morganton after being flown to a nearby Air Force base in a military plane (courtesy of the White House), he thought it was too late to call. He said he hadn't spoken to anybody since the meeting the day before in the Oval Office and that I was the first "human being" he talked to about the meeting.

I went right to the point. "The President has issued a statement concerning an agreement he made with you and Senator Baker, and frankly, Senator, I cannot see how you could have found this acceptable."

"Read me the statement," Ervin demanded. I read the release in the Washington *Post*, which called for the committee to receive the President's summary of the Watergate portions of the tape which would be authenticated by Senator Stennis.

"That's not what I agreed to at all!" Ervin exclaimed.* "We were told that the committee would get verbatim transcripts of the Watergate-related material which would be prepared under the supervision of Senator Stennis. The only summaries we would receive would involve conversations on the tapes that Stennis did not believe were related to Watergate, so that we could determine whether we agreed with him."

I then told Ervin about the news reports of Nixon's ordering Cox to accept the compromise Stennis plan and to stop seeking to enforce the orders of the court sustaining his subpoena for the tapes. "This looks bad, Senator," I explained. "The President appears to have used your approval of the Stennis plan as a basis to order Cox not to properly perform his function as special prosecutor."

Ervin sounded furious. "That's outrageous!" he exclaimed. "There was nothing said by the President about Cox or any relationship between what we were talking about and the duties of the special prosecutor."

"I suggest, Senator, that you issue a clarifying statement immediately, both as to the nature of the agreement you understand you entered into, and as to the absence of any relationship you understood to exist between that agreement and any obligations of the special prosecutor. It would be good for you to publicly state your agreement with Cox's position." Ervin told me he would call Fred Buzhardt at the White House to let them know what his clear understanding of his agreement was, and then he would issue a statement to the press.

I called Cox and gave him Ervin's version of his agreement with Nixon, informing him that Ervin would make a statement contradicting the President's release. I also let Cox know that I would support him in every way. Cox thought Nixon's use of Ervin had hurt him and didn't sound hopeful.

Not long after, Cox held his famous news conference in which he defied the President's order directing him "as an employee of the Executive Branch" to cease pursuing court process for the tapes. Richardson resigned his position as Attorney General rather than obey the Presi-

*See the Appendix for Senator Ervin's personal account, which was written at the author's request, of his meeting with the President.

dent's order to fire Cox, and William Ruckelshaus, who succeeded Richardson as Attorney General, also resigned for the same reason. Finally, Solicitor General Robert Bork, serving as Acting Attorney General, complied with the President's order and dismissed Archibald Cox as the special prosecutor. The press aptly described these extraordinary events of October 20, 1973, as the "Saturday Night Massacre," and the label stuck.

The news reached me while I was speaking to the students at Case Western Reserve University Saturday evening. I closed by referring to the principles of the rule of law that the President had violated by his arrogant actions in defying the order of the Court of Appeals. Sara and I stayed over that evening in Cleveland with our close friends Judge Jack Day and his wife, Ruth. Early Sunday morning I called Henry Ruth, the deputy special prosecutor. Ruth told me the President had ordered the abolition of the special prosecutor's office and sent FBI agents to seal off the office space. He said he and his staff had reported to work that Sunday to protect the files. They were not allowed, however, to remove any of the files from the offices.

Ruth pledged that until the matter was resolved, he and his staff would stay on duty and see that the ongoing investigative materials were protected. I assured him of the complete assistance of my staff. The country was fortunate to have him as Cox's top deputy during this chaotic period. Indeed, it was Henry Ruth's quiet and inspiring leadership that kept Cox's staff and investigation together and going forward.

Although the Watergate investigation had been noted for its bombshells, none had created such far-reaching, angry public shock waves as Nixon's firing of Special Prosecutor Cox and the resignations of Richardson and Ruckelshaus. The country erupted in a wave of protest which focused on Washington. An unprecedented half million telegrams were delivered to congressional offices alone that weekend. In large part this public reaction resulted from the keen interest millions of Americans had developed in the Watergate facts during our committee's televised public hearings that summer. Ironically, Cox had tried to stop the hearings. Now he had reason to be glad he had failed.

Congress reacted quickly. Increasing numbers of senators and congressmen were emboldened to call for impeachment. And they meant it. Chairman Rodino's House Judiciary Committee immediately began in earnest to consider the impeachment of Richard Nixon, and its staff met more openly with me and my staff to discuss how they could get access to our investigative material.

The committee itself became energized by the crisis. Ervin was quoted from North Carolina as saying that the Senate Watergate committee would now have to take on some of the responsibility of the special prosecutor—especially the investigations relating to illegal campaign financing. Ervin explained that he was especially interested in the $100,000 Howard Hughes gave Richard Nixon through Nixon's good friend Bebe Rebozo. A sure sign the committee was alive and well was the reappearance of the familiar faces of the Washington press corps and the scramble for statements about the committee's plans.

When the committee met on October 30, it voted to approve the actions of Ervin and Baker on behalf of the committee during the ill-fated Oval Office meeting with the President, but only on the basis of the terms Ervin insisted he had been offered. By this time, however, the President had withdrawn his offer to give the tape transcripts to the committee. Senator Weicker joined in the support of his two colleagues, but made it clear that his vote was not intended to mean that he approved of what had been done. "Let's face it," he said with a smile, "you both were zonked by Nixon on that deal."

A new date for terminating public hearings was set for November twenty-first. Senator Baker hinted that he and Thompson were going over a "witness list" that would involve highly important matters, but the only areas of inquiry that they specified were, first, a probe of CIA responsibility for the Watergate break-in, and second, an investigation of some allegations that Larry O'Brien and other officials of the Democratic National Committee had received advance information of the Republican bugging plan of the Washington headquarters at the Watergate but had allowed it to occur in order to embarrass the Republicans. Neither of these theories was ever substantiated by the minority counsel, but we let them pursue the investigations, even helping out by putting some of our own staff members to work. Later I questioned whether Fred ever seriously believed the Democratic boobytrap theory, since when he was given the opportunity to include a reference to it in Senator Baker's additional views in the final report, he and Baker chose to leave it out completely.

On the other hand, Baker and Thompson spent many committee days and substantial funds in their effort to establish CIA responsibility for the whole Watergate affair. They had become committed to the theory that Watergate was a CIA operation, and I could not help feeling that they had resurrected the early cover-up "game plan" that McCord had complained about. My own study of the CIA files and the reports Thompson prepared provided no support for what Thompson and Baker were doing. Senator Ervin, who took his own look at the material, agreed with me.*

By November 15 we had called everyone on our published witness list, having produced in public hearings a capsule version of illegal and unethical campaign practices and financial contributions. The committee and the Washington press corps continued to demonstrate their indifference and lack of sensitivity to what I considered to be basic acts of political immorality and abuse of powers. The most flagrant example of this involved the politicization of the executive branch revealed by the testimony and written memoranda of a key witness, William Marumoto, who played an important role in the White House's so-called "responsiveness" program, which had been uncovered by Dave Dorsen and his staff, particularly Michael Hirshman. According to this plan, each grant and contract in the various departments of the executive branch was to go through a final political approval to ensure that only the friends of the Nixon administration were recipients while Nixon's enemies were cut off "without a dime."

Marumoto was a candid witness and admitted the accuracy of the memoranda and the role he played in the scheme. Yet he received almost no attention from the press. The reporters had tuned him out, labeling him in their own minds as nothing more than an old-fashioned political "pork barrel" operator. The enormity and scope of the plan, however, and the blatant blueprinting of it as the written "order of the day," made this program much more pervasive and dangerous to a free society.

Not only the press, but the committee itself, which practically boycotted Marumoto's testimony, displayed indifference to the shocking story he told. An exception was Senator Montoya, who blasted Marumoto's activities as an insult to American minority groups because of their focus on buying minority votes through the offer of favored deals. Senator Weicker wandered into the Caucus Room after Marumoto's testimony had been completed, grabbed the microphone, and in contrast to Montoya, made a general statement supportive of

*Two years after our committee had completed its work, another Senate select committee, created to study the intelligence community, issued its reports on the CIA. This committee, chaired by Senator Frank Church and on which Baker also served as a member, focused its attention on the illegal domestic activities of the CIA and found no support for the Baker-Thompson theory.

political favoritism bestowed by an incumbent party. His remarks were completely unresponsive to the facts and dangers revealed by Marumoto's testimony. Senator Baker, presiding in Ervin's absence, complimented Weicker for his statement defending the political system, clearly implying that I had demonstrated extreme political naïveté.

Weicker's surprise comments had been so inconsistent with Marumoto's testimony that I tried to make a statement for the record addressed to Weicker: I pointed out that perhaps he did not have the opportunity to hear all the testimony or read the documents, but that Marumoto's testimony was nothing less than the exposure of the creation in the Nixon administration of a blacklisted enemies group. However, Baker cut me off. Thanking me for my remarks, he said that the record would speak for itself. And so it did. But few read it.

The slump in the committee's work that had developed by mid-November created a general morale problem. The staff developed feelings of uncertainty concerning the committee's intention to vigorously pursue the investigation and to hold the public hearings necessary for the two remaining major subjects of the probe—the Hughes-Rebozo and the Milk Fund matters. What the staff needed was something to boost their morale and enthusiasm. Instead, they received a kick in the pants. It appeared in the form of an article in *Rolling Stone* magazine. With only scant mention of the achievements of the committee, the piece contained pages of anonymous committee staff accusations against fellow committee staff members, who were named, ridiculed, and described in gossipy detail. In the context of the article, I came off lightly by being described by some faceless committee source as an "egomaniac." Fred Thompson was hit hard. But the author demonstrated his lack of partisan bias by quoting unnamed committee staff sources in support of brutal attacks on the legal and investigative abilities of Dave Dorsen and Jim Hamilton.

The only staff group spared the poison pen of the *Rolling Stone* author was Terry Lenzner and his staff. And for those who were bloodied by the article, this special treatment aroused an instant seed of suspicion, which quickly turned into bitter accusations.

The day after the article appeared, Terry burst into my office brandishing a copy of the article and newspaper comments on it, complaining that he had been defamed by the article. When I asked Terry how he had been defamed, he replied that he had been described as a tough, aggressive investigator who had the instinct for the jugular vein.

"That's your staff praising you, Terry," I said, laughing. "Compared to what the article says about other members of the staff, that description of you makes you a hero." Terry grumbled something about not liking to be characterized as a cruel investigator and left my office, suggesting that Weicker's staff must have been responsible for the article.

More real was the storm of protest I received from Dave Dorsen, Jim Hamilton and the staff members who worked for them. They were outraged over the article and bitterly resented what they considered to be unfair and untrue attacks on their competence and contributions to the committee staff's remarkable record of achievement.

"It's an inside job, Sam," Hamilton said. He was especially angry over the article's completely baseless charge that the committee had lost its lawsuit before Judge Sirica because Jim's legal briefs had been poorly researched and ineptly written. In fact Jim's briefs were excellent. And Jim's consistently high-quality legal work on behalf of the committee in its numerous lawsuits was one of the most important of the staff's accomplishments. "I think there is no doubt that someone on Terry's staff dumped this load of shit on us and you can't let them get away with it. The integrity of the staff and the committee is at stake."

About twelve staff members had crowded into my office. Jim's accusation and challenge were picked up by others and the heat of the group's anger grew in intensity. They almost resembled a lynch mob, and I thought that I had only to give the word, and they would descend to the auditorium and engage Terry's staff in hand-to-hand combat.

The staff's suspicions proved correct. Scott Armstrong, Terry's best investigator, came to my office, distraught, and admitted his wrong. He had witnessed the extraordinary effect that the article had produced on the staff's morale, and had decided to confess his responsibility in the hope of resolving the tension and thereby helping the staff to get on with its work.

Scott was genuinely sorry—not for the things he had said about different members of the staff, since he believed his assessments to be accurate, but for the fact that the statements had been published and had caused such harm to the committee. Scott was a brutally honest person, and wanted me to know he was not responsible for the article's reference to me as an "egomaniac." He believed it was a staff member of one of the senators on the committee who was responsible for that epithet.

The significant fact in Scott's statement was that although he had spoken critically about fellow members of the staff to a newsman, he had not leaked any substantive material of our investigation. As he explained it, the conversation he had with the author of the *Rolling Stone* article occurred at the bar of the Carroll Arms Hotel, across the street from the new Senate office building, after work one day, when the two of them were drinking beer and talking about the committee. Scott said he thought he was expressing opinions about fellow staff members confidentially, but now realized it was stupid of him not to have known that criticizing staff members of the committee to a reporter would be juicy meat for a story—especially when the reporter was working for *Rolling Stone.*

Scott offered to make amends by admitting what he had done before the entire staff and apologizing for the harm he had caused. It was a memorable event. In a low voice he admitted his complicity before everyone (except Terry's staff) and heaped blame on himself for doing to the Senate Watergate committee what the White House had been unable to do. He did not, however, apologize for the criticisms he had made about his fellow staff members. There were some angry retorts made by those who had listened to him in stony, unforgiving silence. But most of those who heard him made no response and left the room quietly, leaving Scott still sitting in the chair, a lonely figure. The meeting dissolved without resolution.

I received a separate delegation from Terry's staff who urged me to ignore the demands of many on the staff that I fire Scott and to accept his apology as sufficient punishment. I reported the entire matter to Senator Ervin. He had been angered by the *Rolling Stone* article and had urged me to try to learn who was responsible for it.

When I informed Ervin that Scott Armstrong had confessed his role as a major source, he exclaimed that Scott should be fired—perhaps he was also responsible for the other leaks that had plagued the committee. I did not believe this to be so, and argued with Senator Ervin against Scott's dismissal on the ground that he was one of our most valuable investigators. In addition, I stressed the fact that we would not have known of his involvement in this matter except for his own integrity in coming forward and admitting it. No one had admitted talking to a reporter before.

Ervin agreed, and withdrew his suggestion that Scott be fired. Instead, he accepted my recommendation that he be suspended one month without pay. It would be a significant penalty for Scott because he was a tireless worker who would find a month's suspension difficult to take. Additionally, since we were in the midst of the Hughes-Rebozo investigation and needed Scott's work, any longer suspension would be detrimental to the committee. Frankly, the sooner we got Scott back on the job, the happier I would be.

Besides Ervin and myself, the only other person who believed that the one-month suspension was fair was Scott himself. Terry and his staff were angered by it because they believed it was too harsh. And the rest of the staff were displeased because they believed it was too soft.

When Scott left my office on November 19, the day I suspended him, he exposed an emotional side of his personality I had not witnessed before. He shook my hand and assured me he was looking forward to coming back to work. The next day he dropped a note off on my desk. It read:

Dear Sam,

Through the fog of the last couple of weeks, our friendship has emerged clearly and cleanly. While none of us will ever be fully happy with the events, which we've recently laid to rest, I want to thank you for spending so much time and energy being so fair with a guy who let you down.

I was too choked up to respond on Saturday afternoon, but what has meant the most during this ordeal was your simple statement, "Thanks for being you, Scott." I've never felt closer to anybody in my life than I did at that moment when having stumbled you picked me up and made it so clear that you understood who I was and what I wanted to stand for.

Those few, quiet words made it clear who had stuck by me when the chips were down. Thanks, Sam.

Love,

Scott

Weicker seized the opportunity to make a grandstand play, protesting the suspension. He publicly announced that he was offering Scott a full-time job on his staff. Senator William Proxmire also offered Scott a job, but Scott called me and assured me he had turned them both down.

It was not until two years later that the incident was again brought to my attention—by Scott Armstrong. He called me November 19, 1975, to ask me if I remembered why that particular day was significant. I couldn't remember anything special about November 19.

"It's the day you suspended me," he said quietly. I was surprised he had marked the day to remember. "I didn't know you felt so strongly about it," I said, still remembering the dilemma I had faced.

"Well—it was also my birthday," Scott said.

"How terrible!" I exclaimed. "Why didn't you let me know at the time?"

"Oh, you were doing what you had to do—and I didn't want to throw in something irrelevant." Scott had remained the stoic.

When the committee left Washington for the Thanksgiving Day recess, I began the arduous task of preparing for what we expected would be our final set of public hearings in December—the hearings relating to the Hughes-Rebozo contribution for Nixon and the dairy industry contributions to influence Nixon's decision to raise milk prices. There were other less dramatic investigations under way which could be fitted into the Hughes-Rebozo and Milk Fund hearings. One, relating to campaign financing, was an inquiry Thompson's staff and mine were making into certain irregularities in fund-raising activities of Democratic candidates in the 1972 campaign. The principal targets of these investigations were Hubert Humphrey, George McGovern and Wilbur Mills and some of their campaign aides. Even though Watergate itself was a Republican scandal, I was determined to keep our staff work open and nonpartisan.

Though pressured by colleagues, Ervin never sought to limit our investigation. Other Democratic committee members or their staffs made discreet calls at times, questioning our need to interrogate a certain witness or delve into a particular subject. Usually my explanation was accepted, especially when I reminded the caller there was no party label on the resolution creating our committee. In the rare instances where there was disagreement, I persisted, knowing I was risking hard feelings from a majority senator.

On one occasion, after we had given the senators a draft report on some questionable fund-raising activities of the Humphrey campaign, Thompson and I were called to Inouye's office to confront Senator Humphrey personally with our findings and to hear his explanation—something we had been trying unsuccessfully to do with Humphrey for months. Humphrey was angered by the inferences of his personal culpability in the language of the draft report and protested his ignorance of much of the fund-raising efforts made on his behalf. We conceded that there was no evidence that Humphrey personally knew about the receipt of illegal contributions by his campaign organization. But his campaign manager, Jack Chestnut, did have personal knowledge and was later prosecuted by the special prosecutor and convicted by a jury. Thompson and I agreed to modify the report to make it reflect Humphrey's position.

Another probe which could be briefly presented at the public hearings was the White House comprehensive plan to exploit the incumbency—called the Responsiveness Program—which Jim Hamilton and Dave Dorsen were investigating and documenting. It would dramatically expose an arrogant abuse of presidential power.

Some subject areas, though relating to significant evidence, had to be rejected because the committee's resolution clearly did not authorize us to investigate them. One in particular would have led the committee away from its principal mission of exposing the wrongful and illegal acts of the 1972 campaign. Senator Weicker wanted us to reveal the charges of political use of the FBI (including illegal wiretapping) in the Kennedy and Johnson administrations made by William Sullivan and Cartha DeLoach, the two top aides of J. Edgar Hoover.* Ervin disagreed with Weicker, ruling that not only would this evidence have no relationship to the 1972 campaign, but its use by us would contravene the legislative history of our authorizing resolution. Before the Senate unanimously adopted the resolution, it overwhelmingly defeated a proposed amendment which would have authorized the committee to investigate wrongdoing and abuses in presidential campaigns and administrations prior to the campaign of 1972. Ervin and I took the position that any attempt by the committee to investigate illegal FBI activities of prior administrations would violate the Supreme Court's ruling declaring it unconstitutional for a Senate committee to investigate anything the Senate has not authorized it to investigate.

When I reviewed the status of the Hughes-Rebozo and Milk Fund investigations with Terry and Dave, I found that, unfortunately, neither of them was ready for public hearings. Rebozo had now publicly admitted receiving the $100,000 Hughes cash contribution for Nixon, but he claimed he kept it untouched in a safe-deposit box in his Key Biscayne

---

*In his recent book Minority Counsel Fred Thompson accuses Weicker of opposing the committee's use of this evidence because it would dilute Nixon's guilt and justify the view that he wasn't worse than other Presidents. However, this is not so. Weicker urged that this evidence be revealed and did not oppose its use.

bank for three years and then returned it to Hughes. Terry's investigation assumed that Rebozo had not kept the money in the safe-deposit box, but had used some or all of the cash for Nixon's personal benefit. Yet Terry had not been able to find any evidence supporting this theory. Carmine Bellino's effort to examine Rebozo's financial records had been frustrated by evasive tactics and counteroffensives employed by Rebozo and his lawyer William Frates.

Also, Terry still had not received the $100,000 in cash Rebozo returned to Hughes. He had subpoenaed this cash, which had been kept intact by the Summa Corporation (now comprising all Howard Hughes' business operations), to trace the bills to determine if they were in circulation when Rebozo first received the Hughes cash. But Chester Davis, Summa's lawyer, stalled—not only on the $100,000, but also on producing Hughes records and Hughes employees as witnesses. Davis' obvious strategy was to wait out our committee, which he knew would have to end its investigation before February 28, 1974, when it was required to file its final report to the Senate.

There were also major gaps in Dave Dorsen's Milk Fund investigation. An important part of the evidence involved a chance airport meeting in Washington between John Connally and representatives of the dairy industry at which Connally allegedly told one of the dairy representatives that "it was in the bag"—meaning the President's agreement to increase milk prices. Connally had just come from a meeting with the President.

When Connally was questioned under oath in executive session by the committee, he denied that the chance airport meeting had ever taken place. Alan Weitz, a brilliant young lawyer who was Dave's principal assistant in this investigation, told me that although five dairy industry witnesses observed the airport meeting, he had only had the time to question one. If Connally was to be successfully contradicted, it was clear we would need more than one witness. The others had to be questioned.

It also turned out that Herbert Kalmbach had played a significant role, and he still had to be questioned further. In addition, there were a number of White House memos relating to the decision to increase milk prices which Fred Buzhardt had promised to let us have, but had not yet turned over to us.

Since we weren't ready for public hearings, I recommended to Ervin, who agreed with me, that we postpone the hearings until a later date, when we would be more prepared. The committee met after its return from the Thanksgiving Day recess on November 27, 1973, and agreed to adjourn the public hearings until after the Congress returned in January from its Christmas–New Year's recess. Although Senator Inouye requested that we not continue our public hearings beyond the beginning of February, I asked the committee not to set any more termination dates for public hearings, since witnesses had taken advantage of these dates to stall the committee by avoiding subpoenas until they believed that the dates would expire and the committee would no longer be in public session.

Having gained extra time, we became more aggressive in demanding the production of evidence we needed. Hughes lawyer Chester Davis, who had failed to comply with an earlier subpoena, was ordered to appear before the committee on December 4 and produce the $100,000 in cash Rebozo returned to Hughes. When Davis appeared before Senators Ervin and Weicker in executive session, I asked him whether he was ready to comply with the subpoena and produce the money. Chester Davis was a loud and talkative lawyer, whose contrasting styles between indignation and hilarity masked shrewd and clever maneuvering.

He made a lengthy speech claiming he did not understand the language of the subpoena, arguing that his rights would be better protected if he could appear publicly, in front of the press, when he was asked questions by the committee, and he gave every indication that he was ready to defy the committee. Then suddenly in the midst of his protest he opened his brief case and removed two large brown manila envelopes, which he put on the table. Tearing them open, he poured out bundles of $100 bills in front of Senator Ervin, shouting, "There's your goddamned money. Take it, burn it, do whatever you want with it!"

For a brief period the hearing was in a state of confusion. We had all been taken by surprise. But I quickly made sure the official reporter recorded what had occurred and correctly marked the manila envelopes for identification. Ervin did not want the committee to take custody of the cash. However, we did want a record of the bills for the purpose of tracing them.

I suggested that we immediately make photocopies of all the bills in the presence of one of Davis' assistants and return the actual cash to Davis. Senator Ervin accepted the idea with relief. The bills were counted and photocopied by a committee staff assistant with two Capitol police guards and an aide to Davis standing by. When the cash and the copies were returned to the hearing room, I took the sworn testi-

mony of all who had been involved in the copying transaction to make
a record of the chain of custody of the bills that had been deposited on
the table by Davis—from the manila envelopes, to the photocopying
machine and back to the hearing room. For essential future evidentiary
purposes, no gap in this chain had been permitted.

Now having the photocopies of the $100 bills, Terry's staff was in a
position to trace the money to try to determine whether any of the bills
returned by Rebozo in 1973 were not in circulation in 1969, when the
original $100,000 was delivered to Rebozo. If this could be established,
it would prove that some or all of the money Rebozo gave to Hughes
in 1973 was not the same money he had received in 1969. This would
support the charge that contrary to his sworn testimony, Rebozo had
used the original $100,000.

Our tapes subpoena, still tied up in the lawsuit pending federal court
action, called for the President to produce only four recorded Oval
Office conversations he had with Dean. Before the committee adjourned for its long Christmas recess, I obtained committee approval
to subpoena the President for all the remaining White House taped
conversations relevant to our investigation. Ron Rotunda and Scott
Armstrong were assigned to put together a complete list from our files.
They were assisted by our computer staff to permit them to zero in on
key conversations and to include after such conversations a brief description of what we could expect the conversation to be about. Each
conversation listed was rated A to D in terms of importance to the
committee.

After an exhaustive analysis of the files, with the aid of the computer
search, we produced a subpoena for approximately five hundred presidential conversations. Even so, these represented less than one-tenth of
the presidential conversations with Watergate principals. Also, only
about a hundred of the five hundred were rated A by the staff as top
priority for the committee.

As it turned out, the committee never received any of these conversations. However, we gave copies of our list of conversations with descrip-
tions to the House Judiciary Committee and the special prosecutor, and
practically all of those identified in the priority A group were ultimately
obtained by them.

The most significant item in this omnibus subpoena the committee
served on the President on December 19, 1973, was the conversation
between President Nixon and Bob Haldeman on June 23, 1972—the
so-called "smoking pistol" tape. In the staff list this conversation was

rated A and described as a conversation between the President and Haldeman on how to use the CIA to limit the FBI investigation.

The special prosecutor finally received this tape only after the Supreme Court of the United States, on July 24, 1974, ordered Nixon to turn it over to Judge Sirica, along with other tapes we had asked for on December 19. When Nixon complied with the order, impeachment and conviction became certain, and resignation an irresistible alternative. However, on December 19, 1973, when we served our omnibus subpoena at the White House, we could not have anticipated these incredible events.

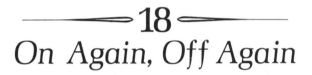

18

On Again, Off Again

BY THE TIME THE COMMITTEE RETURNED FROM ITS LONG CHRISTMAS recess in the third week of January 1974 the Washington press corps had already written the committee off as a continuing significant public investigative body. The focus of attention was swinging to the special prosecutor's office and the House Judiciary Committee's impeachment inquiry. During the recess I had at times found it necessary to telephone Senator Ervin in Morganton and get his approval to issue a statement to newsmen that the committee did indeed plan to hold further public hearings when it returned after the recess.

My principal concern was not what the public believed, for our hearings, when they reconvened, would speak for themselves. Rather, I was concerned with the devastating effect the news stories had on the morale of the staff, which was working around the clock interrogating witnesses and collecting evidence in preparation for public hearings. Much of this work seemed pointless to them if the news stories were correct that the committee had decided to have no further hearings and was planning to close up shop.

A particularly upsetting report came from Dan Schorr, who announced that the committee was ready to wind up its business and would hold no further public hearings. Rufus Edmisten, who was probably anxious to begin campaigning for the office of attorney general in North Carolina, was supposed to be the source for this news. Although Rufus denied this, I made sure he called Dan with his denial. Dan got in touch with me soon afterwards. "Okay, you win this time," he said. "Rufus just called me and told me I was wrong about my report about the committee. But between the two of us, Sam, my announcement of no more committee public hearings was exactly what Rufus first told me."

The committee met on January 23, 1974, in the midst of this confusion of press statements, with mixed personal feelings about continuing in the public limelight as an investigating committee. To the very hour of the meeting, reporters called each of the senators in an effort to poll their votes on the issue of continued public hearings. Although the responses most of the reporters received were hardly encouraging for the position I had been assuring the staff the committee would take, I knew that the final vote would depend on whether Senator Ervin stuck by his position in support of public hearings. If he did, then there would be four votes in favor of public hearings.

Before all the senators arrived, Ervin told me that Talmadge had expressed deep reservations to him about further public hearings. However, Talmadge was a veteran member of the Club and would do nothing to embarrass Ervin. When the meeting began, I found I did not have Weicker's vote. He had lost interest in further public hearings. "Let's quit while we're ahead and cash in our chips," Weicker argued. "This committee's excellent reputation can be ruined if it makes the bad mistake of boring the public."

Baker and Gurney also opposed public hearings. Their reasons, I believed, were partisan. They knew that live TV would return to cover the Hughes-Rebozo and Milk Fund testimony, posing an unpredictable threat of embarrassment for the White House. They welcomed Senator Weicker back into the fold, since now there would be a solid minority vote against the hearings. After some additional debate, the four Democrats voted in favor of continued public hearings and the three Republicans voted against. This was the first and only vote of the committee that divided on party lines.

Three days later I went on a sorrowful journey to attend the funeral of my former boss Richardson Dilworth. I had been his first assistant when he was district attorney of Philadelphia, and had followed him as D.A. to fill his vacancy when he ran for mayor of Philadelphia. As I sat waiting for the beginning of the service, one of Dilworth's long-time aides came to me and told me there was a long-distance call for me.

It was Rufus Edmisten. He apologized for calling during the funeral, but said that Ervin had tried to reach me all morning, and that when he was unable to talk to me, had acted on his own.

"What did he do?" I asked impatiently.

"Damn it, Sam, he postponed the public hearings," Rufus said. "He said he acted on a request from the United States Attorney's Office in New York, based on the claim that our public hearings would prejudice the Stans and Mitchell trial in the Vesco matter, which starts next week. Ervin took a telephone vote of the committee members, and they all supported his recommendation to postpone the hearings."

As soon as the funeral was over, I drove back to Washington and got in touch with Ervin. Ervin assured me that he had merely postponed the hearings and had not canceled them.

Before talking to Ervin I had had a chance to talk to Terry Lenzner, who informed me of a disturbing piece of news which I now gave to Ervin. Tom Corcoran, the powerful Washington Democratic figure, had met with Ervin in the morning prior to Ervin's announcement of his decision. Terry was suspicious that there had been pressure from Democrats to persuade Ervin to call off the hearings for some unexplained reason—perhaps to avoid a public backlash that some people feared the committee might receive if it renewed its appearance on TV in the Caucus Room. "Senator," I said, "Mr. Corcoran was seen visiting with you. Some staff members have wondered whether there have been political pressures brought in this matter."

Ervin replied quickly, "Oh no, no, no, Tommy was seeing me about an entirely different matter. He never even discussed the hearings or the work of our committee. You can be assured that his visit had nothing to do whatever with my decision. The reason was exactly as I have given it to you." Ervin's voice was firm and sincere. I had no reason to doubt him. I told Ervin that I fully supported his decision and respected the reasons that motivated him to make it.

Dan Schorr was the first news commentator to catch me as I started to leave the Senate office building. The initial question put to me by Schorr suggested the kind of interview he was hoping to obtain. "Aren't you disturbed and upset that the chairman of the committee has postponed the public hearings the committee just recently voted to hold?" I refused to bite. I replied that I had spoken to the chairman and was satisfied that he had acted on the highest motives of justice when he responded to the appeal from the prosecutor in New York.

Undeterred, Dan pushed for a fight belligerently. "But the chairman acted without even consulting you, didn't he?" I replied that Senator Ervin was the chairman of the committee and did not have to consult me. I added that Senator Ervin was especially sensitive to issues of justice of this kind, as I was myself, since he had once been a member of the Supreme Court of North Carolina

I excused myself and left Schorr standing holding his microphone with an unsatisfied expression on his face. That evening he ran a garbled version of the interview, which carried his belligerent, accusing question and a brief, unresponsive statement from me, taken out of context from a different part of the interview. It gave the impression that I was halfway agreeing with Schorr's suggested criticism of Senator Ervin. Schorr called me after the newscast and apologized for the manner in which the interview had been presented. He blamed technicians for faulty editing.

Publicly I stuck to my statement that the hearings had been postponed and not canceled, but I knew the momentum had been lost. And there was no new bombshell to thrust the committee back into the Caucus Room. Rather, events moved quickly to transform Ervin's postponement of the hearings to a formal cancellation.

Over lunch at the National Lawyers' Club, the new special prosecutor, Leon Jaworski, voiced his concern to me about our committee issuing a report on February 28, the date our resolution required the committee to report to the Senate. Jaworski confided that he was planning to have the Watergate grand jury return major indictments at the end of February or the beginning of March. A simultaneous Senate report, which would undoubtedly condemn the same persons indicted by the grand jury, could seriously prejudice the indictments, Jaworski thought. At the least the report could give the defendants a basis to file delaying motions to quash the indictments.

For my own reasons, I welcomed an excuse to postpone the reporting date of the committee. We had not yet written our committee report, and needed a few more months for this task. On February 7 the committee unanimously voted to request the Senate to extend its life until May 28, 1974, when its final report would be submitted to the Senate. The committee also voted to request an additional appropriation to finance this extended period.

Although Jaworski had not asked Ervin to call off further public hearings, his reason for requesting postponement of the final report applied with equal, if not greater force, to televised public hearings. Baker and Talmadge did not let this obvious reason to call off further public hearings go unargued. They pressed it on Ervin and he readily agreed they were right.

I was not happy with Ervin's decision. Supreme Court decisions permitted us to hold public hearings despite pending criminal indictments. Besides, the subject of our proposed hearings was unrelated to the Watergate indictments. Also, I believed our hearings would support rather than impede the impeachment inquiry.

At first, Ervin's decision raised a crisis for the staff because we thought we faced an issue of principle. I had been promised by Ervin and had in turn promised my staff that the trail of the facts would be followed to the end and all significant information we uncovered would be publicly exposed. It now looked as if this promise was being broken, and my top aides met with me to discuss whether this issue of principle required us to resign. However, we soon recognized we were too close to the investigation to be as objective as Ervin. We might differ with his decision to end public hearings, but we had no doubts that Ervin had acted with complete integrity. Besides, we all respected Ervin and knew he had not acted unreasonably.

The committee unanimously voted to terminate public hearings at its meeting on February 19. Ervin summed up the committee's position when he spoke before the gathered reporters after the meeting. "Despite the committee's power to hold any relevant public hearings it chooses, the committee believes that it should be careful not to interfere unduly with the ongoing impeachment process of the House Judiciary Committee or with the criminal cases which will soon be prosecuted by the special prosecutor, on which attention of the country appears now to be focused."

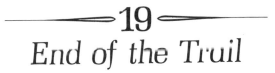

19

End of the Trail

AS MUCH AS TERRY LENZNER AND DAVE DORSEN GRUMBLED WHEN
the committee voted to terminate its public hearings, they were in fact
relieved. Neither of them at the time had the evidence to establish what
he had set out to prove. Dave was more prepared than Terry, since he
could at least show in dramatic detail how the administration had
changed its position on the issue of increasing milk-price supports for
the dairy industry.

But though the evidence Dave and his staff had obtained raised a
strong inference that Nixon's decision was the result of a deal which
included major campaign contributions (some through laundered
funds) from the dairy industry, there were important gaps in the evidentiary proof. Dave still had not been able to obtain a number of White
House documents that were relevant to the milk deal. Also, he was
hindered by not having access to a White House tape recording of a
meeting in the President's office with John Connally and other White
House aides which had occurred just prior to the President's decision
to override the Secretary of Agriculture and authorize an increase in
milk-price supports. Further, a key witness, Jake Jacobsen, counsel for
the Associated Milk Producers, Inc., was negotiating a deal for himself
with the special prosecutor's office. Henry Ruth had asked me to hold
back our committee's investigative efforts concerning Jacobsen so as
not to interfere with the strategy of the prosecution, and on Dave's
recommendation I had agreed. However, by making this agreement, we
had handicapped our own investigation.

Dave never received the White House material. But by the close of
our investigation he had obtained other evidence and pieced together
a mosaic of meetings, testimony and documents to conclusively establish that Nixon's abrupt decision on March 23, 1971, to reverse his
Secretary of Agriculture and increase milk-price supports was return
payment for commitments by the milk producers to make massive

campaign contributions in the amount of at least $2 million. The evidence that was assembled through the interviewing of dozens of witnesses and the examination of the available documents implicated a host of administration figures in the Milk Fund deal, including Haldeman, Ehrlichman, Colson, Mitchell, Kalmbach and Murray Chotiner, a long-time colleague of Nixon's.

To ward off the impact of such a finding the White House issued a White Paper on "The Milk Price Support Decision." It put the blame on pressure by Congress. The White Paper, however, failed to survive the evidence accumulated by the committee and other investigative agencies as well as groups that had picked up on the committee's investigation. Almost none of the evidence developed by Dave Dorsen and Alan Weitz found its way into the newspapers. Ironically, most of it first became public when a letter from the House Judiciary Committee to the White House was leaked in early May 1974, apparently by the House Judiciary Committee. The letter had been sent to the White House to support the Judiciary Committee's request for the tapes and documents that had been withheld from the Select Committee. Front-page stories announced that there was evidence linking Nixon's 1971 milk-price decisions to the $2 million campaign pledge of the milk producers and credited "House Judiciary Committee investigators."

Despite around-the-clock efforts, Terry Lenzner still had little to produce as evidence in his Hughes-Rebozo investigation. The heart of this investigation was the disposition by Rebozo of the $100,000 Rebozo had received from a representative of Howard Hughes. Rebozo's story that he had put the money in a safe-deposit box in his Key Biscayne bank and had kept it there until 1973, when he had returned the identical money to the Hughes people, remained unchallenged. No matter how odd or incredible Rebozo's explanation was, Terry had not been able to develop any evidence that could prove that Rebozo had removed one single dollar of the Hughes money while it was in his custody.

Of course, his task was practically an impossible one. If Rebozo's story was false, how was Terry to prove it in the absence of a confession by Rebozo or the statement of an informer who had been an eyewitness to Rebozo's tampering with the money?

Carmine Bellino suggested a way. He insisted that if he could obtain all of Rebozo's financial records—his private personal records as well as his business and bank records—he could carry out a complete financial audit on Rebozo which would trace all of Rebozo's cash transactions, receipts and disbursements. According to Bellino, this audit might uncover large cash expenditures which could not be tied to identifiable receipts, indicating Rebozo's use of a special cash fund—and the only one known to be available to him was the $100,000 Hughes money.

Desperate for a solution, Terry drew up a subpoena which would command Rebozo to turn over to our Senate Select Committee all his private and business financial records. When Terry sent his subpoena request for Rebozo's records to me for my approval, I was amazed at its scope. It would have stripped Rebozo naked. I knew Bellino's theory and I was as eager as Terry to get at the truth of whether Rebozo had tampered with the Hughes money. However, I also realized how easy it was for investigators to allow their zeal to run away with them, especially when they believed that their cause was right and just. Our committee had to be particularly careful, since our very purpose was to investigate abuse of power of White House officials and there could be no excuse for us to engage in abuse of power.

Senator Ervin had been conscious of this problem from the beginning. He had insisted that all of our investigative methods be not only within the law, but that there not be even the appearance of oppressive or illegal investigative practices on the part of our staff.

There were a number of investigative techniques and strategies that I had ruled out, recognizing that despite their legality they would be inappropriate for our particular committee. For example, we shunned the use of undercover agents or informers, and never employed concealed recording equipment. These were recognized investigative tactics by law enforcement agencies, and would have been available to our committee's investigation. However, Senator Ervin and I agreed from the outset that we would have to give up some of the easier routes of obtaining evidence and confine ourselves to conducting the investigation the hard way—to avoid any suspicion of underhanded or improper tactics.

I thought Terry's subpoena exceeded the committee's power. The Supreme Court had ruled on a number of occasions that a subpoena for all of an individual's personal records could be issued by a congressional committee only if the committee had probable cause to believe that the records were relevant to the committee's legislative purpose. We had no evidence to establish probable cause that Rebozo had dipped into the Hughes money. Therefore we had no right to invade his privacy by demanding all of his private records.

When I told Terry this, he demanded, "What the hell do you mean?

How are we going to be able to show that Rebozo dug into the Hughes money unless we turn Bellino loose to make a complete financial audit on Rebozo?"

I told him I would okay the subpoena if he could show me some evidence to support his suspicion that Rebozo had misapplied any of the Hughes money. Terry was furious. He insisted that I was ruining his investigation, and asked whether he could appeal my decision to Senator Ervin. I readily agreed.

After hearing us both out, Ervin supported my position on policy and law. However, he sympathized with Terry and said to him, "If I had worked as hard as you and your staff to prove Rebozo took the money, I suppose I might want to grab all those records myself to try to clinch the case. But that's the trouble. You're too much like the hound dog close to the quarry to see this matter in proper perspective." Terry was not consoled, and when he left Ervin's office he complained about the obstructions that were being thrown in his path.

Terry ran into another blind alley in his investigation. His staff had developed evidence of a possible quid pro quo for part of the Hughes cash gift made to Nixon through Rebozo. Of course, it may have been enough for Howard Hughes to be purchasing a piece of White House decision-making for so cheap a contribution as $50,000 or $100,000. Handwritten Hughes memos turned over to us by Hank Greenspun revealed Hughes to be sufficiently eccentric to perceive himself as controlling national decisions from his seat of seclusion merely by mandating it in a memo to Robert Maheu while Maheu was still managing his empire out of Las Vegas.

Be that as it may, Hughes did want specific things. He had been buying up Las Vegas hotels and casinos until he was stopped by the Antitrust Division of the Department of Justice. He wanted the Dunes Hotel, and a decision had been made against him by the Department of Justice. Aided by the Antitrust Division, Terry's staff had developed an evidentiary pattern of influence by Hughes on the Attorney General. It showed that at the time of one of the Hughes contributions of $50,000 in cash delivered to Rebozo, John Mitchell overrode the decision of his Anti-trust Division and approved the Dunes deal for Howard Hughes. Ironically, the deal never went through because the transaction soured for Hughes when he learned of the enormous loss operations of the hotel.

Even this evidence, however, did not nail the Hughes contribution to an administration favor on the part of John Mitchell. There was no proof that Mitchell knew anything about the $50,000 contribution at the time he made his decision. The staff was never able to make the connection in a way that would stand up as a matter of evidentiary proof.

In March, time was running out on Terry Lenzner's Hughes-Rebozo investigation and he appeared increasingly morose and secretive. At the beginning of the month the Watergate grand jury had returned the seven major indictments, which included the charges against Haldeman, Ehrlichman, Mitchell and Colson. The limelight would shortly turn to the special prosecutor and his team of trial experts for the spectacle of the criminal trials of the century. In the meantime John Doar was readying his House Judiciary Committee impeachment inquiry for public hearings, which were expected to be carried live on television.

There was little chance remaining for Terry to make a case against Rebozo and Nixon. Our final report was now due on May 28, 1974. With the Hughes-Rebozo investigation remaining an unsolved mystery, Terry's portion of the report would be relatively flat in comparison not only with the Watergate break-in and cover-up section, but even with Dave Dorsen's campaign financing section.

Yet, despite what appeared to be an impossible task at this late date in the committee's existence, the small, loyal band that worked for Terry increased its activity to fever pitch. Headed by Marc Lackritz and Scott Armstrong, this team of investigators continued traveling back and forth between Washington and California or Las Vegas or Florida. I had to approve each trip, and I was routinely told that loose ends were being followed up with Kalmbach, Greenspun, Maheu and persons who had business transactions with Rebozo. I did not press for fuller explanations, because I realized Terry's desperate situation and was willing to allow him a degree of flexibility to work himself out of it if he could.

What I did not know was that Terry and his clan were closing in on a major discovery, which would finally produce the headlines and newspaper credits that had been denied them.

Terry excluded me completely from any knowledge of this activity. He may have been chafing still over my refusal to support his request for a blanket subpoena for Rebozo's private and business financial records. If so, he would have viewed me a potential spoiler. And he did not want anyone to prevent his achieving the prize that was almost within his grasp.

*   *   *

It was not until Friday evening, April 5, 1974, that I found out what had happened, and by then the story was ready to break in the newspapers. Indeed, the first one to tell me about it was Bob Woodward of the Washington *Post*. He called me at home to verify his story. "Sam," Woodward informed me, "we have it from a very reliable source that Kalmbach has told your committee that Rebozo admitted to him that he gave some of the Hughes $100,000 cash to Rose Mary Woods and to Nixon's two brothers, Donald and Edward. This is an important break in the Hughes-Rebozo investigation and your committee deserves a lot of credit for cracking Kalmbach. I just want confirmation that the story is true." I had never heard of the story, and I was certain that if we had received such a statement from Kalmbach I would have known about it. Although I usually refused to comment when a reporter asked about committee investigative information, it appeared to me that Woodward had been given a really wild story and that it was important to scotch it as quickly as possible. I told him that his story was completely wrong, from what I knew, and that he shouldn't waste his time on it. Woodward expressed amazement at my response, although he realized I was being frank with him. He said he knew the story had substance to it and suggested that I check further with my staff. I hung up, somewhat bemused over the story he was chasing. I couldn't help wondering whether he was letting his reputation make him reckless.

However, the next call troubled me. It was from Jack Anderson, and he inquired about the same story. I made the same denial and told him that Woodward had called about the identical story. "Goddamn it!" Anderson exclaimed. "How did he find out about it? He must have got a leak from the White House, or your Scott Armstrong is at it again." When I protested that the story was a fake, Anderson shut me off by saying, "It's true, Sam—I know it's true. I can't tell you my source— but Ervin's got Kalmbach's statement, and Lenzner knows all about it."

I felt foolish and did not know how to respond to Anderson. However, he was more concerned about Woodward's possible scoop of the story, since, as he told me, he did not have another column until the following week, and Woodward would be able to hit the front page of the *Post* with the story the next morning, which was Saturday. "I guess I'll have to go on the radio tonight and break the story first that way to keep from being scooped." With that Anderson hung up.

I felt as if I had just been hit in the face. As chief counsel I needed to be on top of every part of the committee's investigation. Now I was being told I didn't know about important evidence uncovered by some of my staff. This was the first time to my knowledge anything like this had happened to me in my work with the committee, and I was determined to get to the bottom of it.

After a few phone calls I got the number of Terry's hotel in Seattle. Terry was out of his room, but called me back a few minutes later, and in an exaggeratedly pleasant tone of voice that was unusual for him, asked, "What's up, Boss?"

I told Terry about the information I had been given by Bob Woodward and Jack Anderson and asked him if there was any truth to it. Clearly, he had to sense my mood as I bit off my words over the telephone. Instead of answering me directly, Terry matched my anger with his own by exclaiming, "Christ! You mean the story is going to be all over the damn newspapers!"

"Cut it out, Terry," I snapped. "Anderson has already told it all on the radio this evening, with ample references to you. Answer my question. Did Kalmbach tell us that Rebozo used the Hughes money, and if he did, why the hell didn't I know about it?"

"The story is true, Sam," Terry replied quietly. "Kalmbach gave that testimony in a secret session before me and Senator Ervin in Ervin's office three weeks ago. But nobody in the office knew about it except Ervin, me, Marc, and Scott, who had to help me complete the investigation. Ervin ordered the transcript of the executive session hearing with Kalmbach sealed and prohibited me from informing anybody on the committee or the staff about Kalmbach's testimony, except one or two of my own investigators, who, as I said, had to help me."

"That's nonsense!" I exploded. "Any evidence that has ever been sealed by the committee or that Ervin has ordered not to be disclosed to committee members or staff has always been intended by Ervin to be available to me as chief counsel of the committee. You work under my direction, Terry—and I'm in charge of this investigation. How the hell am I supposed to carry out that responsibility if important evidence is withheld from me?"

I told Terry to return the following morning to Washington, where he would report to my office with a copy of the Kalmbach transcript.

When I hung up on Terry, I called Senator Ervin at his Washington apartment. He expressed surprise that I had not known about Kalmbach's testimony. He had simply assumed that Terry had been acting under my direction and had kept me fully informed. When I heard this

I mentioned to Ervin that I was considering firing Terry because of what he had done.

"Oh no, Sam," Ervin said quickly, "don't fire Terry. Why, he and his staff are the hardest workers you've got. They've done an amazing job in the Rebozo investigation. Maybe his zeal has led Terry to do some unorthodox things, but that only means he needs watching."

I was suddenly struck by the irony of our discussion. A year earlier Ervin had stubbornly wanted to fire Terry because he had been told by his political advisers that Terry would be harmful to the committee, and I had succeeded in persuading Ervin that he was wrong.

The Kalmbach transcript turned out to be quite thin. The hearing before Ervin on March 21, 1974, could not have taken more than twenty or thirty minutes. However, when I read it, I could guess at why Terry had gone over my head and concealed the testimony from me. Had I known of his plan, I might have vetoed it.

Kalmbach did not testify voluntarily that Rebozo had admitted to him at a White House meeting on April 30, 1974, that he had taken some of the Hughes money from the safe-deposit box to give to Rose Mary Woods and Nixon's two brothers. Kalmbach had been compelled to reveal that information by an order from Ervin, made at Terry's request over Kalmbach's objection, that he had received the admission from Rebozo as a privileged communication in an attorney-client relationship. When Kalmbach made his objection, Terry argued that the attorney-client privilege did not apply. His argument was clever, but based on a maneuver that was questionable.

Kalmbach had told Ervin that before Rebozo admitted to him he had taken some of the Hughes money from the safe-deposit box, Rebozo said to him, "Can I now go on an attorney-client basis with you, Herbert, in discussing a personal problem that I have?" Kalmbach said he replied to Rebozo that he would "so regard the discussion on whatever followed as that between attorney and client."

On the same day Kalmbach gave this testimony to Ervin, Terry was also interrogating Rebozo under oath in another room, going back and forth between the two private hearings. As part of his strategy to negate an attorney-client relationship between Kalmbach and Rebozo, he pressed Rebozo for the names of the lawyers he had consulted regarding his problems with the IRS and the Hughes money he had received. Rebozo named a number of lawyers, but did not mention Kalmbach.

Shortly afterwards, when Terry appeared in Ervin's office for the Kalmbach hearing he argued to Ervin that Rebozo could not have considered Kalmbach to be his lawyer concerning the Hughes money because he had just testified under oath that he had consulted other lawyers about that subject without making any reference to Kalmbach. Terry also claimed that when he interviewed Rebozo in Florida in October 1973, Rebozo told him that he had mentioned the Hughes contribution to Kalmbach at a White House meeting on April 30, 1973, but that it had been an irrelevant part of the discussion. Apparently to bolster his arguments, Terry pointed to Kalmbach's admission that he had not been paid a fee by Rebozo or done any legal research in the matter. He finally insisted that Rebozo had waived whatever attorney-client relationship that might have existed when he told the committee staff in October of the April 30 discussion he had with Kalmbach.

There may not have been an attorney-client relationship established between Rebozo and Kalmbach, but under these circumstances it is at least doubtful that Terry disproved the existence of such a relationship. It was irrelevant that Kalmbach had been paid no fee or had not been asked to do any legal research. Preliminary discussions between an individual and a lawyer which are intended to lead to an attorney-client relationship are covered by the attorney-client privilege. Frequently such discussions are not consummated by such a relationship and no fee is paid or any legal research done. Yet the attorney is prohibited from revealing what he has heard during these preliminary discussions.

Also, Terry was simply wrong that Rebozo had waived any privileged relationship he may have had with Kalmbach when he spoke to the committee staff in October. He had limited his statements solely to admitting that he had spoken about the subject matter of the Hughes contribution. He had not confided to the committee staff that he had made any particular admissions to Kalmbach. Only if he had related such admissions to the committee staff, would he be considered to have waived his privileged relationship with Kalmbach.

Finally, Rebozo's failure, during his interrogation in another room, on March 21, to mention Kalmbach as an attorney he had consulted would not be determinative of the fact that Rebozo had not consulted Kalmbach as an attorney. In the first place, the questions put to Rebozo were in a context remote from the issue of an attorney-client relationship with Kalmbach. In addition, Rebozo could have overlooked his relationship with Kalmbach in his response—or he might have lied. If he had lied, this would be a basis for a charge of perjury, but would not serve to destroy any attorney-client relationship if one had existed between Rebozo and Kalmbach.

When I finished reading the Kalmbach transcript, I told Terry that if he ever again tried to act behind my back or conceal committee evidence from me, I would fire him, no matter how hard he had worked for the committee. I also reminded him that time was running out on his investigation. Our final report was due May 28.

I gave Terry an April 30 deadline for his investigation and told him that I wanted a draft report on the political espionage phase of his investigation and hearings by May 15. Since he might not have anything to include in the final report on the Hughes-Rebozo investigation, I did not set a deadline for him, but told him he could take up until the last day that the report was due.

I then asked Terry what he planned to do next to follow up on the Kalmbach information. He replied glumly that he appeared to be stymied, since no one corroborated Kalmbach's testimony.

"You are overlooking a whole new investigative opportunity that is now open to you," I informed him.

"What do you mean? Terry asked.

"For God's sake," I exclaimed. "Now with Kalmbach's statement of Rebozo's admission that he took money out of the box—even if it isn't sufficient to prove Rebozo's guilt—it certainly constitutes, under the law, probable cause that would support the kind of subpoena you wanted me to get Ervin to sign in the first place."

Terry's face broke into a broad smile. "Damn it, Sam," he said, "you mean we can let Bellino loose on Bebe now to make a complete audit?"

"As fast as you can get the subpoena drawn up, I'll have Ervin's signature on it," I replied. Terry ran out of my office and returned fifteen minutes later. He had taken the old subpoena I had disapproved and had his secretary change the dates on it to make it a current subpoena. Ervin agreed to sign it when I explained the legal support Kalmbach's sworn testimony now provided the committee for the issuance of the subpoena.

Frates' first response when he received this subpoena in Miami was to call Fred Thompson and to complain that the committee was harassing his client and that he planned to go to court to object to the subpoena. After much discussion back and forth, I finally got Frates to agree to produce Rebozo in Washington on May 9 before the full committee with the understanding that he would have an opportunity to argue his objections to the subpoena. My argument was simple: If Rebozo had an opportunity to prove Kalmbach was wrong but refused to produce this evidence, the committee would be forced to draw an inference of his guilt.

While waiting for the May 9 meeting with Rebozo, Terry recommended an alternative route. The Internal Revenue Service had begun an audit of Rebozo as far back as a year earlier, which had originally been bungled because of the inexperience of the IRS investigators first assigned to the job and the apparent hesitation on the part of their supervisors to do anything that might annoy the President's best friend. Embarrassed by the poor job that was done and alerted to the need for a thorough audit of Rebozo's financial affairs, IRS Commissioner Donald Alexander ordered an exhaustive tax audit of Rebozo and directed that it be carried out by a team of the best investigators the IRS could assemble for this obviously controversial task. By April 1974 the audit was well under way. The IRS had collected or examined most of Rebozo's financial records and the tax investigators had been sharing much of this information with the special prosecutor's office, which had maintained an interest in the Hughes-Rebozo matter.

However, the special prosecutor's office had engaged in only marginal investigation in this area, since it was aware of the heavy concentration of time and energy on the part of our committee staff concerning Rebozo and was receiving regular reports from us with regard to our evidentiary findings. It was understood that once our committee went out of business, the special prosecutor's office would pick up the investigation where we left off.

Terry now suggested that our committee formally seek to gain access to all of the investigative records the IRS had developed through its earlier audit of Rebozo. With these records Bellino would be able to complete his own audit and his effort to make an airtight examination of all of Rebozo's cash transactions. In anticipation of our investigation's need to make use of IRS records, the committee earlier had obtained a Senate resolution, required by statute, authorizing the Senate Watergate committee to obtain tax returns and investigative records from the Internal Revenue Service. We had not initially made use of this resolution in Rebozo's case because we were all sensitive to the privacy questions inherent in seeking access to IRS files. We treated the resolution as a weapon of last resort.

So far we had been thwarted by Rebozo's own actions and we had little time left to carry out the committee's full responsibility to uncover all the facts of Watergate. At my request, Senator Ervin formally implemented the Senate resolution authorizing our committee to have access to IRS records by writing a letter to Commissioner Alexander. I told Terry that as soon as Alexander responded to Ervin's letter, I would set up arrangements for Bellino to begin working with the IRS investigators and the records they had collected.

However, it was not to be that easy. After considerable delay, Commissioner Alexander's legal adviser called me and asked if he could come over to my office with one or two of his assistants to discuss some legal problems that were involved in Senator Ervin's request to Commissioner Alexander. He specifically asked me to arrange to have Fred Thompson present at the meeting. I agreed, but insisted that Terry Lenzner be present, since the matter involved an investigation he was supervising.

When we met the following morning, it was obvious that the lawyers from the IRS were ill-at-ease. They made some awkward expressions of general support for the committee's investigation and stated that Commissioner Alexander would like very much to be of assistance to the committee. However, they informed us that their study of the law had led them to conclude that even under the Senate resolution our committee had obtained, Commissioner Alexander was not authorized to permit our committee to inspect investigative files or financial records that the IRS had obtained from a taxpayer or during an investigation. They thought that, at most, the Senate resolution perhaps would authorize the committee to see Rebozo's tax returns, but none of the back-up records.

"That's nonsense," Terry exploded. "You've been giving all of these records to the special prosecutor's office. Under the Senate resolution we now have an equal right to get access to those records."

The IRS lawyers disagreed with Terry, claiming that the special prosecutor's office was a law enforcement agency of the executive branch of the government and that the IRS served as an investigative arm of the government—or, in this case, the special prosecutor's office. In support of Alexander's position, we were shown some IRS regulations. However, I found them to be quite ambiguous and not applicable to a Senate select committee acting under an authorization resolution adopted by the Senate.

I told the IRS lawyers that I disagreed with their position, but that we would do more legal research on the matter and would be in touch with them as soon as possible. I stressed the fact that time was running against us and it was essential that this question be immediately resolved. Throughout the meeting, Fred Thompson played a passive role, except for stressing from time to time the importance of keeping the committee's access to IRS records strictly within the law for the purpose of protecting privacy. To Terry's consternation, Fred indicated he appreciated Commissioner Alexander's hesitancy to open up his files to a congressional investigating committee.

When the meeting broke up, Terry stayed behind and complained, "Did you hear Fred Thompson? Who the hell is he working for? I'll bet he's back in his office now calling Bill Frates and giving him the good news that the IRS wants to screw us." I told Terry to assign the lawyers on his staff to research the law so that we could get a memo back to Alexander as quickly as possible.

Terry's research at least proved that the IRS lawyers were wrong in their position that Commissioner Alexander was barred by the law from giving our committee access to the records. There was sufficient ambiguity in the legislation and regulations to permit Alexander to comply with Ervin's request under the Senate resolution the Committee had obtained if Alexander wanted to do so. Unfortunately, the same ambiguity would support his refusal. We were left then with the question of the exercise of Alexander's discretion. It was clear that as things now stood, he was exercising that discretion against us.

I suspected that his decision in this regard was motivated in part by a request he had probably received from the special prosecutor's office not to supply Terry and his staff with the records. The special prosecutor's top staff assistants were not sympathetic with the aggressive tactics of Terry's team. They suspected them of being the source of some of the committee's major leaks, and may well have been concerned that IRS records in their hands would find their way to the Washington *Post* or *The New York Times*.

With time running out on him, Terry played a long shot. He prepared a memorandum addressed to the members of the Senate Select Committee complaining about the unwillingness of the IRS to cooperate with the committee. He included a long list of grievances against the IRS, charging the service with carelessness and ineptitude that came close to implying cover-up in the Rebozo investigation and claiming that the present decision of Commissioner Alexander to impede the Senate Watergate committee's investigation of Rebozo was just another indication of ineffectiveness on the part of the IRS.

Terry sent copies of this memorandum, dated April 14, 1974, to the offices of each of the senators who were members of our committee. However, when it was distributed, most of the senators were out of town for the week-long Easter recess of the Senate.

A copy of the memorandum, which Terry claimed he sent to me on April 14, did not appear in my office until a week later, the day after the full memo was revealed in a Sunday front-page *New York Times* story by Seymour Hersh. The story made numerous references to Lenzner and gave the clear impression that he was the only one who would have benefited by the leak to Hersh.

When I read the story in the Sunday *Times,* I had no knowledge of Terry's memorandum. Not only was I angry, but I knew that all hell would break loose. Fred Thompson was the first to call me complaining, "What are you going to do with Terry Lenzner? That guy simply is incorrigible!" I told Fred that the whole thing was a mystery to me and that I was going to find out about it.

I called Terry at his home and demanded a explanation. Terry confounded me by complaining angrily on the phone about the leak. "We can't keep anything confidential inside our committee, Sam!" he exclaimed. "One of the senators or a senator's staff assistant must have given it to Hersh." Terry expressed shocked surprise when I told him that I did not even know anything about his memo until I read about it that morning in *The New York Times.* He swore to me that one of his staff assistants had been assigned to deliver a copy of the memo to me a week ago at the same time it was distributed to the senators.

When I asked Terry why he hadn't cleared the memo with me before he sent it to the committee members, he apologized and explained that he had rushed the memo out to catch the senators before they left for the Easter recess. I then told Terry that he had probably ruined any chance we had to arrange a compromise with Alexander and told him to meet me in my office the following morning.

On Monday I had a meeting with Alexander, fully expecting that we had lost every chance to see the records. However, despite his real anger at Terry, Alexander seemed to be giving in. In the next couple of days the newspapers continued to carry stories referring to Lenzner's memo and with counter-stories quoting Alexander as denying any effort to impede the committee. It was now becoming clear that if Terry had in fact arranged for the leak of the memo, he had succeeded in bringing newspaper pressure on Alexander, forcing the IRS commissioner to demonstrate that he was not engaged in any kind of cover-up—which meant granting our committee access to Rebozo's records. In short, this may have been a leak that worked a good purpose, even though Lenzner took plenty of heat as a result of it.

Bill Frates turned the May 9 meeting of the committee into a trial of Terry Lenzner, Scott Armstrong and Carmine Bellino. He was assisted in this strategy by supportive remarks from Senator Baker and Fred Thompson. Baker was especially angry that most of Terry's Hughes-Rebozo investigation had been carried out in secret, and that some of the evidence obtained had been withheld up to that very day from the minority senators and staff members of the committee. He kept calling on Terry to report on what files he had hidden away in his office safe. Fred Thompson did not make matters any better when he interjected the remark: "Even Sam Dash, the chief counsel, doesn't know what Terry has squirreled away!"

Except for the Kalmbach incident, Fred's charge was not really true. Terry had kept me fully abreast of his investigation and findings. I knew the substance of the materials he had collected and had authorized his operating secretly, without sharing the investigation of witnesses or the collection of evidence with minority staff members or committee. The reason was obvious. It stemmed from the information about Baker, Gurney and Thompson which John Dean had given me. I knew that Fred Thompson was in constant communication with Fred Buzhardt at the White House and with Bill Frates in Miami. Senator Ervin had been fully informed of my decision not to share investigative material with minority staff and he had agreed with my reasons and approved my actions. At the May 9 meeting Weicker raised more objections than Baker or Thompson. He had always supported our investigation and Senator Ervin's goals at committee meetings. However, he was visibly upset at the charges made by Frates that Terry had violated Rebozo's rights in his maneuvering to nullify a client-attorney relationship with Kalmbach. "For Christ's sake!" Weicker snapped. "We're not bloody prosecutors after somebody's hide. We should treat people decently. That's the whole point of this investigation. We shouldn't act like the bunch of blockheads in the White House who knew only one way to treat people—indecently!"

On Senator Montoya's motion, the committee went into executive session, and Frates and Rebozo were excused from the meeting temporarily. Fred Thompson then suggested to me that I join him in talking to Frates outside the meeting. After fifteen minutes of discussion between Rebozo and Frates in a private office Frates agreed that we could have the records Bellino thought would be sufficient for the purposes of his audit. I said that I would draw up an understanding of our agreement for our signatures and Frates could forward the records to me when he returned to Miami.

Frates replied that he was late for a meeting in the special prosecutor's office and that he would like to be excused with Rebozo to attend that meeting. As soon as he was through, he would come back and sign my statement of agreement. Naturally, I agreed to this request and we all went back into the hearing room.

While I was out of the room, Terry had been able to make his peace with Weicker, and the meeting ended with Weicker complimenting the work of Terry and his staff and stating that the record should show that they had done a good job and that the committee did not accept the allegations Frates had made against him. Carried away with the spirit of Weicker's statement, Senator Ervin said, "That is a fine statement, Lowell. These men have worked harder than anyone. If I were Terry, I would certainly want to get my work completed as successfully as I could. I have great respect for the character and zeal of his fine staff."

I glanced at Jim Hamilton and Dave Dorsen and noticed their long faces. The meeting had been converted from a trial of Terry and his staff to a testimonial—not completely deserved, in Jim's and Dave's opinion. I added the statement that although Terry and his staff worked hard, all of the committee staff worked just as hard, and also deserved the committee's commendation.

I went back to my office with Terry and Carmine Bellino and prepared a statement of agreement for Frates' signature. Frates had said he would return in an hour. We waited two hours and Frates did not appear. I called Fred's office and asked him if he had heard from Frates. Fred said he had not.

Terry suggested that he call the special prosecutor's office to learn whether Frates and Rebozo were still over there. Perhaps they had been detained. He made the call and reported back: the special prosecutor's office had no record of any meeting scheduled with Frates and Rebozo that day and the security guard had not seen them come in.

I called Fred again and told him what I had just learned. Fred expressed surprise and told me that he would call Frates' hotel. He called me back in a few minutes and told me that Frates and Rebozo had checked out, and the hotel clerk had told him that they had taken a cab to the airport at least an hour ago.

When I announced the news to Terry and Bellino, Terry threw down his file on my desk and exclaimed, "The bastards!" I looked blankly at the unsigned statement of agreement. The committee never had a chance to enforce its subpoena against Rebozo; he left the country shortly after returning to Florida, and did not come back until the committee's investigative powers had expired.

As the deadline for completing his investigation closed in on Terry, he never could prove that Rebozo misappropriated some of the Hughes money. A thorough and tedious effort was made to trace the serial numbers of the $100 bills Chester Davis had delivered to us, but the evidence turned up here was ambiguous because of conflicting versions of when the original Hughes cash contribution was given to Rebozo.

Even if Carmine Bellino could not prove that Rebozo had tampered with the Hughes money, he did perform a remarkable piece of accounting detective work. Working with Terry's staff up to the last week of the committee's investigation, Carmine expertly peeled back the shielding covers of a number of trust accounts through which Rebozo had laundered a political contribution he had received for Nixon. Exposed in this process at the very end was Rebozo's use of a $5,000 cash fund to enable the President to purchase a birthday gift of diamond earrings for his wife, Pat.

When our report became public, Pat Nixon's diamond earrings were treated nationally as a front-page news sensation. Bellino was also able to establish that Rebozo had paid out approximately $50,000—mostly in cash—for luxury additions to Richard Nixon's Key Biscayne home. Bellino queried where Rebozo, who was always borrowing money to keep his own affairs afloat, had been able to find the money for these contributions to the Nixon home. However, Bellino could not find the answer, and was unable to corroborate his suspicion that this money came from the safe-deposit box and the Hughes cash.

When our final report was filed and the Senate committee closed down at the expiration of the time allotted to us under its Senate resolution, we turned over to the special prosecutor all the evidence we had accumulated in the Hughes-Rebozo investigation. After months of investigation the special prosecutor's office closed the Hughes-Rebozo file without any indictment.

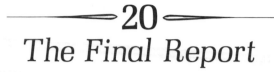

The Final Report

THE COMMITTEE HAD FOCUSED PRACTICALLY ALL OF ITS ACTIVITIES and efforts on its public hearings and accumulation of evidentiary facts through a network of nationwide investigations. I believed this was a proper choice of priority while the committee was functioning as a public-informing and fact-finding body, and we had indeed informed and awakened the public through our public hearings in the summer of 1973. These hearings had set the stage for the House Judiciary Committee's impeachment proceedings and helped provide the public support for the special prosecutor's efforts.

As important as our hearings had been, if the committee were to go out of existence doing nothing more, it would leave for history only the record of these hearings and the raw documentary evidence it had accumulated. Others would certainly interpret this material in writing the history of this extraordinary period. However, I believed it was crucial that the committee leave behind its own analysis of the evidence and recommendations for reform as a contribution to history, even though such an analysis could only be tentative because of our closeness to the subject matter.

The Senate resolution that had created the committee called for the submission of a final report. Such a requirement was frequently fulfilled by congressional committees by submitting a superficial narrative of the committee's history, accompanied by the chairman's lofty statement of unattainable goals.

By April and May of 1974, both committee members and staff had reached a state of exhaustion and were not eager to undertake the task of writing a thorough final report. However, Senator Ervin gave me the strongest support for my recommendation that we could not afford to disband without preparing as complete a final report as possible. Ervin thought that this report not only should present an analysis of the committee's work, but should also contain conclusions and findings of fact involving the complicity of individuals in the Watergate affair. During the spring of 1974, in Ervin's early statements about the final report, he even suggested that there be a separate chapter on the involvement of President Nixon in Watergate on the basis of our evidentiary findings.

Senator Baker at first supported the general concept of a final report. But he was very much opposed to the committee's making findings of fact regarding individuals, and strongly argued against including any special section of the report devoted to the President. He claimed that the committee would be usurping the prerogatives of the House Judiciary Committee's impeachment function if it had a Nixon chapter. And he warned that the committee would be charged with prejudicing the criminal trial if it issued a final report containing accusations.

While Terry and his staff were busy completing the Hughes-Rebozo investigation and Dave Dorsen and his staff were finishing up the Milk Fund probe, I undertook to draft the first part of the report dealing with the Watergate break-in and the cover-up. Initially, Ron Rotunda with a staff of research assistants were assigned to feed me fact memos analyzing testimony and the documentary evidence the committee had received. But it soon occurred to me that a much more reliable source of data would be our computer tapes. Not only could the computer help us retrieve all our evidentiary record, but it could also assist us in organizing this material. I drew up an outline for the first phase of the report indicating the topical and chronological organization in which I wanted the material presented. The computer staff went to work and submitted print-outs of the abstracts of our evidence selected by the computer in accordance with my organizational plan.

I found that the computer gave me remarkable assistance when I wrote the report. Not only was I confident that I was receiving all the essential data, but the abstracted format saved us many hours of condensing the vast material in our files. Using the print-outs made it less of a chore to write a narrative of the evidence and to present an analysis and a listing of findings of fact and conclusions which logically flowed from the narrative.

Jim Hamilton worked closely with me in the preparation of this part of the report, and he proved to be an excellent editor. He has a talent for taking a clumsy sentence or paragraph and tightening it, and he also brought to the task a special sensitivity and judgment which served as a balance in portions of the draft where I had allowed myself to be carried away by rhetoric.

When I had completed the draft of this first part I gave it to Fred Thompson to review. He in turn showed it to Senator Baker. Shortly Fred returned it to me with portions of the report underlined in red, indicating Baker's or his own objection to a conclusion or statement. In some instances, the disagreement was a matter of semantics—I found I could say practically the same thing using phrases that were acceptable to Fred and Senator Baker.

There were a number of objections, however, which challenged statements I considered fundamental. These included interpretations of the testimony and inferences I believed could properly be supported by the evidence. I decided that I would ignore the red underlining of these statements and seek Ervin's support for my draft. Ervin liked the report as I had written it, and told me he would back the draft against any objection Baker might make. "If Howard still has any disagreement," Ervin said with finality, "he can just file his own minority report."

The draft of the first part was circulated to committee members in preparation for a meeting where it could be reviewed. As could be expected, no sooner had the draft been circulated to the members of the committee than it was leaked to the press, and major news stories appeared on the findings of fact and conclusions concerning the break-in and cover-up phase. When the committee met, Ervin expressed his disappointment that the draft of the report had been leaked. Except for Senator Talmadge, who angrily protested the looseness of the committee's security procedures, the rest of the committee seemed little concerned over the incident.

The committee showed no inclination to go over the report in any detail. It was willing to accept the chairman's expression of satisfaction with the draft. However, Senator Baker renewed his protest against the report containing any conclusions and findings of fact. He stressed the harm that these findings might do to both the impeachment inquiry and the special prosecutor's criminal trial. Even greater harm, he claimed, would come to the reputation of the members of the committee, who would be accused of meddling in the responsibility of other investigative bodies.

This time Baker hit a nerve. The consensus was beginning to form around the committee table for a report that would omit specific findings of fact against individuals. Ervin sensed the temper of the meeting and agreed that the report should be written solely as a factual narrative, objectively stating the evidence obtained by the committee. "Frankly," he concluded, "I don't think it really much matters. If you state the facts clearly and logically enough, the conclusions will naturally flow from the facts." Then Ervin smiled and said, "In fact, the unstated conclusions might even be stronger if they spring out of a factual report that is presented in an objective way."

Shortly after this meeting, Ervin began to have second thoughts about a separate chapter on Nixon. He did not reject the idea completely. He asked me to have a draft just in case the committee decided to include it. Although Ron Rotunda was busily working on the Nixon chapter, and fervently urged that the staff fight to include it in the final report, I suspected that the committee would prefer the exclusion of a special Nixon chapter.

My own view also had changed on the question. It made sense to me that our committee should avoid making a special finding with regard to President Nixon in view of the pendency of the House Judiciary Committee's impeachment inquiry. If the House Judiciary Committee should vote articles of impeachment, and if the House of Representatives did impeach Richard Nixon, the Constitution called for the United States Senate to try Nixon on the impeachment charges. The Senate members of our committee might have to disqualify themselves from such a trial if they joined in a report condemning the President for involvement in the Watergate cover-up prior to a Senate impeachment trial.

Although the nature of our final report was gradually changing, I was not prepared for the next suggestion Senator Baker made at a committee meeting. He questioned the wisdom of the committee filing any final report at all, until after the impeachment proceedings, and perhaps after the criminal trial itself. I told Baker that if we waited until the impeachment proceedings and the criminal trial were through, our report would have little or no impact on legislative reform. Congress would no longer be under any pressure to act. Besides, I also knew Senator Ervin would no longer be in the Senate then. He had decided not to run for reelection, and without him the spirit and drive would be removed from the committee's actions.

Baker pushed for his suggestion. He claimed that he did not think the committee staff had sufficient time to prepare a thorough report on all the matters investigated by the committee, or to make the kinds of constructive recommendations which should be included in the report. After the meeting I met with Ervin and told him that I thought Baker was maneuvering the committee into a position in which it would never file a final report. Ervin believed this might be possible. I then recommended that my staff and I use the Memorial Day recess to write the final report. Fred and his staff would be told that they could take the recess as a holiday, and while they were gone we could complete the report. When they returned, they would find a *fait accompli.* Ervin agreed with me that it was absolutely essential for the committee to file a final report before the June 27 deadline now set by a recent amendment of the committee's resolution. He approved my plan and told me to go ahead with it.

I assembled my top staff aides and alerted them to my strategy. I told Terry, Dave and Jim that they and their staffs would have to work around the clock every day to complete their portions of the report so that I could review them and then clear them with Senator Ervin. Next I met with Fred Thompson and told him that the Memorial Day recess appeared to be a fine time for him to meet with his family in Nashville, and that he ought to let his staff have a vacation. Fred readily accepted the suggestion and left town almost immediately.

The plan worked. The draft of the report was completed over the next two weeks. Ervin reviewed it, section by section, while he was in a hideaway seashore resort. As was his practice, he thoroughly read every line of the draft we sent him by messenger, and telephoned his corrections or suggestions.

We were now writing under the committee's instructions to prepare a report that merely stated the evidence objectively, without conclusions. At times Terry and his staff found it difficult to live with this decision. Strong conclusions would appear in sections following the setting forth of a series of events that made the conclusions obvious.

When Ervin had completed reviewing the draft of Terry's report, he gave me a call. "Sam," he said, "I have had to strike out a number of conclusions that Terry insists on putting in the report. He's like the fellow who was told there are two ways to draw a horse. The first and best way is to just draw the horse and know that any damn fool looking at it will see that it is a horse. The second way is to draw a horse and then write underneath it the word 'horse.' Terry seems always to want to write 'horse' under the horse." From then on, in reviewing drafts of the report, all of us used Ervin's horse story to good purpose when we wanted to strike out a conclusion.

When Fred Thompson and the committee returned from the Memorial Day recess, we had a draft of the final report ready for them. Fred seemed resentful and insisted on his staff going over each section, line by line. We began a procedure whereby we met around a table in my office and negotiated chapter by chapter.

The issues debated, however, frequently dealt with phraseology and emphasis. Most often we were able to agree on a change of language that did not change the meaning of the report. In some cases there were compromises on matters of substance in an effort to obtain a report that would be signed by every member of the committee. However, none of us who had written the report thought that any of the changes affected the integrity of the report itself.

When the table negotiations were completed, the committee quickly approved the report. The senators knew that Ervin had read every word of it and had approved the drafts. Although Baker expressed reservations, he elected to join in a unanimous committee report. The only absent member was Senator Gurney, who by this time had been indicted in Florida and stopped coming to committee meetings.

We did not release the report on June 27, 1974, the day required for the filing of the report by our resolution. Ehrlichman and Colson had just gone on trial for the Ellsberg break-in and the committee voted to delay the public release to avoid any prejudice to the trial. Technically, Ervin was able to meet the filing requirement by handing a dummy cover of the report to the clerk of the Senate on the Senate floor. I joined Ervin in this little, unnoticed ceremony.

I chose Sunday, July 14—my wedding anniversary—for the public release of the report. The committee met for the last time in the Caucus Room for a press conference on the report on Thursday, July 11. In advance of the press conference Ron Ziegler had declared that our report would be "full of baloney." To add a little fun to our last official meeting with the press, Scott Armstrong purchased a huge twenty-pound kosher baloney, and Senator Ervin held it up and waved it at the press as he announced the release of our report. The baloney was cut up and eaten by reporters and the staff after the press conference.

Before Ervin left office, he made sure that the more important legislative recommendations of the committee were incorporated in bills drafted by the staff of the Committee on Government Operations, which he also chaired. The bills were sponsored by most of the Senate Watergate committee members and were consolidated as the Watergate Reorganization and Reform Act of 1975. Although our committee made more than forty recommendations which ranged the full extent of its mandate, the Watergate Reorganization and Reform Act sought to implement the major recommendations directed more at institutional change than at creating new criminal laws.

For example, the legislation provided for a permanent special prosecutor, a special counsel for Congress and financial disclosure by high executive branch officials and members of Congress.* The committee's recommendation for a Federal Elections Commission had already been implemented by Congress. The Government Operations Committee, now under the chairmanship of Senator Ribicoff, did not get around to holding hearings on the Watergate legislation until the end of July 1975. Senator Ervin could not attend, but Baker and I appeared as witnesses, while Weicker sat as a member of the committee to hear us. Weicker had not lost any of his youthful enthusiasm and complained that Congress had done very little to implement the Senate Watergate committee's recommendations.

Indeed, what I had feared when I opposed Baker's suggestion for postponing the committee's final report had occurred. Even though we had prepared and issued a report, it had been shelved until now. Ervin was no longer in the Senate; the Government Operations Committee was under new leadership; the criminal trials were over and there was no public pressure on Congress for action. Baker in his testimony, as if to add the final touch to his earlier strategy of postponing the committee's report, countered Weicker's impatience by saying, "I think sometimes that the country is tired of being outraged and indignant. I think sometimes we run across a theorem of public life that says you may only be moral once a week."

I thought I had to respond to Baker when my turn came to testify. I said, "I was a little disappointed in hearing the vice chairman of the former Senate Select Committee say that as time goes by he feels that the American people may have become a little tired of being outraged and indignant. I think one of the remarkable things that I noticed of Senator Weicker's participation this morning and during the Senate Watergate committee hearings is that throughout these hearings and investigations he has been outraged and indignant. I have seen from his questioning and statements this morning that he remains outraged and

*Our committee had recommended financial disclosure provisions only for the President and Vice President. And we had called for a special prosecutor only when needed, suggesting in the interim "a public attorney," appointed by the court, who would serve more like an ombudsman.

indignant. I am also. I hope the American people do not tire of being outraged and indignant at the kinds of things that occurred in Watergate. Only if they do not, will we be able to see perhaps a change in some of the things that occurred that were so tragic and dramatic in our country."

The Justice Department under a new Attorney General resented the suggestion that they could not be trusted to prosecute high executive branch officials, and disapproved the concept of an independent special prosecutor appointed by a court. After some modification of the special prosecutor provision that made it an ad hoc rather than a permanent office, but with specific procedural devices to create it when needed, the Watergate reform bill was voted out of committee.

President Ford, still sweating out the struggle for delegates on the eve of the Republican National Convention, maneuvered to avert confrontation with Congress on a bill labeled "Watergate reform." In a last-minute switch he overruled his Attorney General and backed the bill after obtaining overwhelming Senate approval for a compromise. The President proved to be the shrewder bargainer. Instead of the truly independent special prosecutor appointed by a special court when really needed that was provided for in the bill before Ford's change, Ford won acceptance for a permanent official to be appointed by the President and located in the Justice Department. True, there is language that calls him independent and says he can't be fired by the President except for extraordinary improprieties. But these are the same safeguards that "protected" Professor Archibald Cox. As this book is published the crippled Watergate reform bill now moves to the House Judiciary Committee, chaired by Peter Rodino.

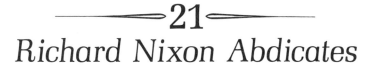

═══21═══
Richard Nixon Abdicates

FOR THE SENATE WATERGATE COMMITTEE THE SUMMER OF 1974 contrasted dramatically with the previous summer. The exhilarating atmosphere of a thriving investigation and the excitement of the televised hearings which electrified all America were gone now. In the summer of 1974 the committee worked in the shadow of the impeachment inquiry and the special prosecutor's criminal investigation.

We were winding up our work, which meant completing the task of drafting and obtaining committee approval of the final report, reducing the size of the staff to a core final team and getting ready to pack up the committee's files and close our offices. Nevertheless the committee was still alive, and would remain so under the terms of its resolution for three months, until September 27, 1974, after filing its final report on June 27. Despite this fact, the Senate Rules Committee was eager to regain control over the valuable space we had begged, borrowed and stolen, and as early as June of 1974 I received a message from the Rules Committee inquiring when we would be ready to relinquish our space. That such little courtesy was afforded us angered me. Indeed, when the staff of one Senate subcommittee jumped the gun and began to move some of the furniture out of my office on a Saturday morning in August, I was outraged and ordered them out. Then I called the chief counsel of the Senate Rules Committee and emphatically informed him that we needed our office space until the committee went out of business in accordance with our Senate resolution. There were no further raiding incidents after that.

If the public interest in Watergate had waned, it was rekindled by the April 30 release by Richard Nixon of his edited transcript of presidential conversations. Even Nixon's own version, with its numerous omissions and distortions, of what some of the tapes revealed was terribly damaging to him.

He had resorted to another "game plan" and it backfired. Confronted by subpoenas from the special prosecutor and the House Judiciary Committee for more and more tapes, Nixon hit upon a grandstand play to make it appear he was releasing all of the relevant information on the tapes. He chose the familiar Nixon strategy of a simulated "frank and candid" television disclosure to the American people. Behind him, as he told the television audience he was releasing the tape transcripts to the public, was a large number of loose-leaf binders, each bearing the seal of the presidency, giving the appearance that a huge amount of transcript material was being exhibited. In fact they contained the edited transcripts of only a few of the subpoenaed tapes. Nixon announced that a fair reading of this material would lay to rest all the false charges against him and prove once and for all that he was innocent of any wrongdoing in the Watergate affair, as he had repeatedly asserted to the American people.

Doubtless, Nixon believed this was all he had to do to escape the specter of the White House tapes. Having shown his willingness to make public their contents through his edited transcripts, he must have believed that the great majority of Americans—the ones he liked to call so frequently "the silent majority"—would not even bother to read the transcripts, but would accept the word of their President. As when he caused the firing of Special Prosecutor Cox, Richard Nixon once again demonstrated how much he misjudged the aroused interest of the public in the issues of Watergate.

He misjudged as well the attention his edited transcripts would receive from the news media in cities and towns in every section of the country. Nixon's opinion that only the large Eastern newspapers, such as *The New York Times* and the Washington *Post,* would cover the material was just plain wrong. The press in "Peoria" was equally interested.

Even while Nixon was appearing to be candid with the country, he was once again engaging in deception. The transcription of the tapes had been falsified in a number of places, and substantial portions of damaging conversations had been omitted with the misrepresenting explanation that the omitted material was unrelated to Watergate. It was a clumsy effort at deceit. Both the special prosecutor and the House Judiciary Committee had copies of some of the tapes included in the President's transcripts. They were able to make a comparison and to detect the alterations and omissions. The Rodino committee printed the comparison of what the actual tapes contained side by side with the President's account of these tapes. The differences were startling, and public anger mounted over this additional effort of the President to deceive them.

Two days after the President released the transcripts the U.S. Court of Appeals issued an interim order in our tapes lawsuit. Referring to the President's action and also to the fact that the House Judiciary Committee had received the same White House tapes our committee had subpoenaed from the President, the court ordered the Senate committee to file a response indicating whether the committee still had a sense of need for the tapes. If the committee did, it was directed to inform the court "in what specific respect the transcripts and the material that can be obtained from the Judiciary Committee are deficient in failing to meet the Select Committee's current need."

We were being put on the spot. The Court of Appeals was asking the committee: "Why are you subpoenaing the President for tapes when you can read the transcripts he released or get the tapes from the House Judiciary Committee?" It was a good question.

Could we get the tapes from the House Judiciary Committee? As I thought about it I could see no reason why we couldn't. Rodino had begun his impeachment inquiry by asking our committee for all the evidence we had collected. The Senate committee promptly agreed and I worked out a procedure with John Doar which permitted his staff to photocopy, over a six-week period, 100,000 evidentiary items. In addition, I provided Doar with a duplicate copy of our complete computer tape which gave him access to our entire data bank. In a letter written March 25, 1974, Doar thanked us: "Without the help of you and other members of your staff our inquiry could not have progressed to the extent it has to date."

In return for all this I thought the House Judiciary Committee could let us listen to the White House tapes we had subpoenaed from the President. In any event, we could not proceed any further in the Court of Appeals without first requesting access to the tapes from the House Judiciary Committee. On the same day I received the order from the Court of Appeals, I wrote John Doar a letter referring to the order and attaching it. I asked him "whether the five tape recordings which the Senate Select Committee subpoenaed from the President may be obtained from the House Judiciary Committee by the Select Committee."

Four days later, on May 6, 1974, I received Doar's brief, official reply:

Dear Mr. Dash:

This is in reply to your letter of May 2. The Judiciary Committee is conducting its impeachment inquiry under strict rules of confidentiality. A copy of these rules is enclosed. As you can see from these rules, there would be no way that I could release to you the materials.

I know of no way the materials could be obtained from the House Judiciary Committee until the Judiciary Committee decided in the course of its own inquiry to make them public.

Sincerely,

JOHN DOAR

Special Counsel

I was astonished. It seemed we had come full circle in our quest for the tapes. Even though the refusal of the House Judiciary Committee could be defended on technical grounds—it had received the tapes from the grand jury through Judge Sirica's order—once it had the tapes, it was in control of what it did with them. Certainly, it could have played the tapes publicly at its impeachment hearing. Also, no matter how understandable it might be for the committee to want to appear to be bending over backwards to reassure the public that it could be trusted to maintain sensitive evidence in a confidential manner, Chairman Rodino and John Doar should have been able to work out a plan with Senator Ervin and me for the confidential review of the tapes.

The refusal was especially stinging for two reasons. It came from a committee that had taken most of its evidentiary material from us. And it was our committee that had uncovered the existence of the White House tapes. Without this investigative contribution, nobody, except Richard Nixon, would have had any White House tapes at all.

Despite our report to the Court of Appeals that we could not obtain the tapes from the Rodino committee and that the President's edited transcripts were inadequate, the court ruled against us, holding that we had not made out a showing of "paramount need" for the tapes. The court's decision, if used as a precedent, could cripple future congressional investigations. However, Ervin, Hamilton and I thought that the case would be restricted to the unique factors surrounding the Watergate investigation and we decided not to recommend to the committee further appellate review by the Supreme Court. Not only were we close to the end of our committee's extended life span, we also did not want to risk a Supreme Court ruling that would restrict congressional investigations.

The special prosecutor, as before, fared better in the courts than we did. Unsatisfied with Nixon's transcripts, he pursued his subpoena for additional White House tapes and Sirica ruled in his favor. When Nixon appealed Sirica's order, the special prosecutor by-passed the Court of Appeals and asked the Supreme Court to review the case directly under an expedited schedule because of the urgency of time. The Supreme Court agreed, and the stage was set for an historic constitutional decision on the President's claim of executive privilege.

In the meantime, the House committee's impeachment inquiry seemed to have bogged down. Chairman Rodino had not yet opened the proceedings to the public. Instead, under the guidance of special counsel John Doar, the inquiry was proceeding laboriously, with Doar reading to mostly bored and sometimes slumbering committee members the raw evidentiary data selected from the thousands of pages of documentary exhibits and transcripts of testimony we had given him. Doar read the material without emphasis and in a monotone, purposely making an effort not to indicate bias or prejudice concerning the evidence. However admirably objective this approach may have been, its impact on the House impeachment committee was deadly in its soporific effect.

Reporters received from committee members daily versions of what they had heard and wrote disjointed and sometimes conflicting accounts about the evidence the impeachment committee was receiving from its counsel. In the opinion of a number of columnists, the momentum of public interest was being lost, and I was concerned that the evidence we had contributed to the impeachment committee might be wasted.

From my own experience with the Senate Watergate committee, I knew that to keep the committee's or the public's interest alive the staff had to do more than disclose a mass of loosely organized and detailed facts. The facts had to be presented as a cohesive narrative and frequently explained or summarized as to their possible or probable interpretation and meaning. This did not imply a partisan presentation, as Doar evidently believed, since the summaries and interpretations could include a fair balance of competing versions.

I was not the only one who was growing impatient with Doar's approach. A number of the congressmen serving on the impeachment committee began to voice their complaints of being overwhelmed and confused by the mountain of unevaluated facts being daily droned into their ears by the committee's special counsel. It was inappropriate for me to give advice to Doar directly, but I did express my opinion to Senator Ervin in the hope that he would have occasion to talk to Rodino.

Whether it was Doar's own strategy or he was heeding the advice of others, he switched from the dry drawn-out presentation of facts to a dramatic summary and explanation of the impeachment case against Nixon. The effect of the change of pace on the committee and the press was remarkable. The stage was now set for the House committee's debate on articles of impeachment which Rodino announced would be held at a public hearing open to all the people through television and radio. From then on events moved rapidly.

On June 28, 1974, when Nixon's lawyer James St. Clair made his final argument before the House impeachment committee, Senator Ervin and I were officially filing a dummy copy of our final report on the floor of the United States Senate. On July 17, 1974, when the House impeachment committee heard the testimony of its last witness, our completed final report had just been released to the Senate and the public. And during the period of July 24 through July 30, 1974, when the House committee held its famous televised impeachment debate, our Senate committee staff was beginning the tedious job of packing up the files and closing down the committee's activities. Some of us remarked how extraordinary it was that we had now become observers instead of participants, and found ourselves in front of television screens instead of being on them.

The House impeachment committee voted three articles of impeachment against Richard Nixon. The first charged him with violating his presidential oath and constitutional duty to preserve, protect and defend the Constitution of the United States, and to take care that the laws be faithfully executed, by participating in the Watergate cover-up and obstruction of justice. The second article of impeachment charged him with the same violations of his presidential oath and constitutional duty by his abuse and misuse of the agencies in the executive branch of the government, including the IRS, the FBI, and the CIA. The third article of impeachment charged Nixon with violating his presidential oath and constitutional duty to see that the laws are faithfully executed by failing to produce papers and other evidence lawfully subpoenaed by the House Judiciary Committee in its impeachment inquiry.

The evidence that had been produced by our Senate committee and the House impeachment committee was overwhelmingly against Nixon. But White House loyalists, including Senate Minority Leader Hugh Scott and Vice President Gerald Ford, predicted that the House of Representatives would not support the articles of impeachment voted by the House Judiciary Committee. And even if it did, they were certain the Senate could not muster a two-thirds vote to convict. A substantial number of impeachment supporters pessimistically agreed. Many doubted that either the House or the Senate had the courage to follow through on the historic and distasteful task of impeaching a President.

On July 24, 1974, the Supreme Court gave Congress little alternative. It decided the tapes case against Nixon and ordered the President to turn over to Judge Sirica the subpoenaed White House tapes. Nixon and Fred Buzhardt knew that this group of tapes included the June 23 tape, which recorded a conversation between Nixon and Haldeman in which Nixon conspired with Haldeman six days after the Watergate break-in to use the CIA to head off the FBI investigation of the break-in. Soon Alexander Haig and James St. Clair learned of the existence of this tape and they were convinced that it would guarantee Nixon's impeachment in the House of Representatives and conviction in the Senate. Contents of the June 23 tape were quietly circulated among the leadership of Nixon's defense in the Congress and to a few top Nixon aides in the White House, such as Pat Buchanan and Ron Ziegler.

The decision had already been made by Nixon to obey the Supreme Court's ruling and surrender the tapes to Sirica. The June 23 tape began to be called "the smoking pistol" because Nixon's defenders had earlier claimed that his accusers had not produced any direct evidence, such as a smoking pistol, to prove that Nixon had been involved in any wrongdoing. Now those who were aware of the contents of this tape knew that it represented just such direct evidence of Nixon's criminal involvement, and that the President's only alternative to impeachment was resignation.

On Thursday, August 8, 1974, I went home early. President Nixon was going to announce his resignation that evening. On my way out of the Senate office building I stopped by the auditorium. The Capitol police guard at the entrance said, "You won't find many people in there, Mr. Dash." He was right. The room was strangely silent, almost empty of staff. It seemed eerie. I could recall the scene only a few months back. This huge room had been crowded with lawyers, investigators, research assistants and secretaries; witnesses, accompanied by their lawyers, waiting to be interviewed; reporters, cameramen, hovering at the entrance, watching for a story, a picture.

At 9:04 that evening, Sara and I watched the TV image of Richard Nixon announce to the American people and the world that he would resign his office of President of the United States at noon the following day.

On September 8, 1974, the eve of the criminal trials of his top lieutenants, Richard Nixon was pardoned by President Gerald Ford. Although never indicted for any crime, and at most mentioned by the Watergate grand jury in its major Watergate indictments as an unindicted co-conspirator, Nixon was pardoned for any crime he might have committed during the period when he first took office as President in 1968 until he resigned the presidency on August 8, 1974. Ford had earlier publicly stated that he would not interfere with the work of the special prosecutor and would reserve judgment on the question of executive clemency for Nixon until a later time. Now, suddenly, he changed his mind.

Having learned from Jaworski that Nixon, now a private citizen, would be indicted by the Watergate grand jury and that Nixon could not be brought to trial on criminal charges for about a year, Ford faced the specter of serving out Nixon's unexpired term in the shadow of Nixon's criminal trial and the continuing raging controversy of Watergate.

On the basis of Jaworski's communications, President Ford felt assured that he would receive no protest from the special prosecutor if he pardoned Nixon, even though by taking such action he would, in a sense, be firing the special prosecutor from the investigation and prosecution of Richard Nixon—if a President pardoned all of the targets of the special prosecutor's probe, then the prosecutor would be just as effectively dismissed as if he had been fired, since he would have nothing left to do. And it is logical to believe that in Ford's desire to put Watergate behind him and begin his presidency with a fresh start, he was ready to pardon all the indicted Watergate defendants after he had pardoned Nixon. This would even have appealed to a perverse sense of equal justice.

The instant public outcry, however, against his Nixon pardon—which came from every part of the country—surely shook Ford and would have stayed his hand from any further exercise of the pardon power. Having assumed the presidency with such universal good will after Nixon left Washington in disgrace, Ford now experienced an instant credibility gap as a result of the pardon. His popularity plummeted in the polls. Ford must have been truly surprised, since he had never understood the meaning of Watergate or its impact on the people. He had never bothered to look at the evidence, and even shortly before Nixon's resignation he had performed the loyalist's role of team player by proclaiming Nixon's innocence in public statements.

Ford's pardon of Nixon demonstrated more than a failure to understand Watergate. It reflected his insensitivity to the concepts of equal justice and did more to undermine the public's confidence in its system of justice than any single act in recent history. His own explanation that "Nixon had suffered enough" was more a convenient cover than a humanitarian statement; it concealed, for his own political purpose, his desire to rid himself and the public of the constant reminder of Nixon's Watergate.

Senator Ervin was outraged by Ford's pardon of Nixon and spoke out publicly against it. He said, "In granting to former President Nixon an absolute pardon exempting him from all the legal consequences of all crimes which he may have committed against the Constitution, the laws and the people of the United States while serving in the highest office in the land, President Ford did infinite injury to the indispensable principles of good government embodied in the phrase 'equal justice under the law.' "

Jaworski himself had no stomach for a trial of Nixon. Instead of complaining about President Ford's interference with the special responsibilities of his office, he publicly supported the pardon, despite the contrary views of the Watergate grand jury and much of his staff. Indeed, although the prosecutions had not begun and the special prosecutor's final report had not been written, Jaworski announced that his work was completed and he resigned his position as special prosecutor to return to the large law office he headed in Houston, Texas.

Most of the Watergate defendants were convicted after a trial by jury. CRP attorney Kenneth Parkinson was acquitted. Gordon Strachan had been severed from the trial on his claim that it was unfair to prosecute him because he had testified to the grand jury under a grant of immunity. Later, the special prosecutor's office dropped criminal charges against Strachan.

In order for John Dean, the prosecution's principal witness, to appear credible, the special prosecutor had insisted that he plead guilty and be sentenced prior to the trial so that defense counsel could not question his expectancy of a lenient sentence as a motive for his testimony. Just before Dean was to plead guilty in August 1974 he called me and asked to see me to get my advice. Although Sara and I were on our way to Ocean City for a much needed weekend of rest, I invited John to join me there. On the beach, looking at the ocean, Dean and I talked throughout a warm Saturday afternoon about his fear of the sentence Sirica might impose. He was in a state of panic and even threatened to change his position and plead not guilty. I told him I thought it was too late for that, but suggested he seek his lawyer's advice before deciding on any course of action. Since Shaffer was out of town, Dean wanted to go to the special prosecutor's office to talk it out with the people there. It was my view that he should wait until his lawyer returned and was in a position to guide him. Dean took this advice and shortly afterwards pleaded guilty and was sentenced by Sirica to a period of imprisonment of one to four years.

When Shaffer had asked me what I thought Dean would get, I had guessed one to three years. Even though Ervin and I had each written Sirica a letter recommending a lenient sentence because of Dean's cooperation with our Senate committee, I suspected that Sirica wanted to appear harsh enough so that the jury would not believe that Dean's testimony had been induced by any considerations of leniency. After the trial, Ervin and I each wrote Judge Sirica again on behalf of the committee recommending a reduction of the sentence. Sirica did reduce the sentence and Dean was released from imprisonment after serving four months.

In December 1974 Seymour Hersh of *The New York Times* broke the CIA scandal. This was the exposé of illegal CIA activities in domestic intelligence and assassination efforts against foreign heads of state—and not related to Senator Baker's claim that the CIA was responsible for the Watergate affair. Hersh's *Times* story resulted in the creation of a new Senate select committee to investigate the intelligence community. The House of Representatives ultimately created a House select committee for the same purpose. President Ford sought to jump the gun on the investigations by appointing a presidential commission under the chairmanship of Vice President Rockefeller to look into the charges against the CIA.

These investigations revealed a list of horrors involving illegal activities on the part of the CIA, the FBI, the Secret Service, the military intelligence agencies and other federal intelligence and police agencies. The catalog of illegal behavior included break-ins, wiretapping, bugging, assassination attempts and terrorist activity. Targets of this illegal behavior were so-called radical or extremist groups within the country and individuals, including heads of state, identified as enemies or threats to the United States outside of the country. Under this onslaught of illegal federal intelligence and law enforcement activity the United States Constitution had been violated thousands of times.

During the Watergate investigation we had uncovered some suggestions of illegal CIA activities, but had not been in a position to verify or investigate them. A number of tips had been received by us concerning political assassinations and tie-ins between government agencies and organized crime figures. However, many of these tips were anonymous and referred to activities that occurred clearly prior to the presidential campaign of 1972. Our mandate under Senate Resolution 60 was to investigate solely illegal or improper activity concerning the presidential campaign of 1972. There was so much for us to do under this mandate alone, and we were spread so thin, that even if our curiosity had tempted us to explore some of these tips, we neither had the time nor the manpower to do it.

More recently, as the Senate Select Committee on Intelligence, chaired by Senator Frank Church, filed its findings and reports, some columnists—still seeking to retrieve Richard Nixon's image—wrote pieces noting the fact that abuses of official power occurred in other administrations, including some of the more popular Democratic administrations. They asserted that Nixon wasn't as evil as he was portrayed, and that if the Church committee findings had been known at the time of the Senate Watergate committee hearings or the House impeachment committee inquiry, Richard Nixon would still be President today. There was little response to these columnists, but I suspect a number of people silently though reluctantly concurred.

Of course, even though other Presidents have been guilty of similar transgressions, it is idiotic to suggest that Richard Nixon was treated unfairly when, because of his criminal acts, he was subjected to impeachment proceedings, which led to his resignation. The cry of Nixon's apologists was that "everybody's done it." So what? It is saying the obvious to point out that because some robbers and murderers get away with it, it doesn't mean that those who are caught red-handed should not be tried and punished.

But in fact Watergate represented something worse, much worse than the violations revealed by the intelligence committee reports. Although abuses of power occurred on numerous occasions during the earlier administrations, there is nothing in these revelations that approximates the dominance of the Nixon White House in police-state activities and the pervasive role in illegal conduct played by the President of the United States and his top aides.

The intelligence committee investigations do in fact reveal that prior Presidents must have acquiesced in, condoned, and even at times directed, illegal acts on the part of federal authorities. But if this had been a regular procedure on the part of White House occupants prior to Richard Nixon, there would have been no need for the Huston memo. The Huston memo made official recommendations for interagency intelligence activities to suppress internal dissent by means of burglaries, wiretaps and mail covers. President Nixon was warned in this memo that these activities were illegal. Yet he gave his assent to them. There was the difference. An American President in violation of his oath of office and his constitutional duty overtly authorized unconstitutional police-state practices.

We do not have all the facts, and perhaps we never will, but it is likely that presidential involvement in illegal action in the past occurred on an ad hoc basis with the Presidents fully aware that they had no authority to permit such conduct. Richard Nixon carried this practice to the extreme. What had been ad hoc became systematic and pervasive. The essential difference was that Nixon believed he was a sovereign who had the authority to act above the law and approve or authorize illegal acts. This mentality in a President brought us close to dictatorship.

Perhaps it is a good thing that congressional investigations have revealed that there have been no heroes in the White House in recent American history. Abuse of power is not a partisan matter. Whether the public official, especially if he is the chief executive, is Republican or Democrat, there can be no rationalization to defend his betrayal of the people's trust. The power of the executive branch of government is great, and for a world power like the United States it must of necessity be so. An essential check on that power is accountability. Over the past fifty years the presidency has grown more powerful and less accountable. Secrecy has been substituted for openness. Mighty bureaucracies of police and intelligence agencies—equal in their capability for terror and harm to those of totalitarian countries abroad—have grown within the executive branch; they are incompatible with constitutional government or with the free society the founding fathers bequeathed to us two hundred years ago.

The Constitution entrusts to Congress the responsibility of oversight of the executive branch as a check against abuses of power. But Congress has failed to effectively perform this role. When one examines the mass of evidence based only on admitted violations of individual rights by federal police and intelligence agencies, one must wonder how remarkable it is that we still remain the free society we are today.

Out of this period of increasing executive power, there emerged a President who believed he had absolute, unreviewable power. And it was this perception of the American presidency that produced Watergate. It can happen again if we do not learn the lesson of Watergate, which is the same lesson of history the framers of the Constitution knew well and built into our system of government. A free republic can best be preserved through checks and balances applied through the separation of governmental powers. But they also knew this system doesn't operate automatically. The essential force to make it work is an alert, informed and active citizenry. That force and, consequently, a responsive, accountable government were absent for at least a half century. Momentarily, in the crisis of Watergate, we the people asserted ourselves and witnessed the remarkable impact on representative government. We turn away again at our peril.

Appendix

A PERSONAL ACCOUNT BY SENATOR SAM J. ERVIN, JR., OF HIS MEETING WITH PRESIDENT RICHARD NIXON REGARDING THE RELEASE OF TRANSCRIPTS OF THE WHITE HOUSE TAPES

ON WEDNESDAY, OCTOBER 17, 1973, JUDGE SIRICA HANDED DOWN HIS ruling to the effect that the Court had no jurisdiction of the suit brought by the Committee against the President for the tapes recording his conversation with John Dean. That ruling removed any possibility that the Committee was likely to get any access to the tapes which were crucial to the determination of the truth at any time in the immediate future.

On Friday, October 19, I was at the airport in New Orleans about to take a plane to Charlotte, North Carolina. While at the airport I received a long distance telephone call from Fred Buzhardt saying that President Nixon wanted to see Senator Baker, who had been summoned from Chicago, and me that afternoon.

At Buzhardt's suggestion, I took a Delta plane to Washington and was met at the Friendship Airport by a White House automobile which took me to the White House sometime late in the afternoon.

On my arrival at the White House, I found Senator Baker in a room outside of the Oval Office in company with General Haig, Professor Wright, and Fred Buzhardt. They informed Baker and me that the time for appealing to the United States Supreme Court the order of the United States Court of Appeals for the District of Columbia affirming Judge Sirica's ruling in the District Court ordering President Nixon to surrender the tapes would expire at midnight, and that they hoped that they would be able to reach some agreement with Special Prosecutor Cox about the tapes before that happened. They did not tell us that they had theretofore tried to reach some agreement with Cox and that he had rejected their proposals. We had no notice whatever of this matter.

Both Baker and I informed General Haig, Wright, and Buzhardt that we had nothing whatever to do with the Cox investigation, but that on the contrary, the Senate Select Committee was acting under entirely different constitutional principles and laws from those relating to the Special Prosecutor.

After this conversation occurred we were summoned to the Oval Office and had a conversation with President Nixon. President Nixon informed us, in substance, that he wanted to settle amicably his controversy with the Committee over the tapes recording his conversation with Dean; that he desired for the Committee to receive what these tapes said about the Watergate matter, but was unwilling for them to know what the tapes said about non-related matters which he said affected national security, proposed federal appointments, and proposals for obtaining federal legislation at the hands of Congress; that Senator John Stennis of Mississippi was an expert on national security problems and enjoyed the complete confidence of everybody who knew him; that he was willing to entrust these particular tapes to the custody of Senator Stennis and let Senator Stennis furnish the Senate Committee everything these particular tapes said in respect to the Watergate affair; and that he had not talked to Senator Stennis about the matter personally, but one of his aides had, and that Senator Stennis said that he was a "Senate Man" and would agree to this only if it was satisfactory to Senator Baker and me.

Senator Baker and I thereupon interjected ourselves into the conversation and advised the President that we were only two members of a seven-man Committee; that in consequence we could not make any agreement with him on the point; but that on the contrary we would call a special meeting of the Committee to pass on his proposal. I said at this point that the public might question the authenticity of the tapes, and that I would not agree as a member of the Committee to any proposal unless it was understood that in the event the Committee had any doubt as to the authenticity of the tapes in question after receiving Senator Stennis' statement of what the tapes said about Watergate that at the instance of the Committee Senator Stennis could have the aid of electronic experts to aid him in determining the authenticity of the tapes.

President Nixon replied, in substance, that he had no objection to such an understanding because the tapes "had not been doctored."

Senator Baker and I made it plain to everyone present that we had no authority to make any agreement with the President and would not attempt to do so; but on the contrary would call the Committee to meet within the next few days to pass on the President's proposal.

After so stating, we left the White House, and I was returned from Andrews Air Force Base to the commercial airport at Hickory, North Carolina, about 20 miles from my home by military plane.

Before we left the White House, President Nixon asked Senator Baker and myself not to make any statements about the meeting until the White House had issued a statement concerning it. We agreed to this request.

Upon reaching home, my wife advised me that I had received scores of long distance phone calls from representatives of various media of communication throughout the nation as well as a phone call from you [Samuel Dash]. In order to keep my promise to the President to refrain from making any statement, I operated a mechanism which I had had installed on my phone in August 1973 which prevented any telephone calls from reaching my residence. I kept this mechanism on all night, and although I heard a meager television report at 11:00 about the meeting in the Oval Office, it gave no details and was insufficient to acquaint me with the tenor of any statement which the White House may have made during the evening of October 19.

On the following morning, Saturday, October 20, I called you and you read to me a statement which the White House had issued asserting, in effect, that Baker and I had agreed to accept the President's summary of the tapes in controversy as authenticated by Stennis. At that time, I informed you about our conversation with the President, and stated emphatically that I had not made any agreement whatever on behalf of the Committee, but had told the President that Senator Baker and I would call a meeting of the Committee as soon as reasonably convenient. As you will further recall, we did call a meeting for Thursday, October 25, to pass on the President's proposal to Senator Baker and me. I also told you in this conversation that I had never agreed and would never agree to accept any summary of the tapes, and would be opposed to the Committee accepting any proposal which did not make it certain that the Committee would receive verbatim exactly what the tapes said about the Watergate affair.

Immediately after talking to you on Saturday morning, October 20, I called Senator Stennis by long distance telephone and asked him what he understood the proposal of the White House to be. He informed me that he understood he was to have custody of the tapes in controversy, and was to transcribe verbatim exactly what the tapes said about the Watergate affair, and that the Committee under the proposal would receive such verbatim transcripts.

During the late afternoon of Saturday, October 20, 1973, I drove to Asheville to attend the Vance-Aycock Dinner, an annual event of the Democratic Party for fund-raising purposes. Immediately after my arrival at the hotel, I was called to the telephone and received a long distance telephone inquiry from Fred Buzhardt, one of the White House Counsel. Fred asked me to inform him what I understood the President to propose. I informed him that I understood that the President proposed to entrust the tapes to Senator Stennis, and to let Senator Stennis listen to the tapes and give the Committee a verbatim transcript of exactly what the tapes had to say about the Watergate affair. Fred Buzhardt informed me in the phone conversation that that was in accordance with his understanding.

While the dinner was in progress I received information of what has become popularly known as the "Saturday Night Massacre"—that is the firing of the Special Prosecutor.

On Sunday, October 21, my secretary, Mary McBryde, drove my wife and myself by automobile from Morganton to Homestead, Virginia, where I was to speak to a business organization on Monday evening, October 22. This automobile trip occupied about 6 hours of time on Sunday, and we did not hear any news about recent events until after I reached Homestead and was registered in the hotel there. During that evening and on the following day, Monday, October 22, I received a number of inquiries from newsmen by long distance telephone and in person as to what had transpired at the White House during the meeting there between President Nixon, Senator Baker, and myself. I informed them that Senator Baker and I had disclaimed any power to make any agreement with the President, but had assured the President that we would take up his proposal with the Committee and let them make the decision in respect to it, and that the President's proposal as I understood it was that the President was to entrust the tapes in controversy to Senator Stennis, who was to listen to the tapes in person and give the Committee in the event it approved the proposal verbatim transcripts of exactly what the tapes said about the Watergate affair.

To my surprise, Fred Buzhardt called me by long distance shortly after I reached the Homestead and repeated to me the same question he had asked me by long distance in Asheville the night before. The ensuing conversation between him and me was identical to that we had had the night before.

On Monday morning, October 22, 1973, I called my office in Washington, and dictated a telegram to the President to one of my secretaries, Eileen Anderson, in which I made the following statements:

> There seems to be some confusion in the news media as to the nature of the proposal which you made to Senator Baker and me at the White House on Friday afternoon. I have called a special meeting of the Committee to pass on your proposal. In order that I may present your proposal to the Committee correctly, please advise me in writing what your proposal is. As I understand it, you proposed that you should deliver the tapes the Committee is seeking to Senator Stennis and permit him to take from the tapes verbatim transcripts of what they say about the Watergate affair, and furnish such verbatim transcripts to the Committee. I am unwilling to take anything less. I would not be willing to take or have the Committee take anybody's summaries or interpretations of what the tapes say.

My office forwarded this telegram to the White House. I never received any personal reply from the White House concerning it. However, sometime after it was sent to the White House someone on the Committee staff—as I recall it was you—called me by long distance telephone and said that the White House had called the Committee and informed the Committee that the proposal had been withdrawn. My personal recollection is that I received this phone call advising me of the withdrawal of the proposal by the White House on Tuesday morning, October 23.

In retrospect, I suspect that Senator Weicker was right and that Senator Baker and I had been "zonked" by President Nixon. While I cannot furnish any proof for this suspicion, I strongly suspect that President Nixon never had any intention of surrendering the tapes to Senator Stennis in accordance with the proposal made to us, and that the summoning of Senator Baker and myself to the White House and the subsequent White House statement were stage-played solely for the purpose of giving the President a pretext for firing Cox. Unknown to Baker and myself, Cox had repeatedly refused to accept any summaries of the statements on the tapes and the summoning of Senator Baker and myself to the White House gave the White House an excuse for representing to the American people that Special Prosecutor Cox was an incorrigible person who refused to accept substitutes for the tapes which two reasonable men, Senator Baker and myself, were willing to accept.

I believe that what transpired in the meeting between President Nixon, Senator Baker and myself can be understood best if one bears in mind the background then existing. This background may be stated as follows:

Senator Baker and I complied with President Nixon's request to visit him at the White House because we believed that a decent respect for the institution of the Presidency required us to do so. As stated above, only two days before, that is on Wednesday, October 17, Judge Sirica had handed down his ruling in the District Court of the District of Columbia to the effect that the court was without jurisdiction of the suit of the Senate Select Committee against the President for access to the tapes, and in consequence, all hope on the part of the members of the Committee of obtaining access to the tapes of President Nixon's conversations with John Dean at any time in the foreseeable future had vanished. President Nixon still held complete control of the tapes and the true contents of none of them had been revealed to anyone. Besides the Supreme Court decision that President Nixon was required to make the tapes available to the District Court was not handed down until many months later in a suit instituted by the new Special Prosecutor Jaworski.

President Nixon had steadfastly maintained that he was entirely innocent of any complicity in the Watergate affair and that the tapes would so disclose. No one except John Dean had given any testimony implicating President Nixon personally, and his testimony had been sharply contradicted by that of Haldeman, Ehrlichman, and Moore. Moreover, Haldeman had given his incorrect version of the contents of the tapes entrusted to him by President Nixon but withheld by Nixon from the Committee, and Haldeman's version sharply contradicted Dean's testimony on most crucial points.

I had steadfastly maintained from the time of the creation of the Committee that the President of the United States owed the Committee and the country assistance in developing the facts, and as a consequence, President Nixon's assurances that he wanted to give the Committee the information it was seeking manifested that the President was at long last doing the intelligent thing which he should have done many months before.

Index

About The Author

SAM DASH has had a distinguished legal career since graduating cum
laude from Harvard Law School in 1950. Among other things he has
been a trial attorney for the Criminal Division of the Department of
Justice, the district attorney of Philadelphia and director of that city's
Council for Community Advancement, in addition to serving as chief
counsel for the Senate Watergate committee. He is now professor of law
and director of the Institute of Criminal Law and Procedure at Georgetown University Law Center. He has received awards as president of
the National Association of Criminal Defense Lawyers and as chairman of the Section of Criminal Justice of the American Bar Association. Another book, *The Eavesdroppers,* was written by Sam Dash in
1959. He now makes his home in the Washington, D.C., area.